IMAGES
of America

LOST LITTLE ROCK

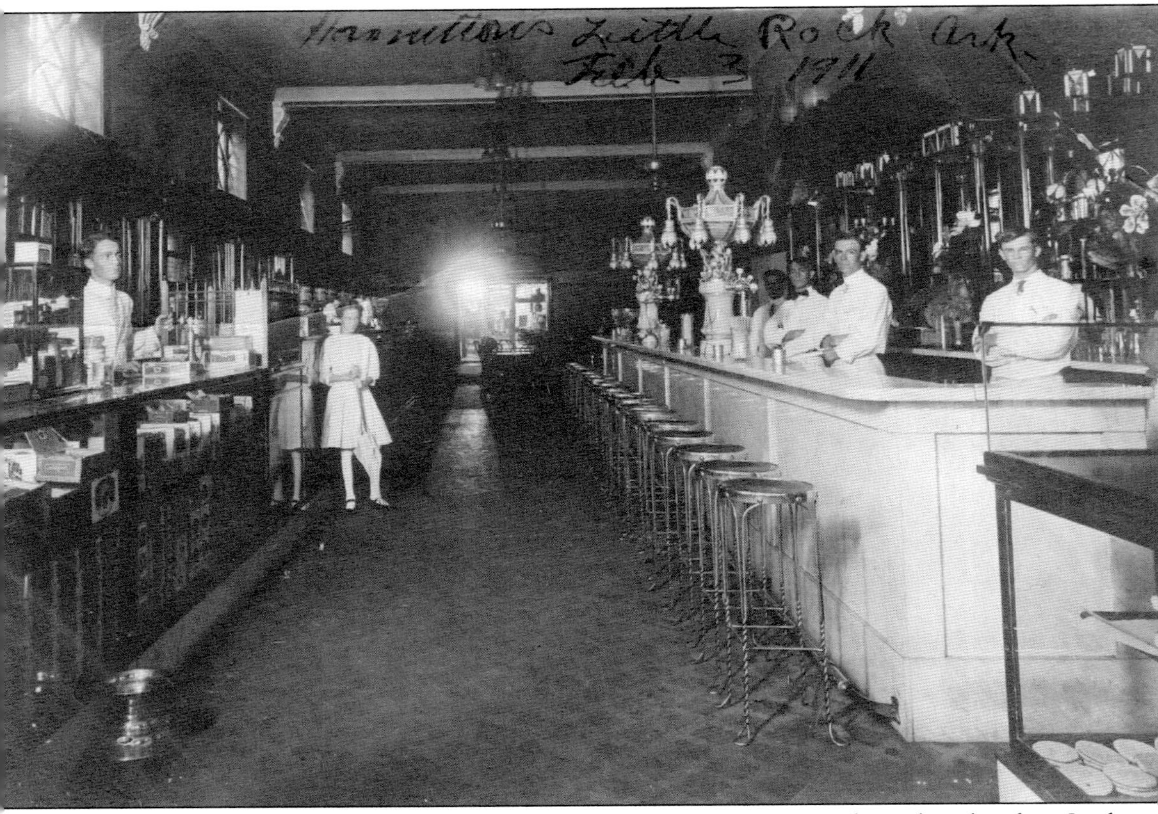

Hamilton's Drug Store at Fifth and Main Streets is a testament to two things long lost from Little Rock's Main Street: independent pharmacies once common before the rise of chain stores, and the handsome soda fountains found in these establishments, like the one shown here in 1911. White-uniformed employees wait to serve up a milk shake or other treat. Across the aisle is a large display of cigars and a brass spittoon, and a young lady stands nearby holding her parasol. (Author's collection.)

ON THE COVER: At the crossroads of Arkansas, the intersection of Capitol Avenue and Main Street, two men are seen crossing. Today, everything on the right is gone, replaced by a large parking lot and modern office buildings a block down. (Courtesy of UALR Center for Arkansas History & Culture.)

IMAGES
of America

LOST LITTLE ROCK

Ray Hanley

ARCADIA
PUBLISHING

ISBN 978-1-4671-1394-6

Published by Arcadia Publishing
Charleston, South Carolina

Printed in the United States of America

Library of Congress Control Number: 2014955048

For all general information, please contact Arcadia Publishing:
Telephone 843-853-2070
Fax 843-853-0044
E-mail sales@arcadiapublishing.com
For customer service and orders:
Toll-Free 1-888-313-2665

Visit us on the Internet at www.arcadiapublishing.com

To all the leaders, both public servants and many in the private sector, who are investing time and a great deal of money in saving and restoring significant Little Rock landmarks.

Contents

Acknowledgments

Thanks are owed to Lydia Rollins at Arcadia Publishing, for seeing the merit in this project and for making the decision to put it into print, and to Julia Simpson at Arcadia, for editing and other help. Locally, special thanks go to Brian Robertson at the Butler Center for Arkansas Studies for helping provide some wonderful photographs and for looking up a number of addresses from his trove of city directories; to Kaye Lungren at the University of Arkansas at Little Rock Center for Arkansas History and Culture for her help with a dozen wonderful photographs; to Joe Fox of Community Bakery for some vintage images of south Main; and, lastly, to my wife, Diane Hanley, for editing assistance. Unless otherwise credited, all images are from the author's collection.

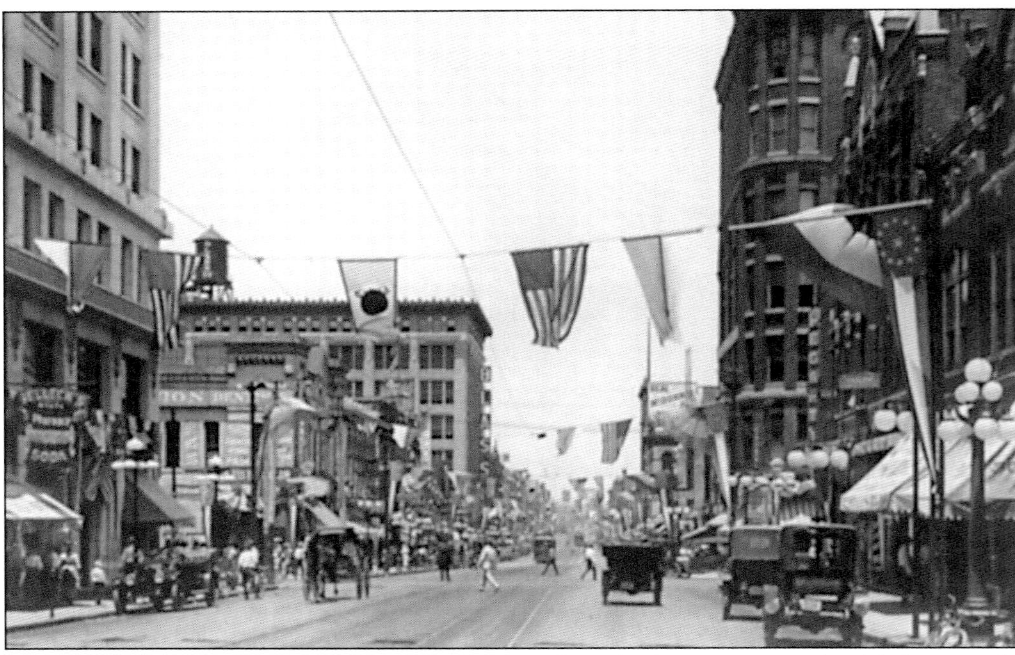

Little symbolizes the lost past of Little Rock more than the former crossroads of Arkansas, the intersection of Capitol and Main Streets. This photograph, taken at the time of World War I, looks north up Main Street through the busy intersection. Automobiles have begun to crowd out horse-drawn vehicles. The entire block just past the buggy is today a large parking lot. The towering Masonic temple on the right fell victim to fire within a few years.

Introduction

"You don't stumble upon your heritage. It's there, just waiting to be explored and shared." So said Robbie Robertson, a Canadian songwriter credited with penning the lyrics to "The Night They Drove Old Dixie Down." The quote seems fitting for the subject of this book, *Lost Little Rock*. The capital city of Arkansas, a rural Southern state, began the first decade of the last century with a robust, architecturally diverse city center filled with wonderful buildings and iconic businesses created by self-made men, often of German and Jewish heritage.

Lost Little Rock seeks to showcase the history of the city center as it was a century ago and to share why so much of what could have been the heritage for the modern citizens of the city has been lost. Because of fires and, especially, repeated decisions to tear down wonderful buildings, it is only through illustrated books like this one that the heritage can "be explored and shared." At the same time, the reader will find a few examples of restored and repurposed buildings saved from the wrecker's ball to inspire what is possible.

The streets of Little Rock began to be laid out in a grid pattern not long after Arkansas gained territorial status in 1820. Advancing from the Arkansas River, near the literal "little rock" for which the city was named, commerce crept up Markham and Main Streets. The population reached 700 by 1830, and the key business streets were lengthened to accommodate commercial growth.

By 1860, on the eve of the Civil War, the city was still a collection of mostly one- and two-story frame structures lining dusty (or muddy) Main and Markham Streets. Commercial business still extended only to about Third and Main Streets. The Civil War would slow progress of the developing city, but a bright future waited.

The 1870s saw the population grow, in part from Northerners who had seen the state and its potential during the war. Brick buildings begin to rise, most at least four stories, including the building on Markham Street known today as the state's only five-star hotel, the Capitol. By the 1880s, the streets were being paved, and the railroads brought in merchandise and building materials, while business grew south on Main Street and east on Markham Street.

By the 1880s, iconic retailers like Gus Blass were making Main Street a shopping mecca, not only for Little Rock residents but for those from surrounding communities who had easy passenger train access to the growing capital city.

By 1900, Little Rock, with a population of 37,000, was by far the largest city in the state, solidifying its position as the center of retailing, banking, and government. Fires were claiming older wooden buildings on Main Street, affording the chance to rebuild under the direction of leading architects like George Mann, who would design a new state capitol building. Soon, an unbroken line of handsome buildings housing upscale merchants, hardware stores, pharmacies, music stores and bookstores, and lawyers and doctors offices stretched for a dozen blocks south on Main Street from the intersection at Markham Street. Just beyond that point began what is today the Quapaw Quarter historic district, where fine homes arose, fueled by the profits from the prosperous Little Rock business district. At the same time, Markham Street was seeing the rise of hotels and restaurants and to the east a booming area of warehouses, stables, and wholesalers.

By 1920, the buildings were larger on Main Street, and new commerce had opened on Capitol Avenue (Fifth Street). Streetcars rumbled off Main Street a dozen blocks up to the new state capitol, which rose on a hill where a Civil War prison once stood. The most significant architecture was the new Blass Department Store building on the 400 block and the remodeled Rose Building, which sported a neoclassical terra-cotta facade imported from Italy. It was in this era that the "window shopper" concept dawned on retailers and contractors; both groups profited from remodeling, expanding, and lighting the front windows of Main Street businesses. Merchants believed the more attractive arrangement of merchandise would lead the public to "stop, look, and buy." A trip "downtown" became a great adventure for families.

The Great Depression and World War II deterred the growth of both business and population in Little Rock, but recovery was rapid after the war, when the economy boomed across the nation. Downtown streets were crowded with cars and people at a time when highways began to open up and the first suburbs started to rise. Developments like Broadmoor and Oak Forest afforded returning GIs the ability to buy small tract homes for a few thousand dollars with easy financing. Change was coming for the historic central district of Little Rock in ways that few imagined.

The 1950s saw the first suburban shopping centers rise to compete with downtown merchants, including the Town and Country Shopping Center on Hayes Street (now University Avenue). Residents of nearby housing developments began to find it more convenient to shop close to home rather than drive downtown, where lack of parking became a familiar refrain.

Urban renewal, one of those government programs that sound good in name, hit Little Rock in the 1950s and 1960s, and with it came the clearing of areas deemed run down and not worth refurbishing. The construction of freeways and high-rise apartment buildings and the demolition of historic structures only accelerated the rush to the suburbs by residents and retailers.

Fast-forward to 2015, and the downtown district has far too many gaping holes on Main Street, Markham Street, Broadway, and Capitol Avenue that have been filled with either parking lots or functional, but bland, buildings. At the same time, Little Rock is seeing a remarkable resurgence of investment and interest in reclaiming or repurposing many of the surviving buildings. This book includes much that has been lost, but there is hope for a brighter future. With shared interest, investment, and effort, it is hoped that no more of historic downtown Little Rock will slip away, and a valuable heritage will be preserved for future generations.

One

Main Street South to Capitol Avenue

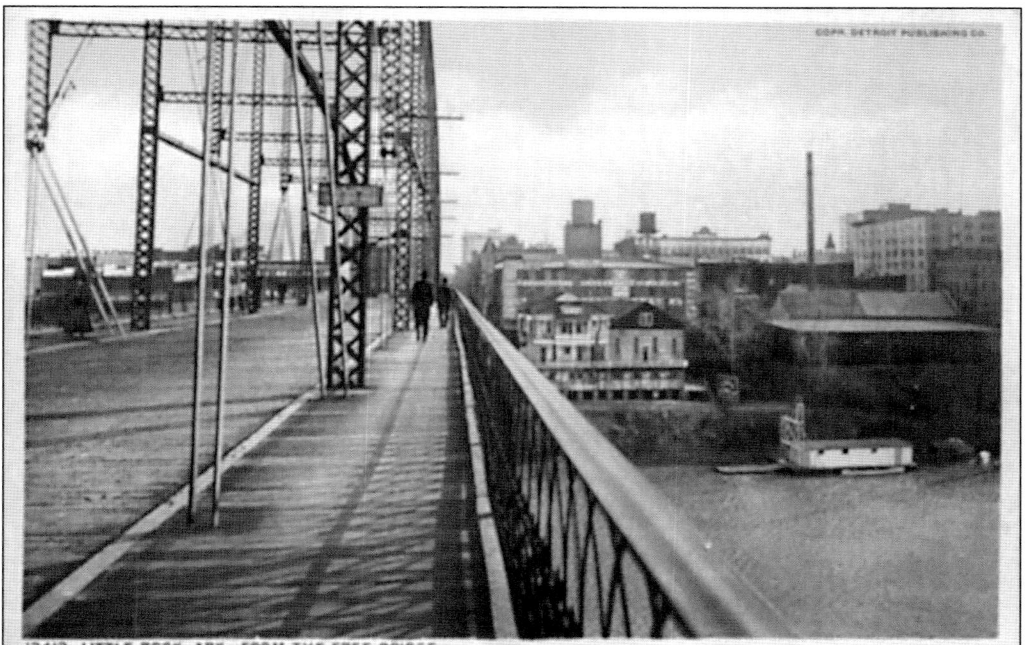

A century ago, entry onto Main Street began at the foot of the "Free Bridge" linking downtown with what was then the city of Argenta, located across the Arkansas River. "Free" denoted that the new bridge had replaced a previous toll crossing, a wooden-planked span. Little Rock's lost past is well captured along the city's Main Street, which started where pioneers began a crude city upon the south bank of the Arkansas River.

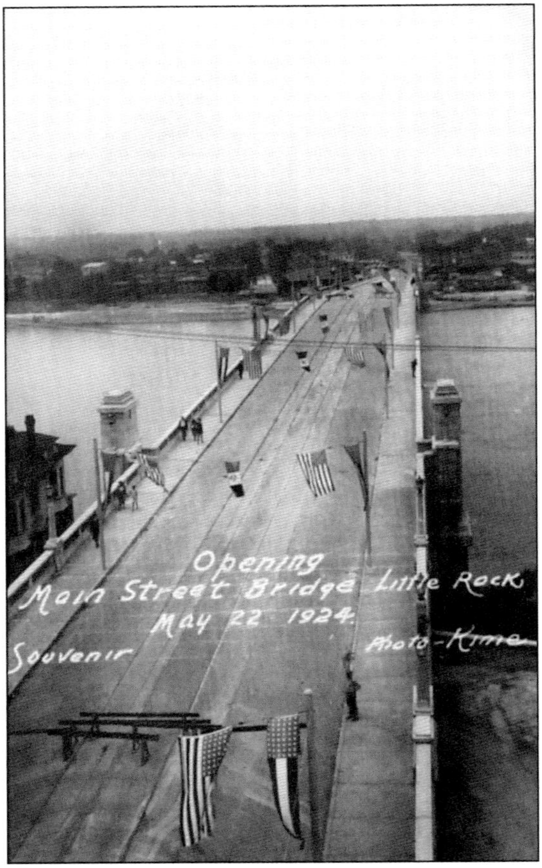

The age of the automobile began in earnest in Little Rock in 1924, when the broad and stylish Main Street Bridge opened to replace the old "Free Bridge." This photograph from the occasion affords a view toward North Little Rock. The 1924 bridge is gone, having been replaced by a newer bridge just downstream that empties traffic onto Scott Street rather than Main Street.

This 1918 photograph was taken from the south end of the Main Street Bridge, where the historic street began its long path through the heart of Little Rock. Motorists passing under the "welcome" banner would have navigated around a variety of construction projects. Less than a century later, every building shown here would be gone. (Courtesy of Arkansas History Commission.)

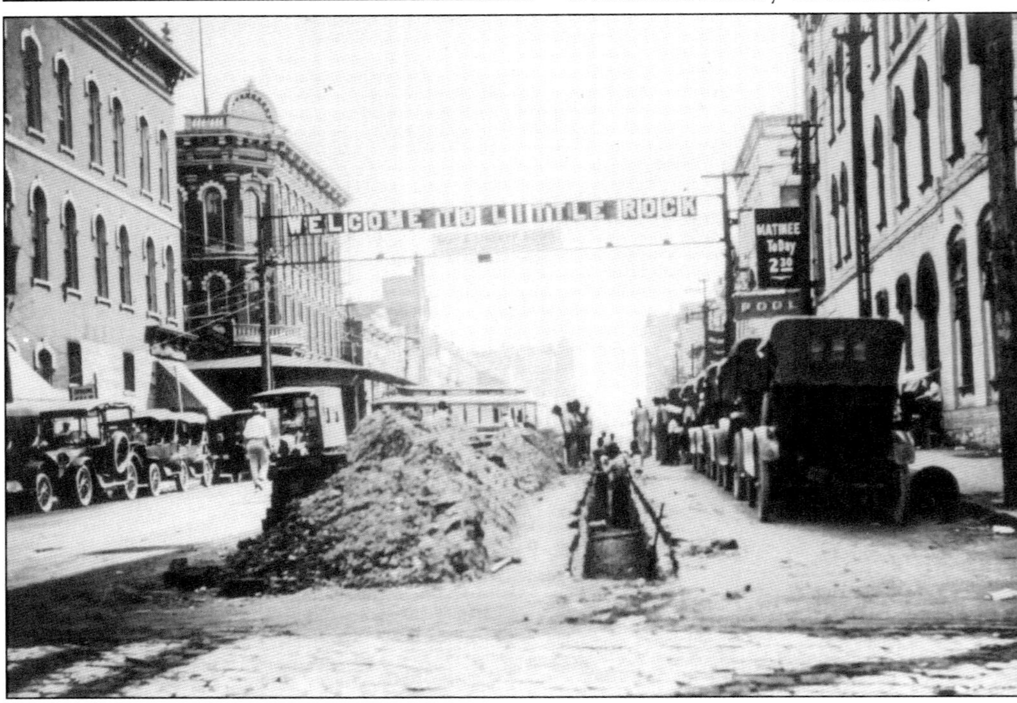

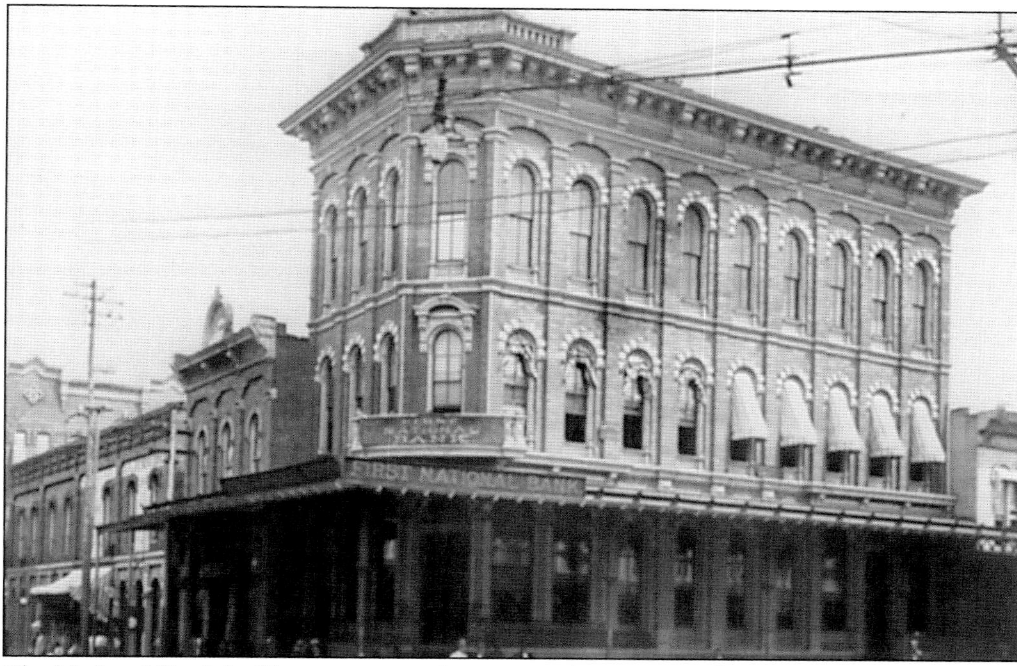

The National Bank building, seen at a distance in the previous photograph, is shown here in 1900. The building, erected in 1866, stood at the southeast corner of Main and Markham Streets. Awnings mark a second-floor lawyer's office over the shaded sidewalk. Since the 1920s, the Wallace Building has occupied this corner. (Courtesy of Butler Center for Arkansas Studies.)

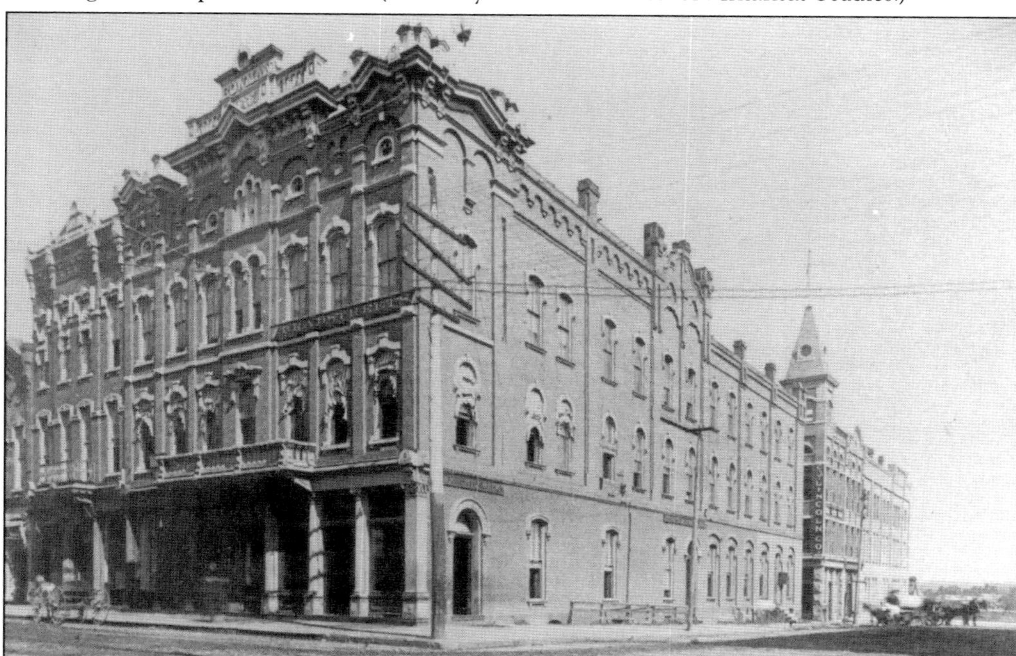

Across the street from the National Bank building, on the northwest corner of Main and Markham Streets, was the Victorian-era New Metropolitan Hotel, which had been erected in 1877. It had replaced the "old" Metropolitan, which was destroyed by fire in 1876. Though it was perhaps the town's finest hotel when it opened, the structure would be gone by the 1920s.

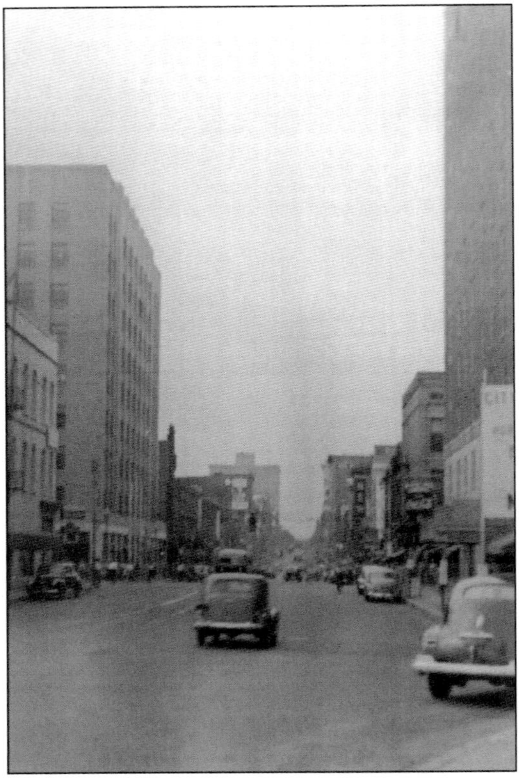

By 1940, the view from the top of Main Street had markedly changed from two decades earlier. The buildings on the west side had been razed and replaced by the Grady Manning Hotel (right), which towered over the street. The sturdy Wallace Building (left) had replaced the 19th-century National Bank building. Today, the three blocks of buildings past the Grady Manning Hotel are gone, as is the hotel itself. (Courtesy of Butler Center for Arkansas Studies.)

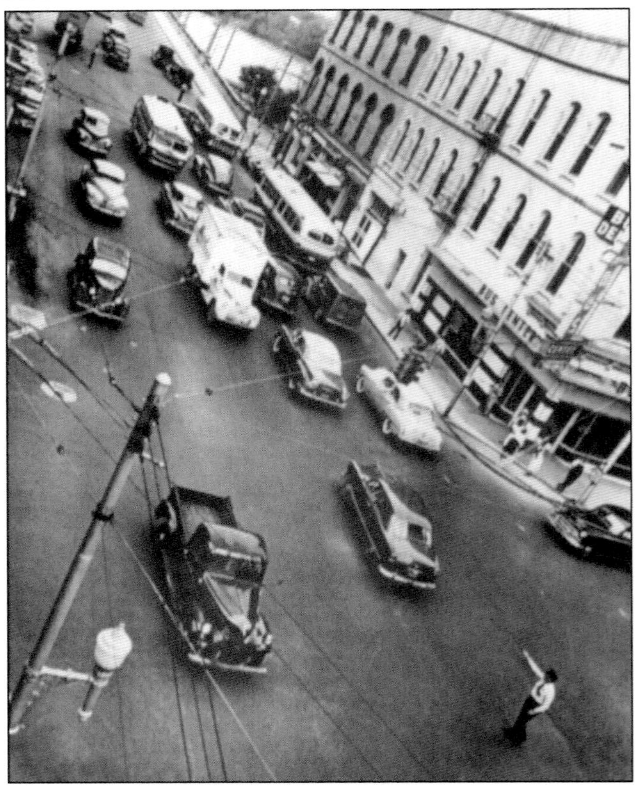

This photograph, taken a half block farther south and 10 years later than the previous image, looks back to the Main Street Bridge. The large building on the right, dating from the late 19th century, housed the busy bus depot, a taxi station, and offices. It was razed years ago; today, the entire intersection is gone, replaced by the Little Rock Convention Center. The Main Street Bridge was relocated a few blocks east.

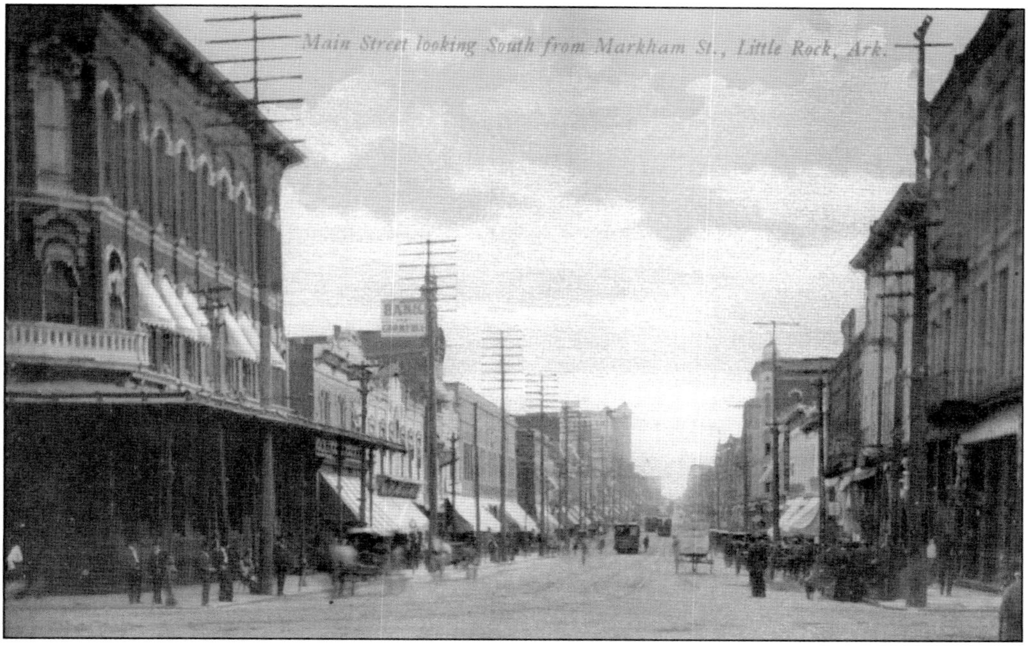

This 1915 postcard image is another view from the end of the Main Street Bridge, facing south. Anchoring the 100 block was the Markham Hotel (left), which had been converted from the National Bank building, including the addition of a corner balcony. Everything on the 100 block has been replaced since this postcard was made; the area on the right was converted to a parking lot for the Capital Hotel.

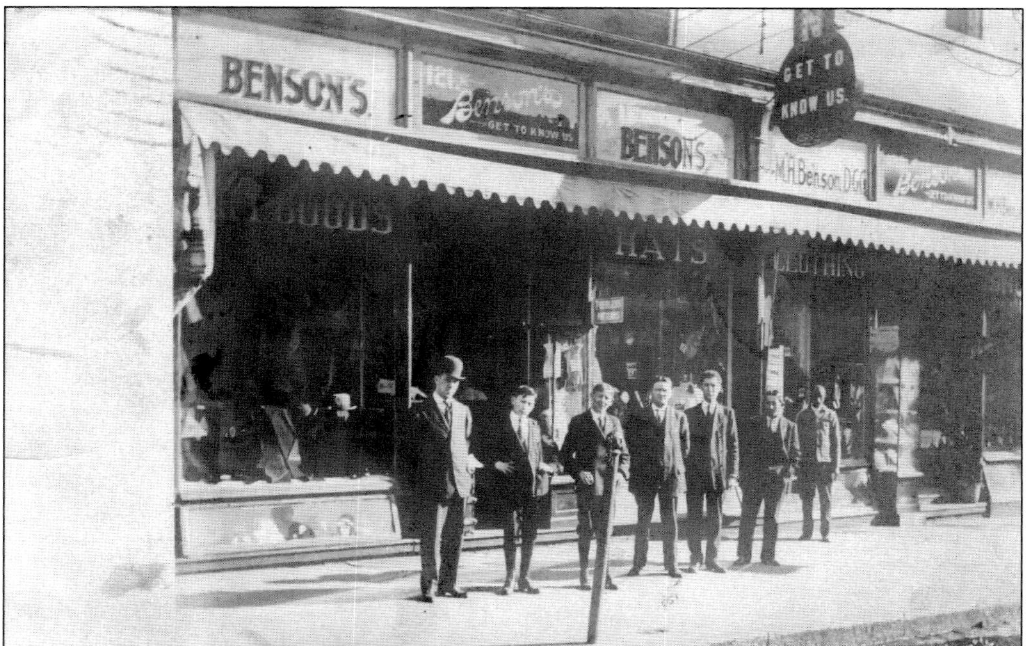

Just beyond the Markham Hotel, at 121–123 South Main Street, was Benson's Clothing Store. The group of well-dressed men posing here in 1908 very likely included the store's sales clerks.

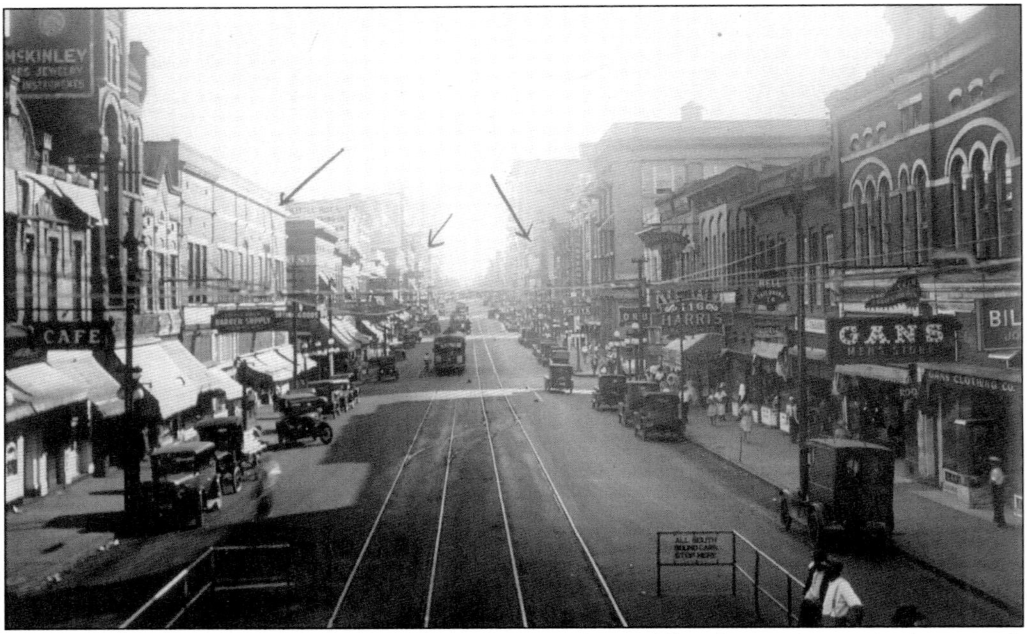

The photographer stood on an elevated platform in the middle of Main Street, looking south from the intersection with Markham Street, for this shot. At the time of this c. 1920 image, Main Street was an unbroken line of commerce stretching beyond the reach of the camera's lens. Shiny streetcar tracks reflect in the sun, and the three streetcars seen here were challenged to cope with a growing number of automobiles. (Courtesy of Arkansas History Commission.)

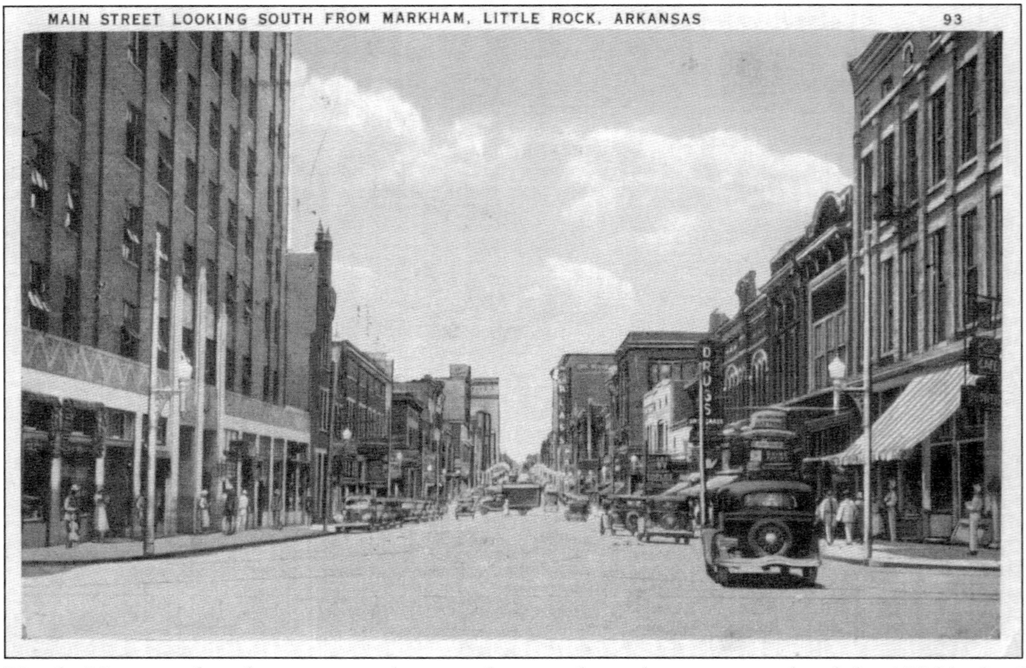

Nearly 20 years after the previous photograph was taken, the western side of the 100 block of Main Street was still intact. The east (left) side had lost the Markham Hotel building, which had anchored the corner since the late 1800s. In its place had risen the Wallace Building, erected by former governor George Donaghey in 1928.

By the mid-1950s, one of the oldest buildings remaining on Main Street was the former Bank of Commerce, with its stone arched windows and twin spires. A bar had replaced the banking facilities on the ground floor, with office or living space presumably on the upper floors. Except for the Wallace Building, partially visible on the far left, everything in this photograph is gone. (Courtesy of UALR Center for Arkansas History and Culture.)

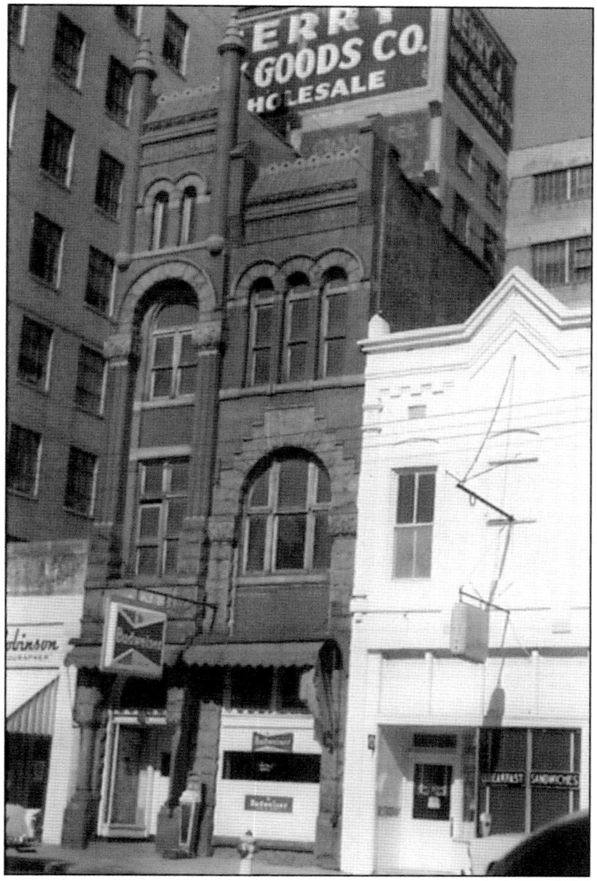

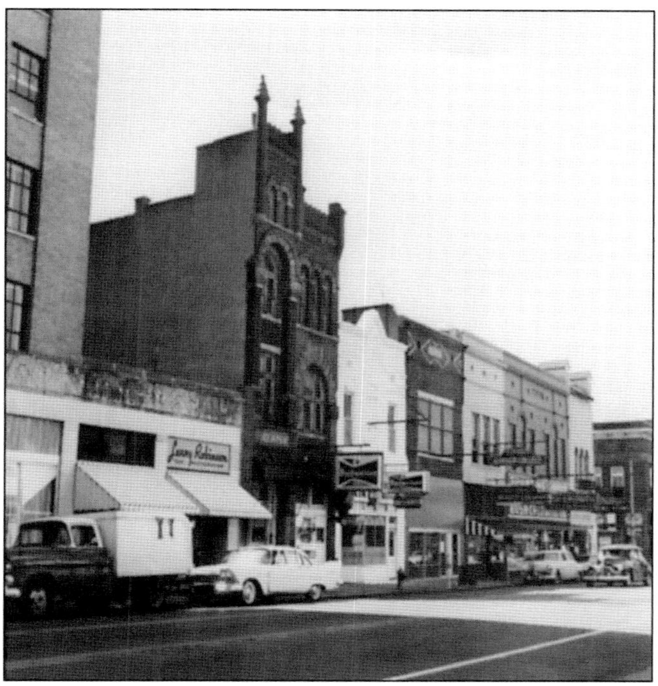

This 1957 photograph looks south from the east side of the 100 block of Main Street. The corner of the Wallace Building is on the left. In addition to the former Bank of Commerce building and its ground-level saloon, other nearby businesses include the studios of photographer Larry Robinson and a former café that had been converted to a billiard parlor. (Courtesy of Arkansas History Commission.)

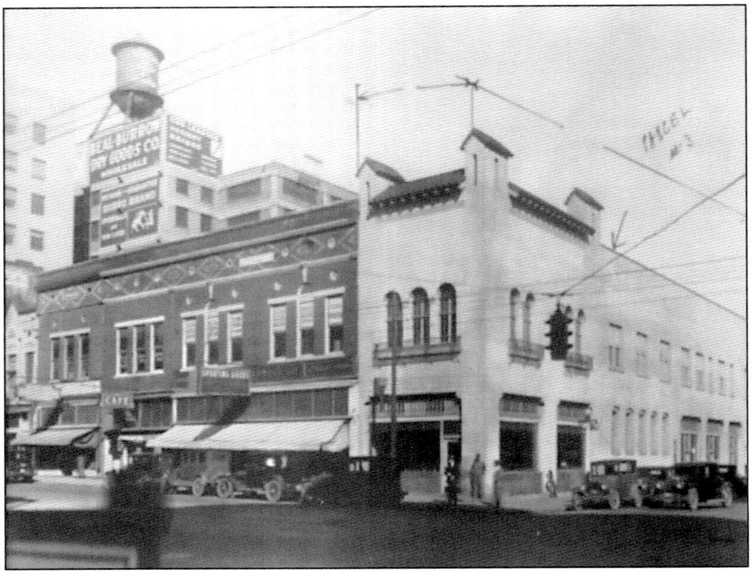

On the eastern side of the 100 block of Main Street in 1925 can be seen the Little Rock Barber & Supply Company, a café, and the Bush-Caldwell Sporting Goods store, which used upper-story windows to advertise its wares. All of these buildings are gone today, including the Spanish-style corner structure. (Courtesy of Arkansas History Commission.)

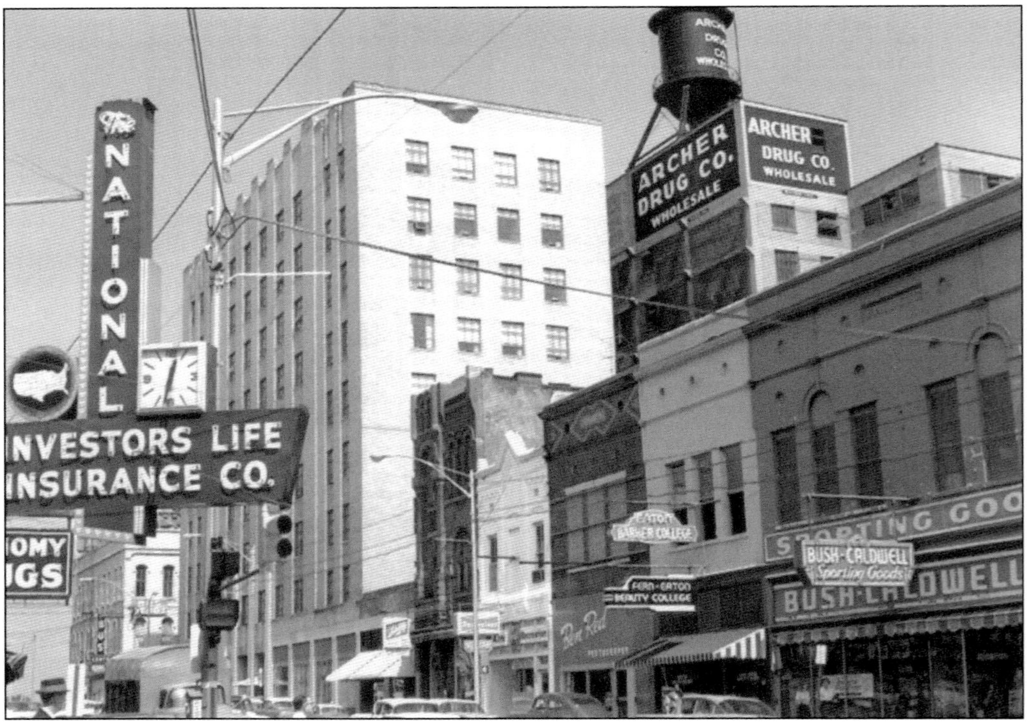

This c. 1960 view looks north up the 100 block of Main Street, with National Investor's Life Insurance in the foreground and the blocky Wallace Building towering over the older structures. Bush-Caldwell Sporting Goods is still thriving, and Eaton's Beauty College has grown from the barber supply company. The Victorian-era bank building has lost its towers, and Ben Red Photography stands next to the billiard parlor. (Courtesy of Butler Center for Arkansas Studies.)

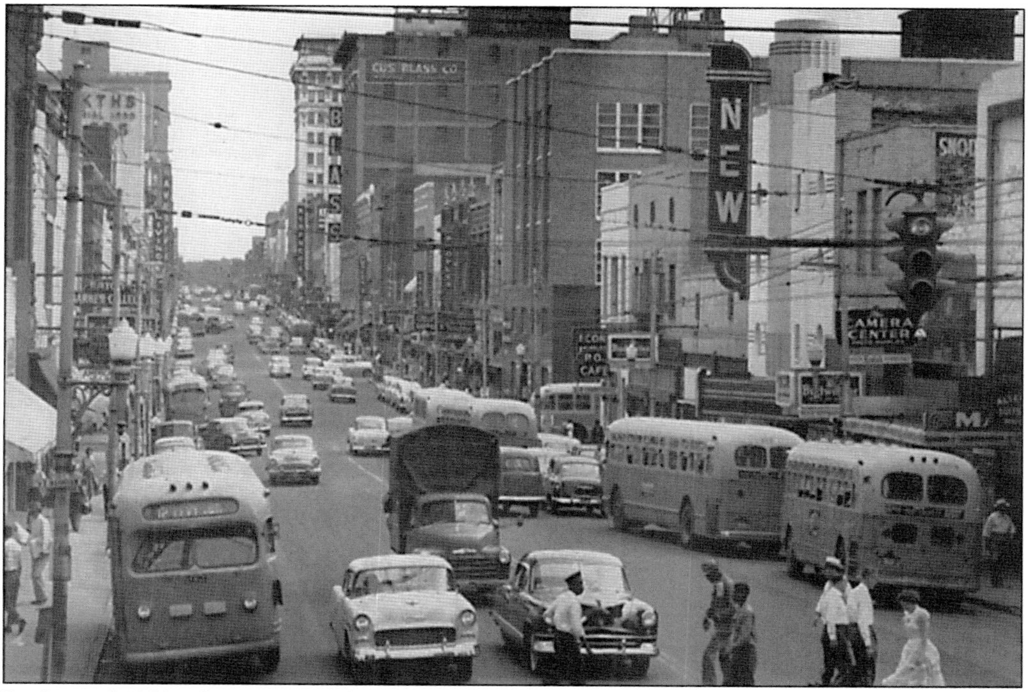

In the mid-1950s, the western side of the 100 block of Main Street was home to a solid stretch of commerce, including Economy Drugs, the New Theater, the P.O. Café, the Camera Center, and the Main Theater, just visible to the right of the two buses. Several citizens cross the busy street. The entire block was razed several years ago and today is a huge parking lot. (Courtesy of Butler Center for Arkansas Studies.)

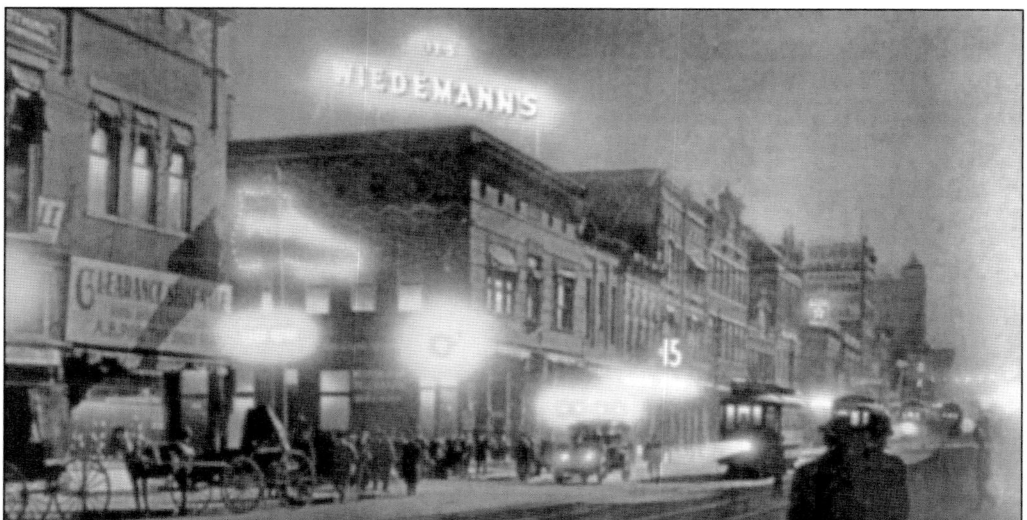

This 1915 "night view" was actually a daytime photograph treated to appear shadowed in order to show off the electrical lighting along Main Street's 200 block. A daytime crowd is still seen, with diverse transportation, including carriages, horse-drawn wagons, automobiles, and streetcars. "A.P. the Shoe Man" promotes a sale on winter shoes beneath an illuminated shoe sign. All of these structures are gone except the Blass Dry Goods building in the distance. The east side of the block is now a parking deck.

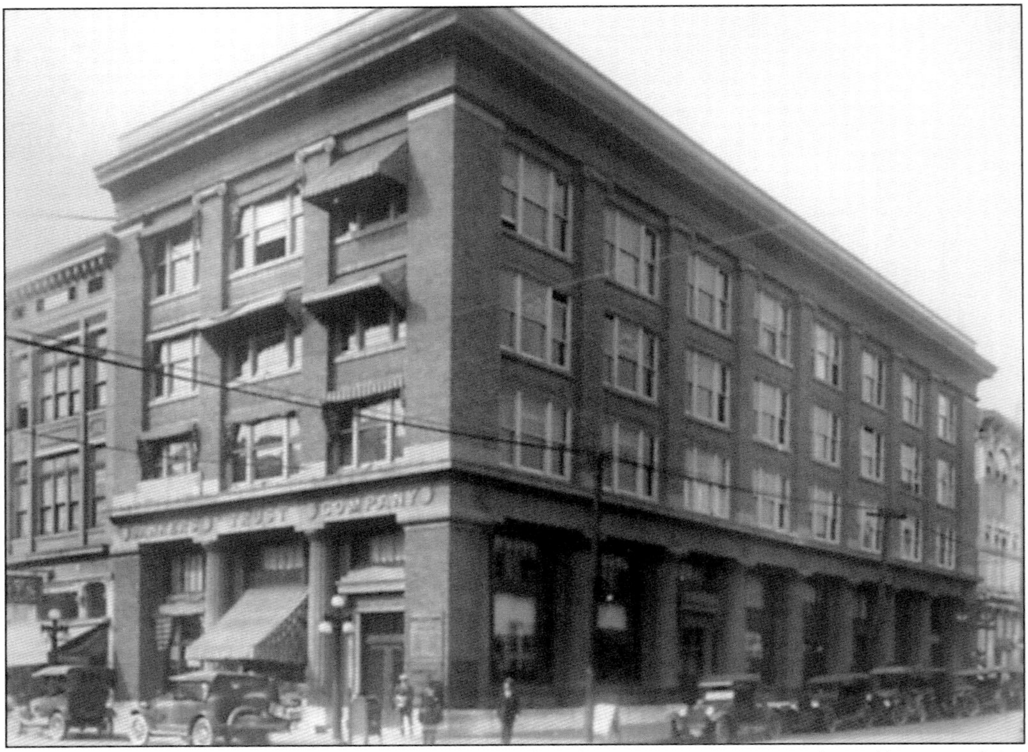

Seen here in 1925, the southeast corner of Second and Main Streets was anchored by one of the more imposing buildings on the street, the Bankers Trust Company. The bank was out of business by the 1930s, and the building was razed a few years later. Today, the corner is one end of a city-owned parking deck occupying the entire square block between Main and Scott Streets.

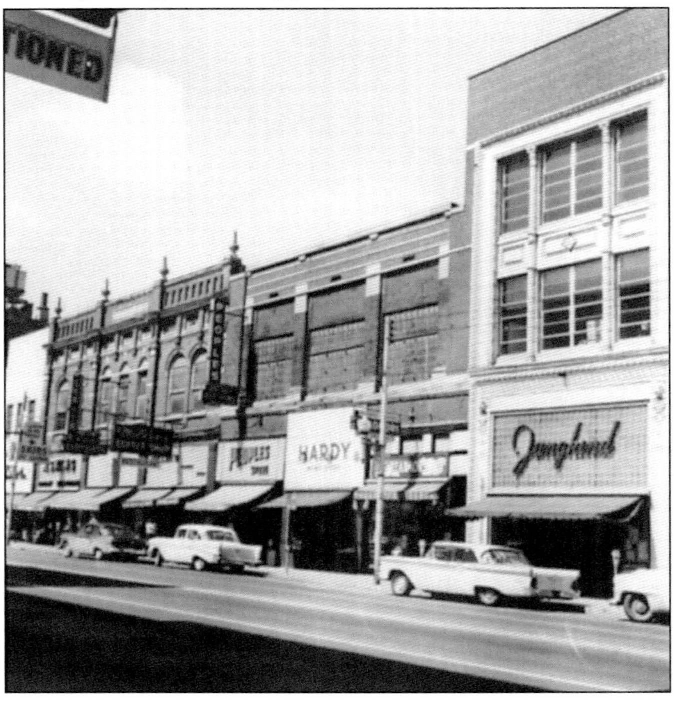

The western side of the 200 block of Main Street was home to Little Rock's best-known camera and photography shop, Jungkind's, along with a host of other locally owned businesses. Many Little Rock residents have memories of shopping at the People's Clothing Store, Hardy Men's Shoes, and Capital Clothiers. Today, the entire block is a parking lot, with all trace of the buildings long gone. This photograph was taken in 1957. (Courtesy of Arkansas History Commission.)

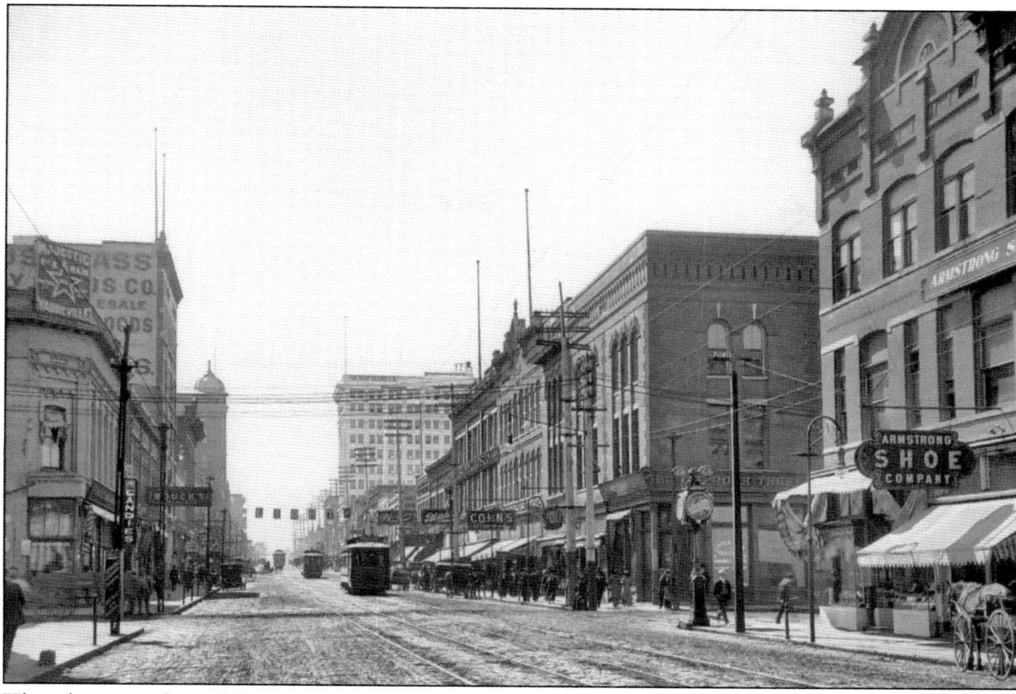

The photographer of this c. 1900 view stood in the intersection of Third and Main Streets with the camera pointed south. The Armstrong Shoe Company building (right), with its Victorian-era arched top, is no more; the site today is a parking lot. The corner building on the left was destroyed by fire and replaced not long after the photograph was taken. Lining the west side of Main Street are three iconic Little Rock retailers: Cohn's, Blass, and Pfeifer's.

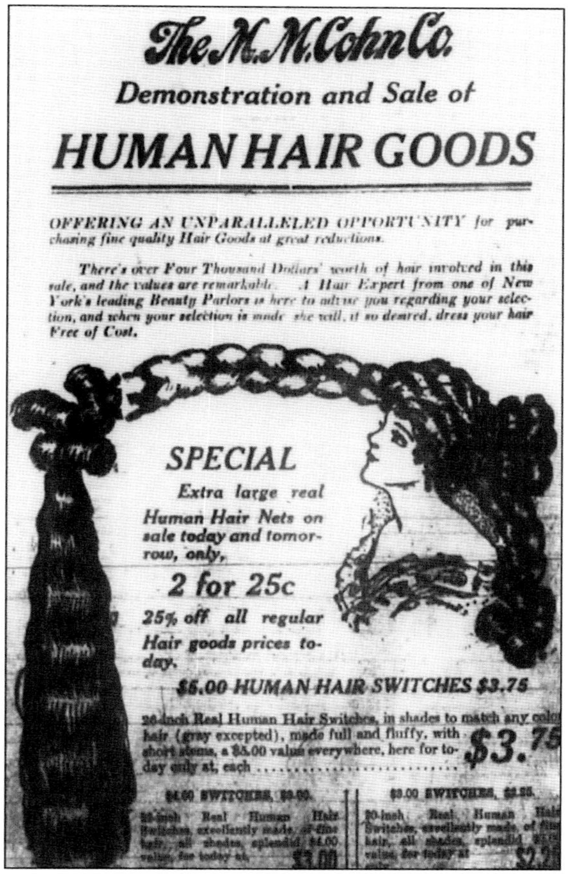

Upscale department store MM Cohn's advertised extensively to attract female customers. This 1911 advertisement from the *Arkansas Gazette* notes, "There's over Four Thousand Dollars' worth of hair involved in this sale." Human hair swatches, regularly $5, were on sale for $3.75, including "26-inch Real Human Hair Switches in shades to match any color hair (gray excepted), made full and fluffy."

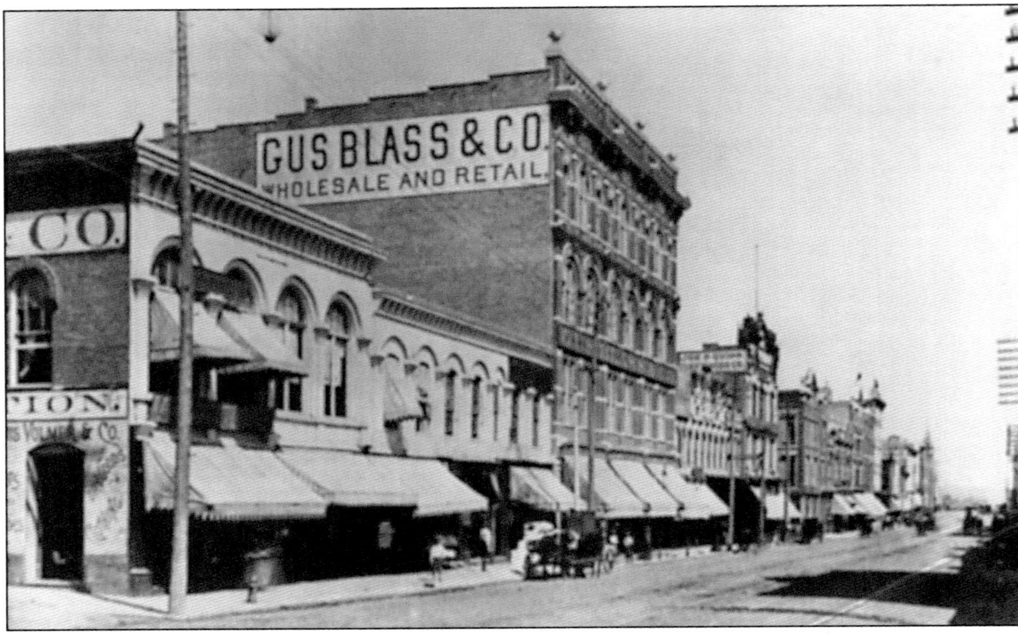

A major fire in 1900 prompted a rebuilding of the east side of Main Street. The centerpiece was the new five-story Gus Blass store, which opened in 1901 and was destined to become the state's largest department store. The Blass Company is long gone, but the building remains and has been restored as a nightclub and loft apartments. It lost all its stone ornamentation and arched windows and today is a much plainer structure.

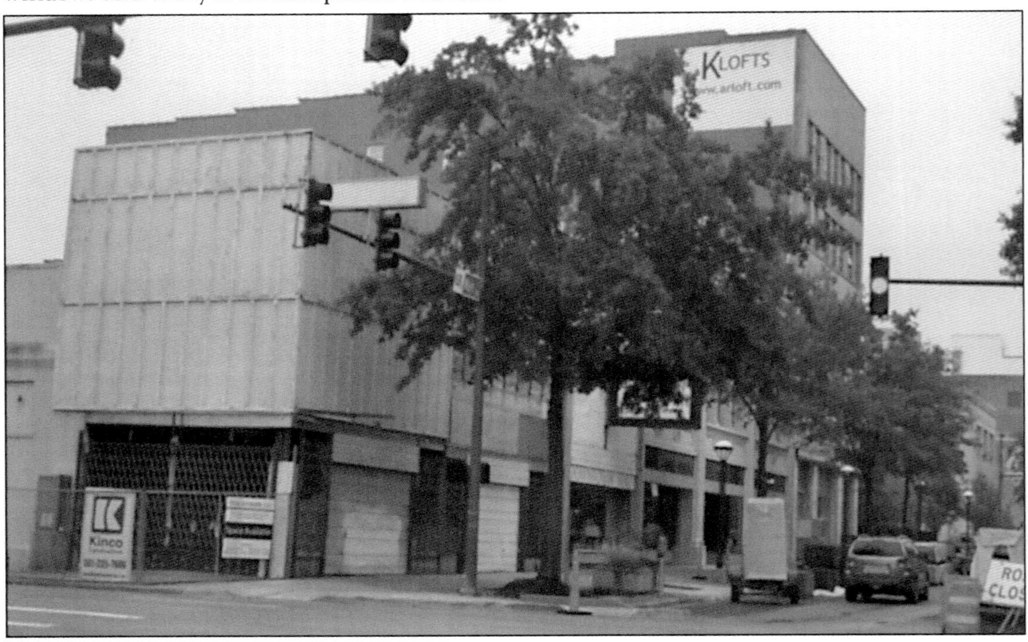

The corner building just down from Blass's had once been a two-story hotel, but after a fire its remaining ground floor served for many years as a retail outlet, most recently as Mr. Cool's Clothing. Deemed too far gone to be restored, the structure's demolition was announced in November 2014. The restored, but much less ornate, former Blass building is seen up the street, labeled as "K-Lofts" apartments. (Photograph by author.)

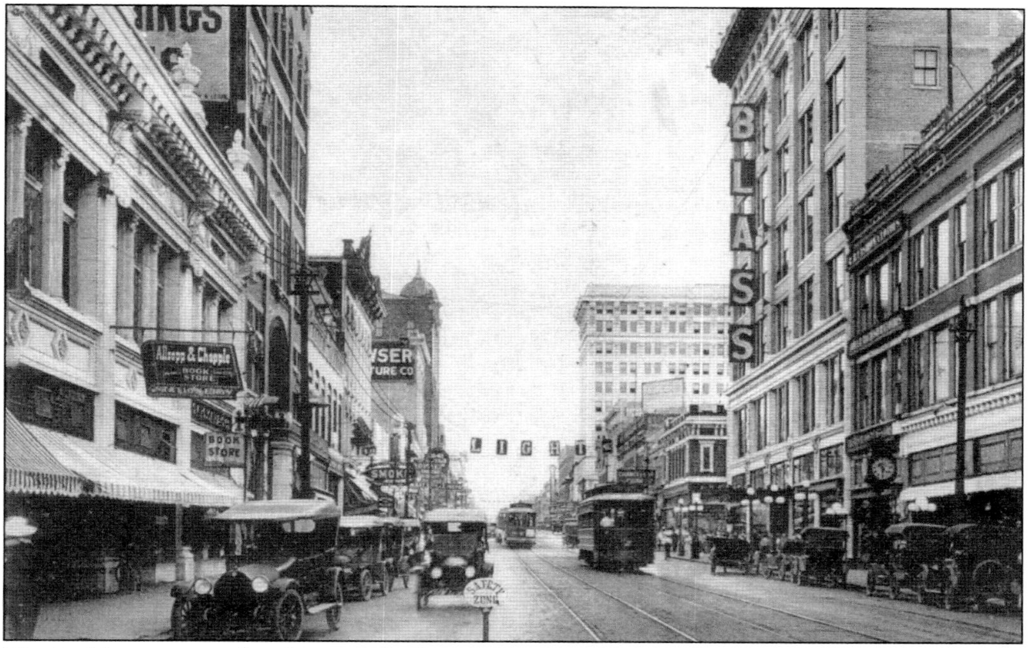

The building seen in the photograph above on page 19, next to the Gus Blass building, was lost to fire and replaced in the early 1900s by the Rose Building (left), which housed the Allsopp & Chapple Book Store. The ornate building, seen here in 1918, was designed by George Mann. It was constructed for office space, but for many years it housed retailers. It still stands today but has been vacant for a number of years.

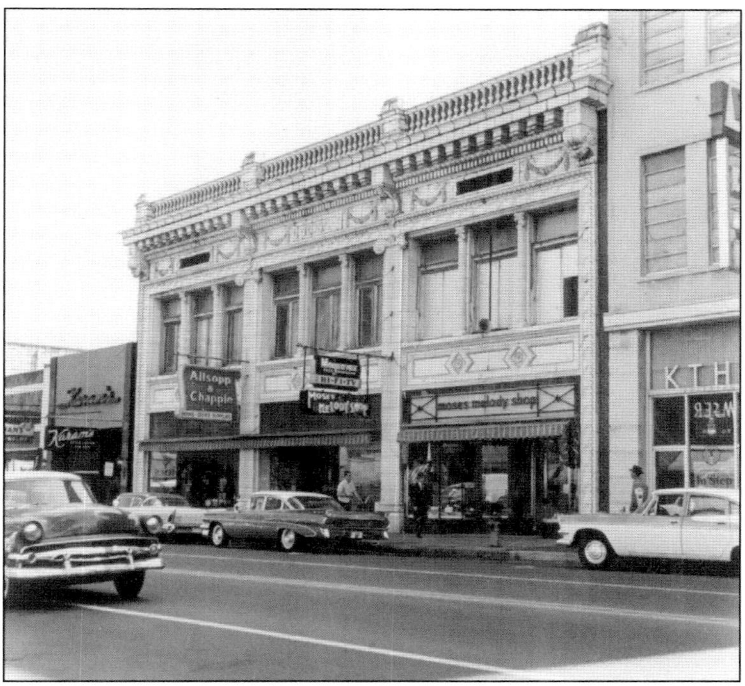

By the mid-1950s, the Allsopp & Chapple Book Store was still selling the printed word, and the Melody Shop had opened in an adjoining part of the Rose Building to sell records and music. Both represent independent businesses of a bygone era. (Courtesy of Arkansas History Commission.)

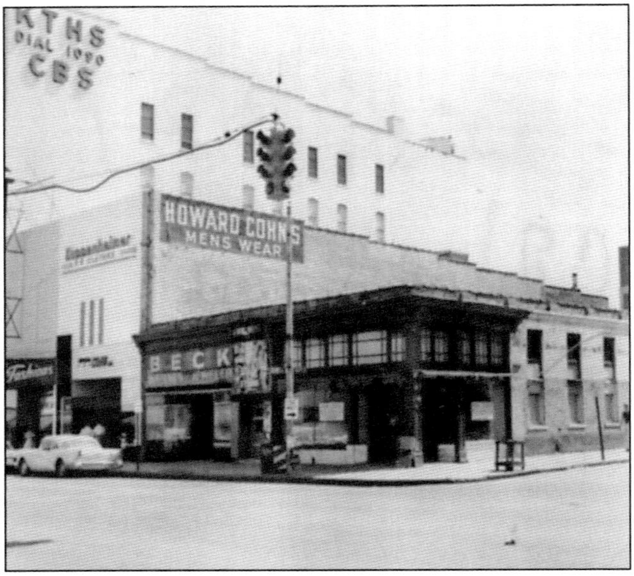

Seen here around 1957, just down from the Blass building, the southeast corner of Third and Main Streets was home to several older buildings with remodeled fronts. Beck's Jewelry store was next to Howard Cohn's Men's Wear, advertising the Kuppenheimer clothing line. The former Blass building housed, among other things, the operations of KTHS Radio and the local CBS television affiliate. Today, the entire corner, down to the former Blass building, is a parking lot.

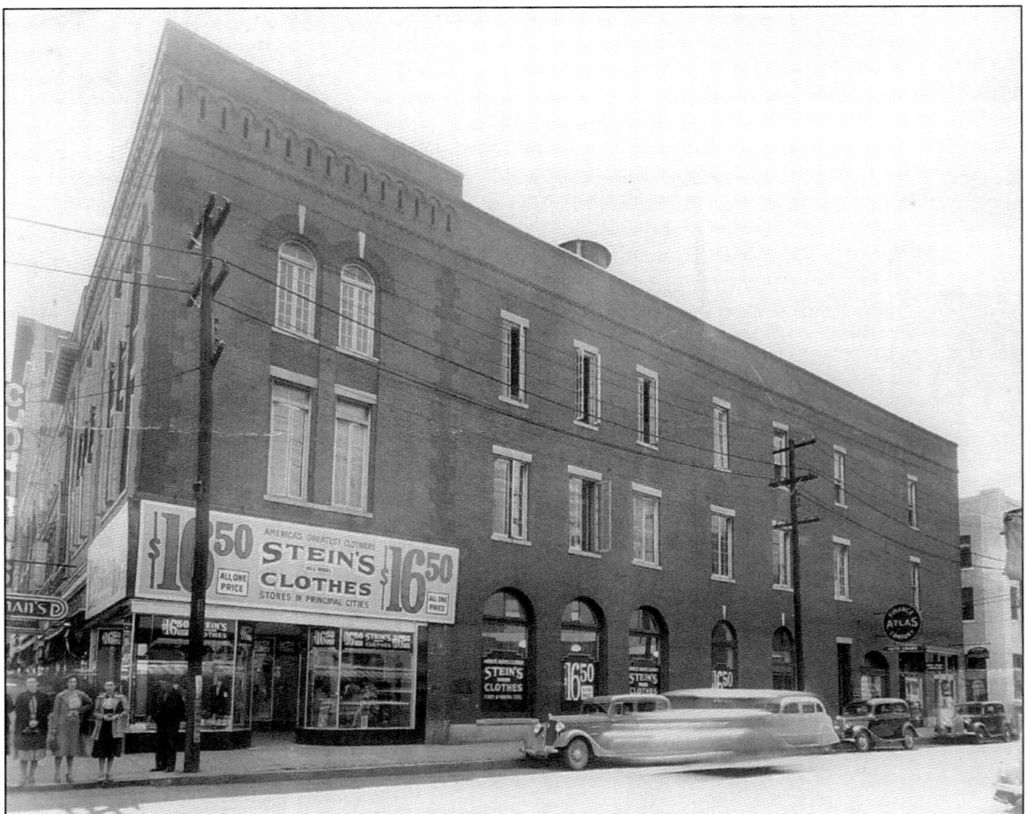

The Fulk building and the adjoining Taylor building arose in 1900 to replace another building lost to fire. For decades, the northwestern corner of the 300 block of Main Street was a retail anchor in the city, offering clothing and shoes at more modest prices than some of the retailers farther up the street. Seen here around 1935, Stein's Clothes advertised men's wool suits for just $16.50 each.

By the 1950s, Bell Brothers had taken the corner, sharing part of the Fulk building with Bauman's upscale men's shop and Green's Furs. The location later transitioned to house Bennett's Military Surplus and Outdoor Supplies for more than 30 years. Today, the century-old building is being remodeled as the offices of an advertising agency. For the first time in its history, the building will have no retail occupant.

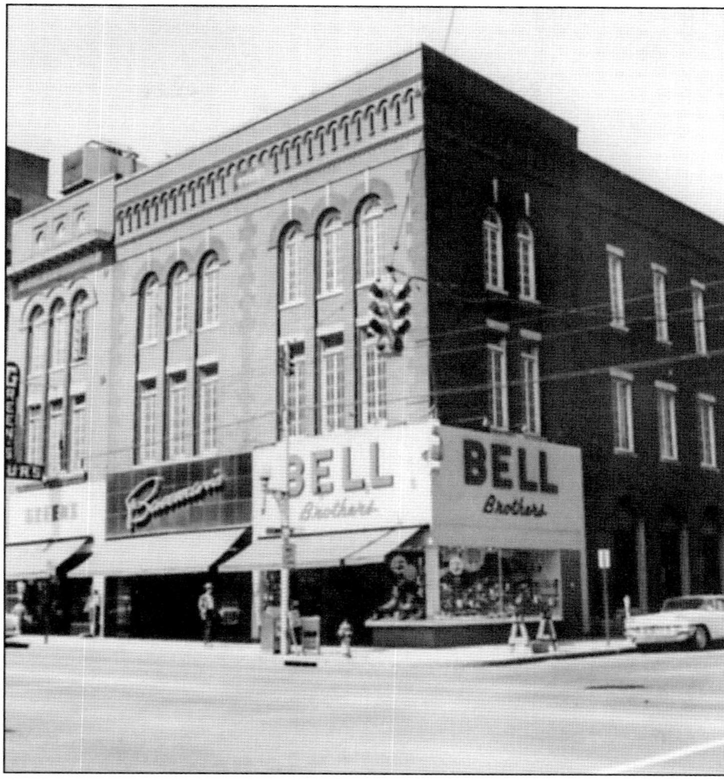

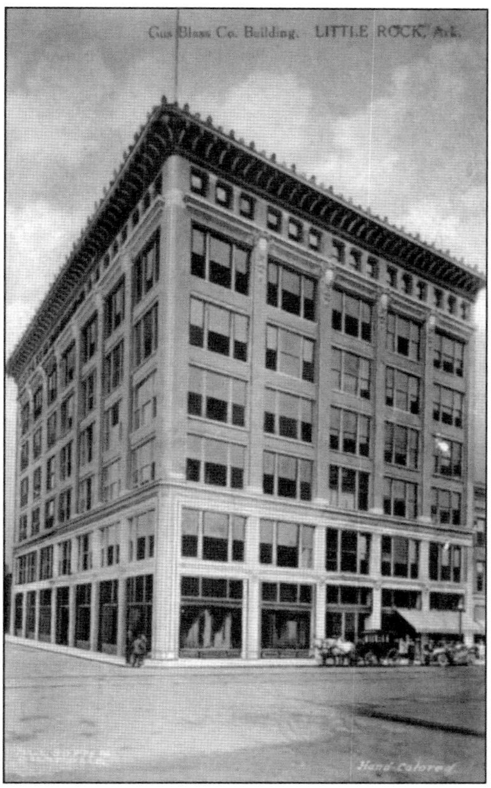

By 1916, Gus Blass had outgrown his store across Main Street, which had been built in 1900. Desiring to set the standard for competitors to beat, he erected a seven-story department store at 323 Main Street, on the southwest corner of Main and Fourth Streets. The store would become a retail icon for decades until being sold to the Dillard's Corporation in 1964; after a merger with Pfeifer's, the Blass location closed in 1972.

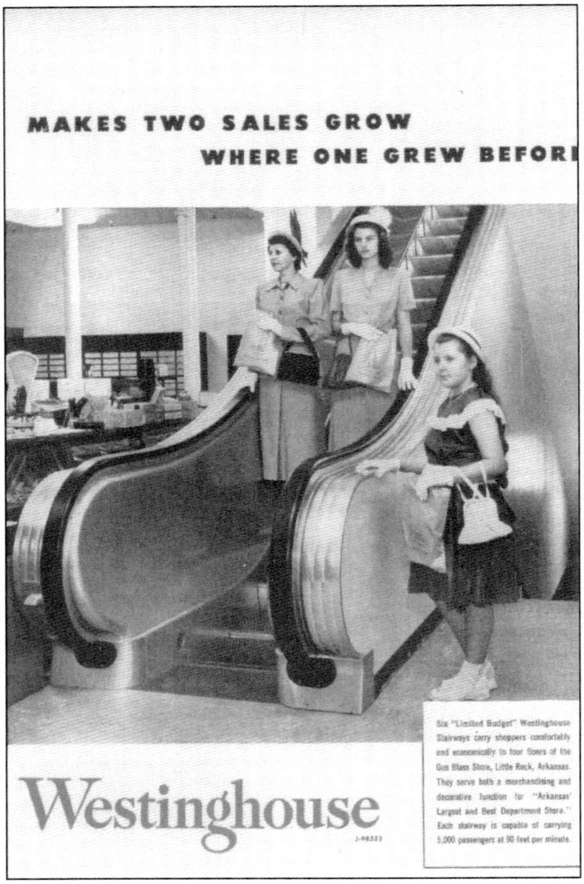

Chain Store magazine in 1950 featured Gus Blass's store in a Westinghouse advertisement showing three generations of women on an escalator the company built. Blass's store was the first in Arkansas to have this feature, just as it had been the first major store to add air-conditioning, in the 1940s. The building survives and is today being renovated into apartments and offices; most retail enterprises are now located farther west.

The northeast corner of Main Street is anchored by the Worthen Bank, a historic but currently threatened landmark. W.B. Worthen founded his bank in 1877 and moved to the new headquarters, designed by George Mann, in 1928. The building, faced in Carthage marble, is today home to the ABC television affiliate. City leaders are considering tearing down the historic building to make way for a planned technology park.

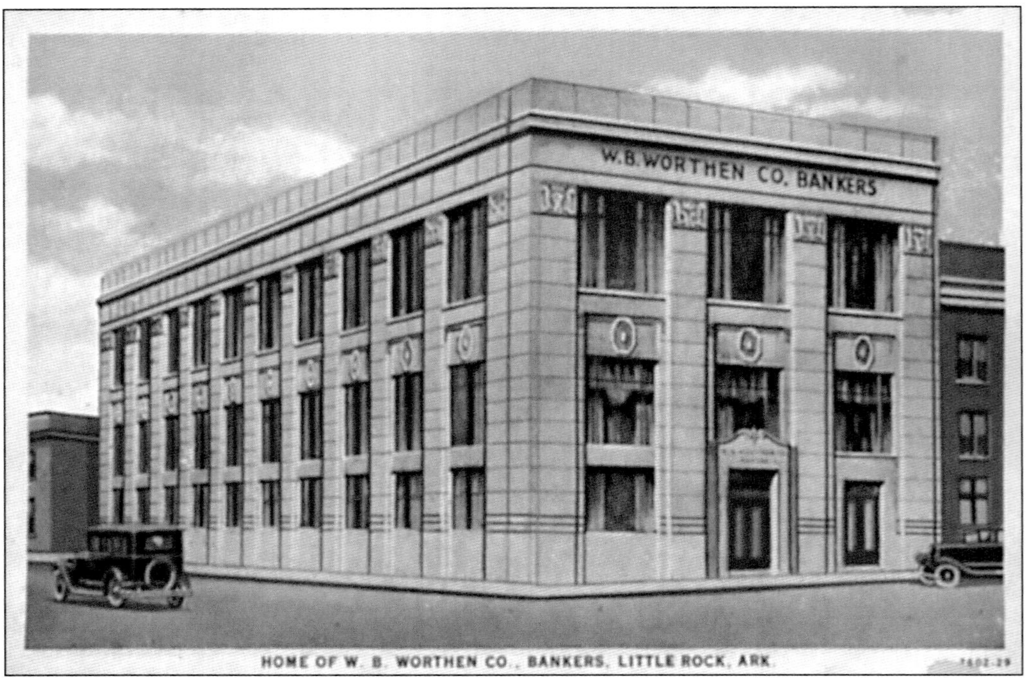

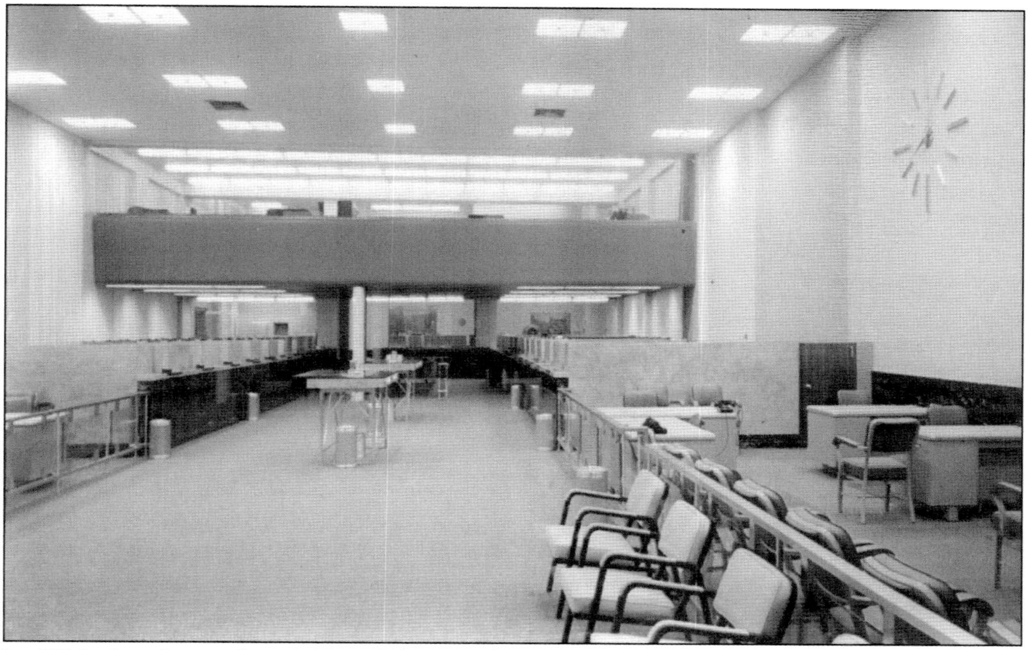

In 1956, the ultramodern lobby of the Worthen Bank is shown on a postcard proclaiming a completely remodeled headquarters in the 79th year of the bank, formed in 1877. The use of the building by KATV Channel 7 did away with the remodeled look of the 1960s.

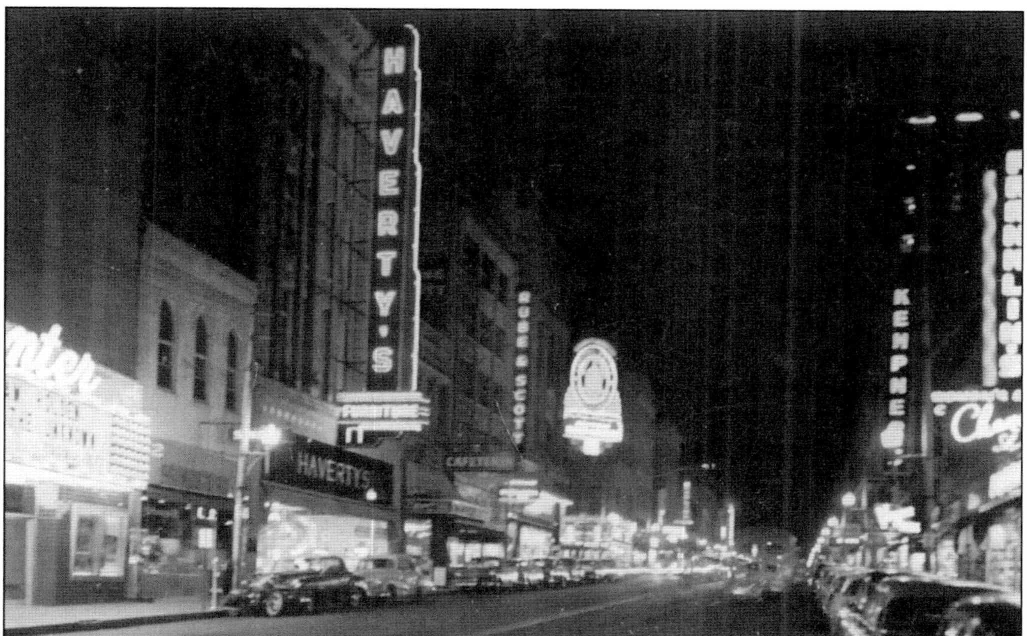

In 1956, neon lights up Main Street, inviting late-night shoppers, especially on Fridays when paychecks were typically distributed. The Center Theater (left) was located on the middle of the east side of the 400 block. Also visible are the Singer Sewing Machine store, Haverty's Furniture, Moore's Cafeteria, and Rube and Scott Men's Wear.

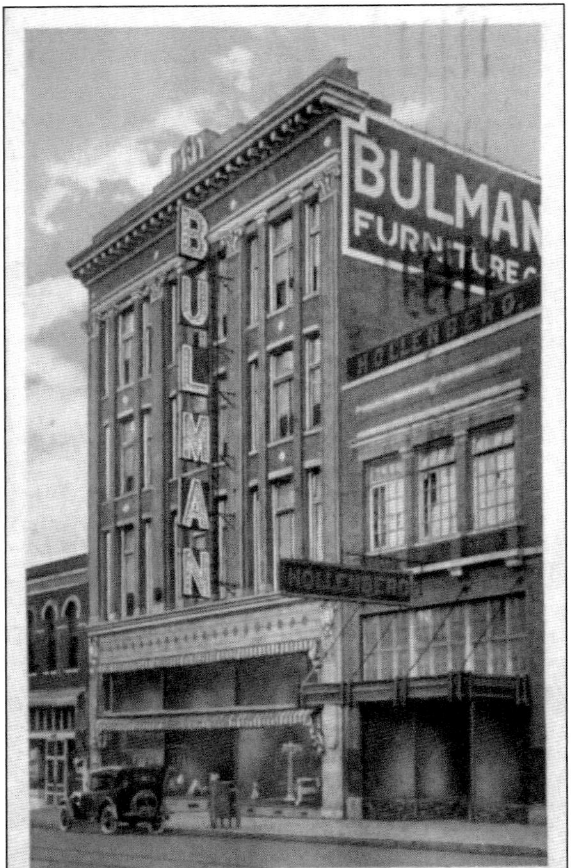

BULMAN FURNITURE CO., 411-413 MAIN ST., LITTLE ROCK, ARK.

Bulman's Furniture at 411–413 Main Street proclaimed in a 1925 advertisement, "Your credit is good at Bulman's, The South's Largest Complete Home Furnishers. We sell everything for the Home, from the Cheapest that's good to the best that's made." The Bulman's store later became Haverty's Furniture (see page 25). The address today is vacant, as is the space of the former Center Theater, both awaiting redevelopment.

Just south of the Center Theater, at 415 Main Street, was Mrs. Adkin's Cafeteria, one of several such eateries serving downtown at the time. The back of this advertising postcard touts, "All women cooks, with personal supervision by Mrs. Adkins," located "in the heart of the downtown shopping district." The building still stands, housing a law firm. The cafeteria concept is now long gone from Main Street.

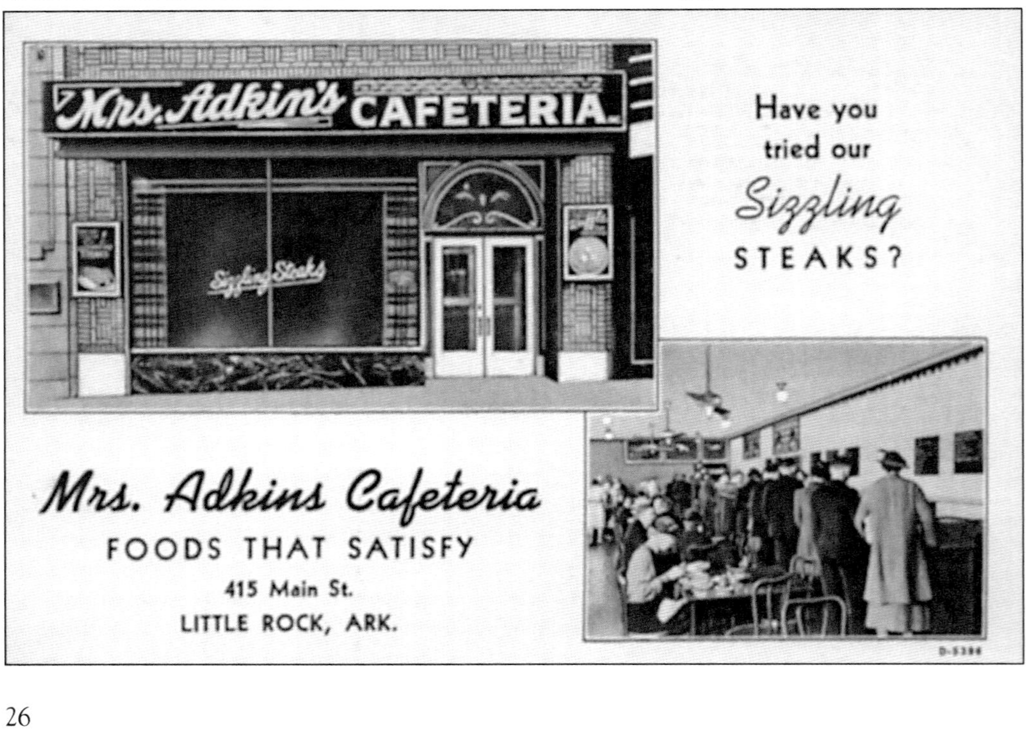

Erected in 1892 at the southeast corner of Main Street and Fifth Street (today Capitol Avenue), the Masonic temple was the city's tallest commercial building. While the Grand Masonic Lodge used a portion of the seven-story building, other floors housed a variety of offices. A drawback to keeping the upper floors rented was the unreliability of the building's steam-powered elevator. This 1905 postcard includes a sign promoting modern "Electric Dental Parlors."

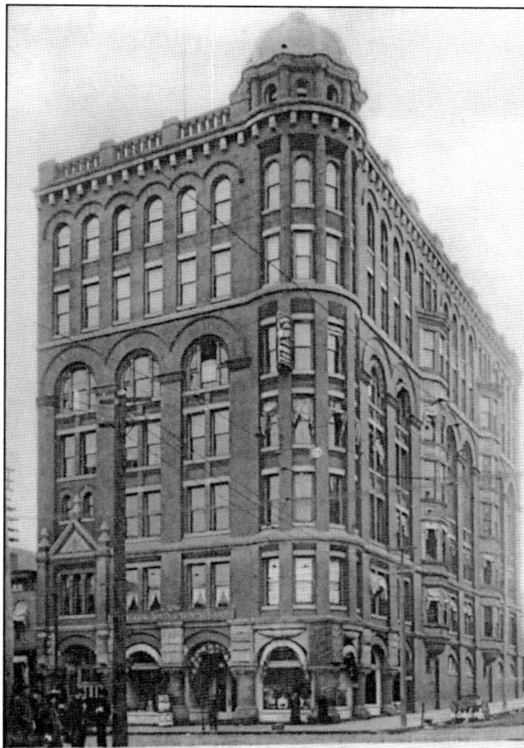

Masonic Temple, Little Rock, Ark.

This 1908 photograph, taken from the upper floor of the Masonic temple building, looks south down Main Street over the end of the commercial district into what is today's Quapaw Quarter of Victorian-era homes. To the right is the back of St. Andrew's Cathedral, the steeple of which was the only man-made structure in the city taller than the Masonic temple. Very little in this expansive view remains today.

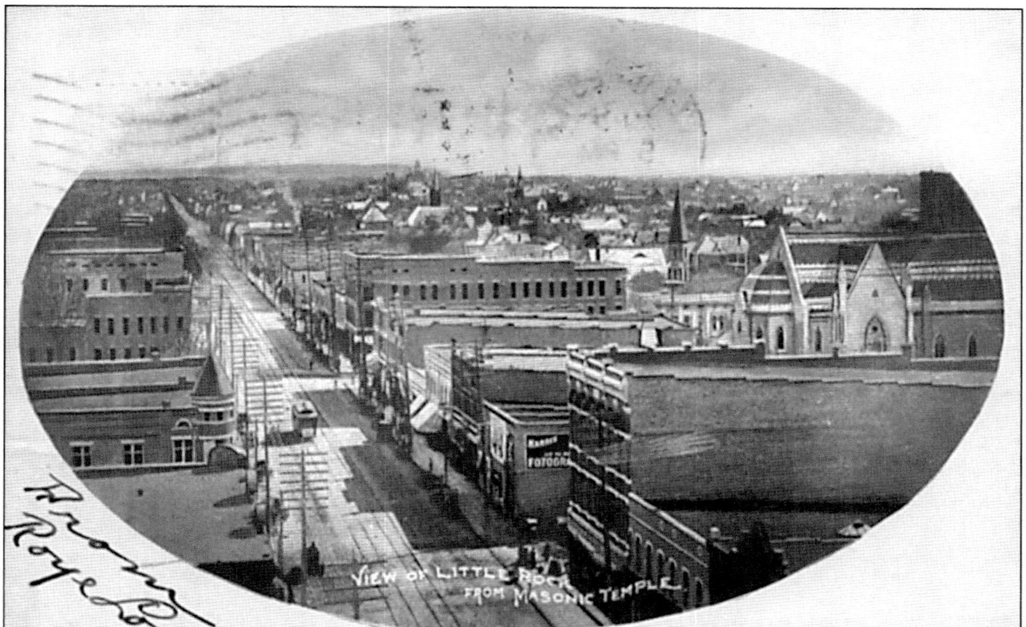

View of Little Rock, Arkansas, from the Masonic Temple.

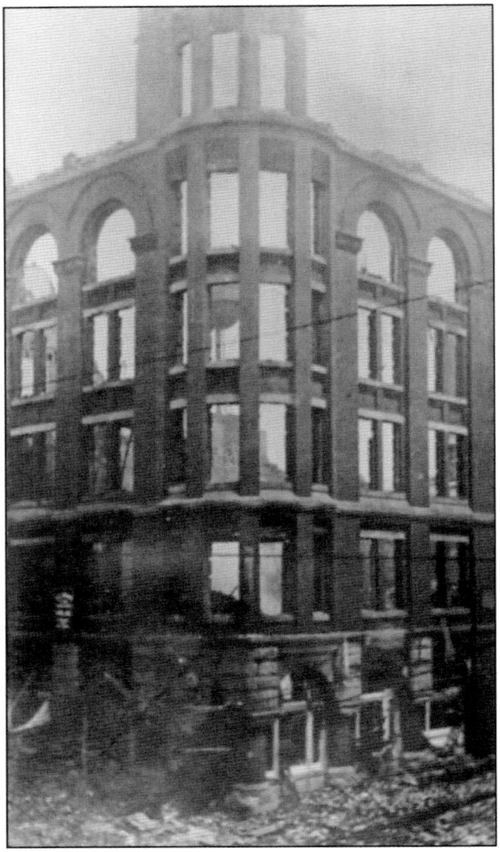

The Masonic temple was destroyed by fire in 1919. Its wooden interior fueled an inferno that engulfed the handsome building. (Courtesy of Arkansas History Commission.)

The Exchange Bank building anchored the southeast corner at 423 Main Street, seen here in 1955. Designed by Charles L. Thompson, the 1921 structure replaced the Masonic temple, which was lost in a 1919 fire. The bank failed in the Great Depression, but the building survived. Today, the vacant structure is threatened with demolition to make way for a technology park, possibly sharing the fate of the former Worthen Bank at the other end of the same block.

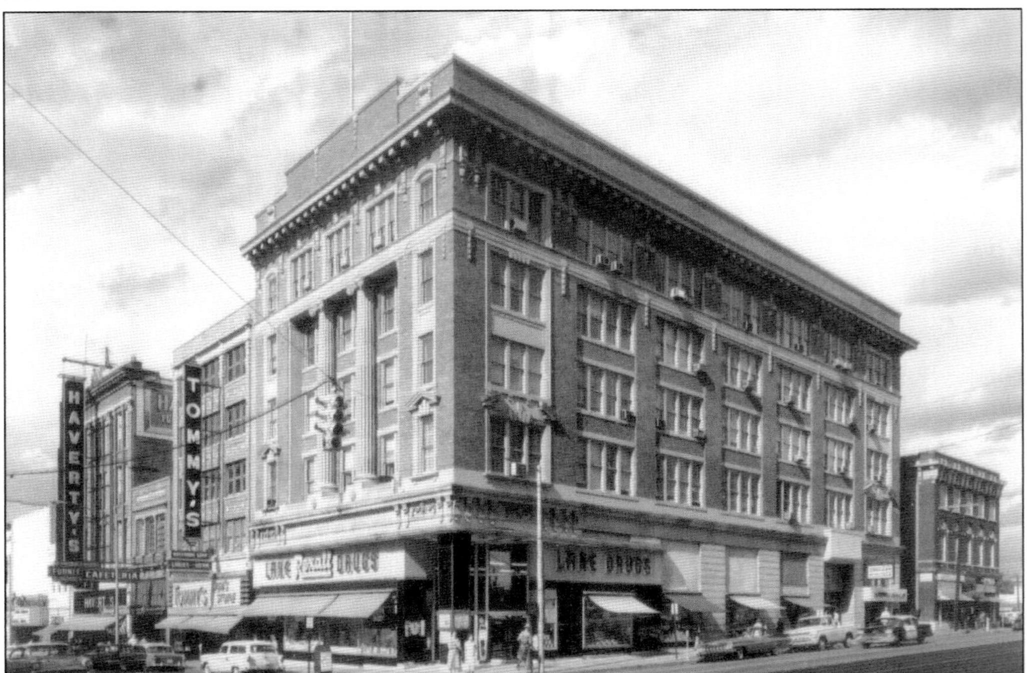

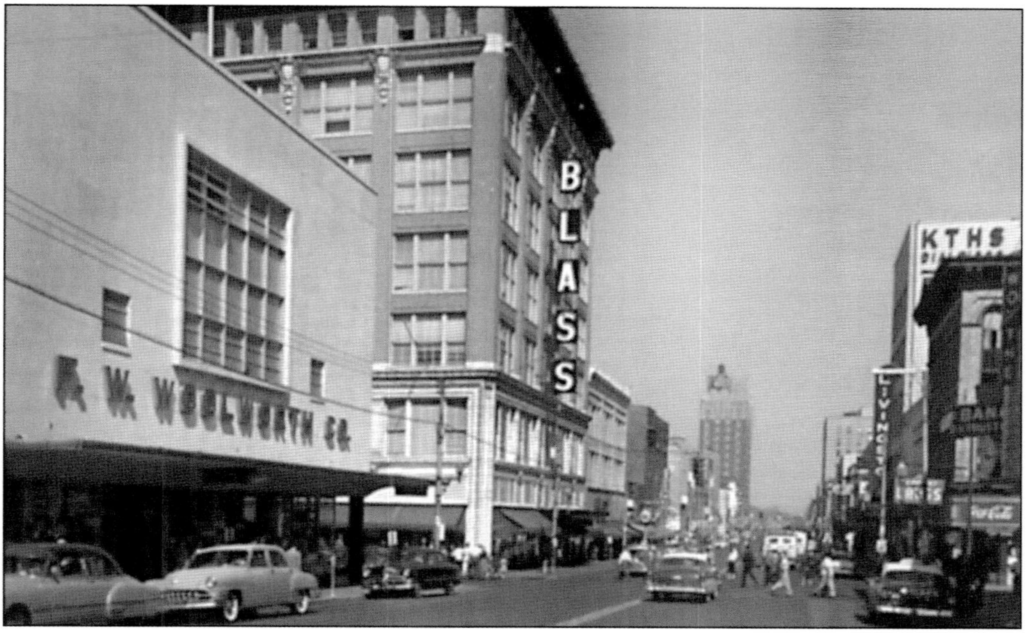

The northwest corner of the 400 block of Main Street was anchored by F.W. Woolworth's, seen here in the mid-1950s. An American main-street presence across the nation for decades, Woolworth's was the site in Little Rock of a civil rights sit-in by 50 Philander Smith College students in 1960. The scene of that protest was lost, along with the store, when the entire block was razed in 2009 for yet another parking lot.

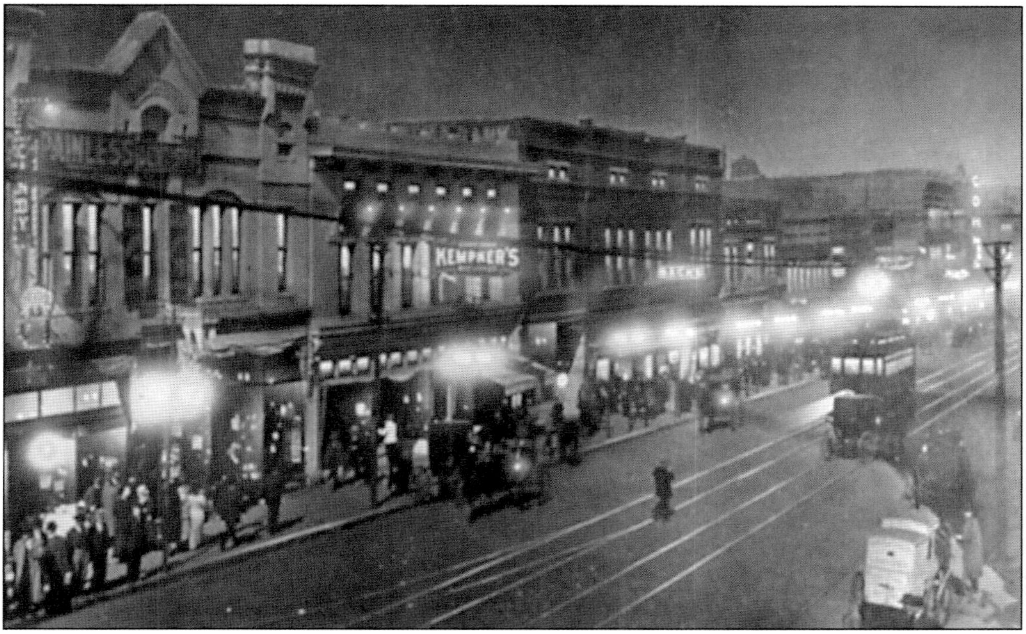

This 1915 photograph, taken in daylight, was altered by the printer to appear as a nighttime view. Looking north up the western side of the 400 block of Main Street, the original Kempner's store is seen before it burned down in 1916. The business was quickly rebuilt and served the city for decades. The entire block was razed a few years ago and today is the site of a massive parking lot between Capitol Avenue and Fourth Street.

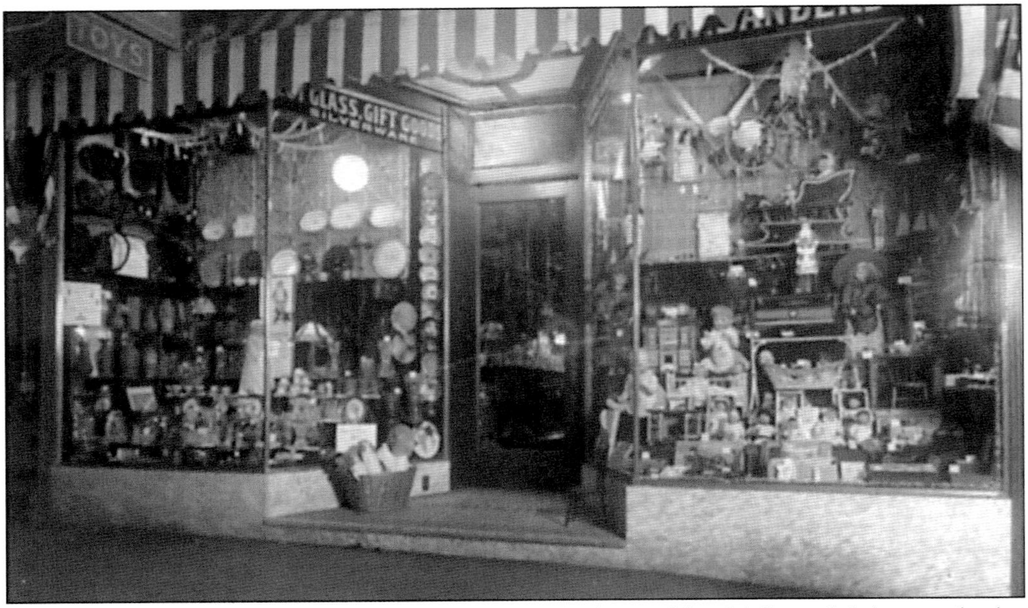

F.W. Sanders gift and toy store at 408 Main Street had a wealth of dolls and dishes on display in 1910. Sander's merchandising methods followed a trend of using smaller doors and displaying merchandise in the windows, thereby appealing to "window shoppers" who, if they stopped to look, would be more likely to come in and buy. (Courtesy of Butler Center for Arkansas Studies.)

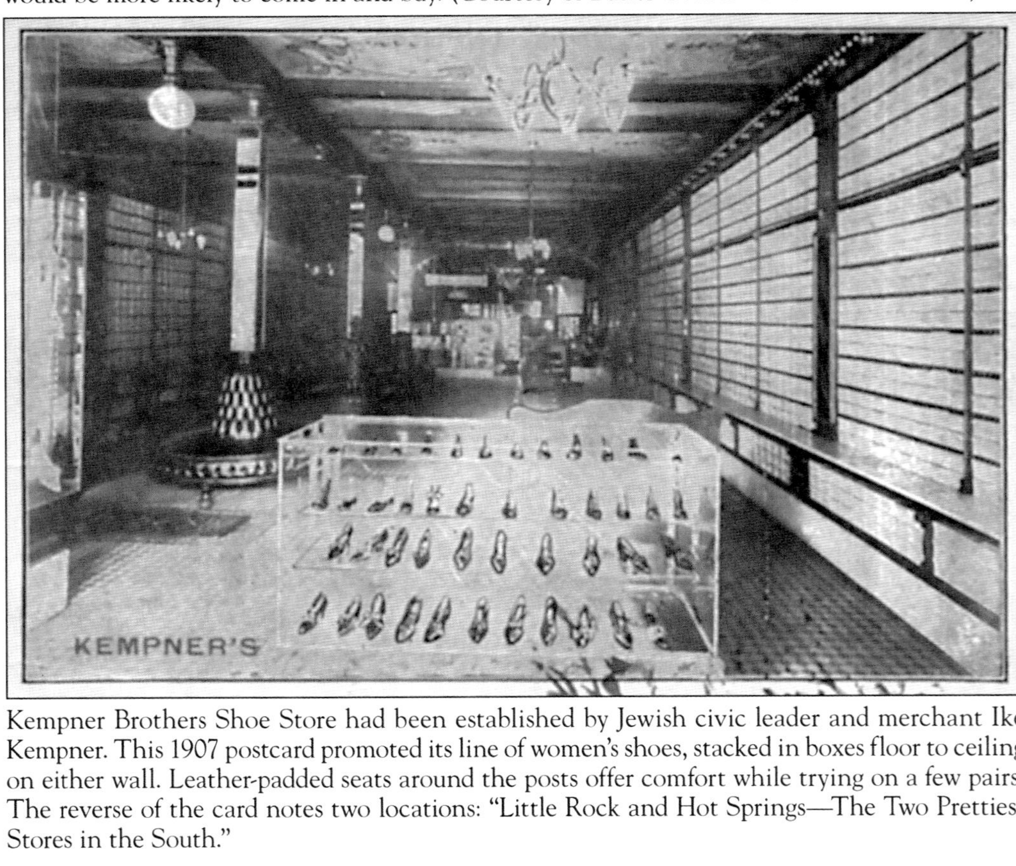

Kempner Brothers Shoe Store had been established by Jewish civic leader and merchant Ike Kempner. This 1907 postcard promoted its line of women's shoes, stacked in boxes floor to ceiling on either wall. Leather-padded seats around the posts offer comfort while trying on a few pairs. The reverse of the card notes two locations: "Little Rock and Hot Springs—The Two Prettiest Stores in the South."

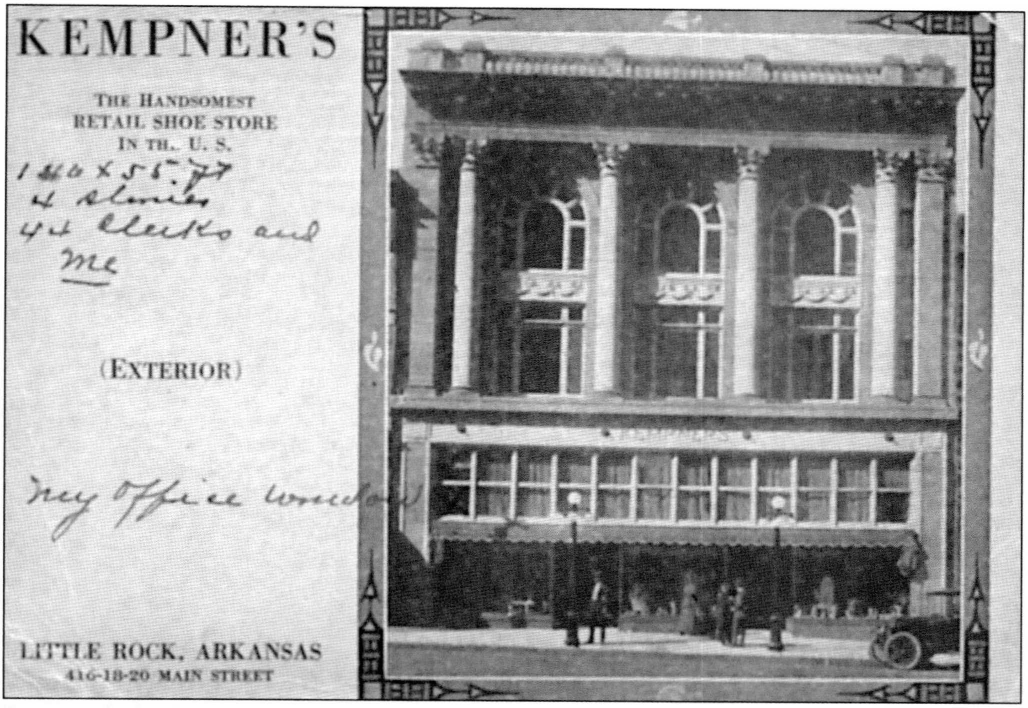

Fire struck the first Kempner Shoe Store in 1916, but a new and grander building opened the following year. "Dr. HJT" sent this card to Missouri, noting that the store had "146 x 55 feet, 4 stories, 44 clerks and Me." He marked his office window with an "X" (lower left) and on the back noted, "At last I've landed in Little Rock. I am with this store as their foot specialist. I have a swell office in the finest shoe store in the U.S."

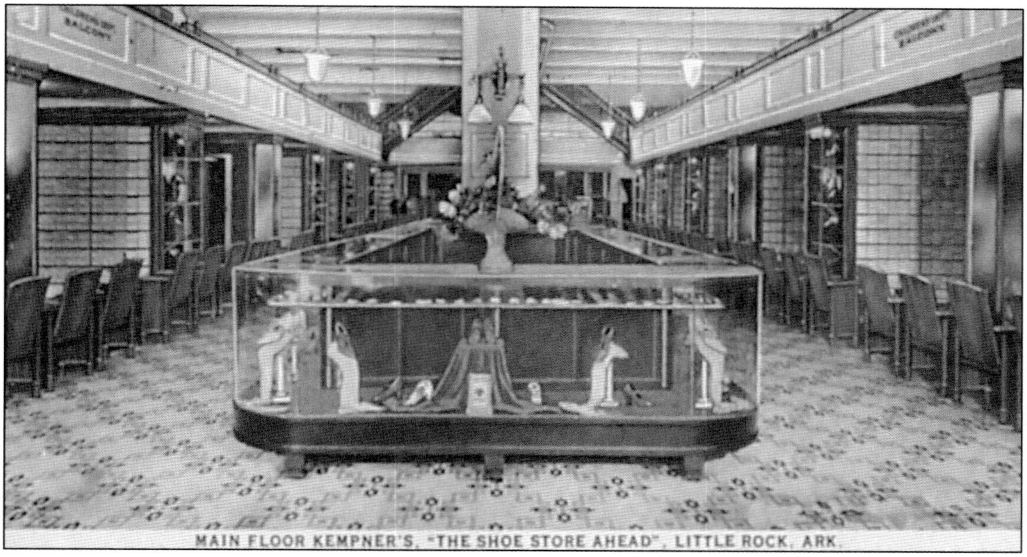

After their first store burned down in 1916, the Kempner brothers rebuilt their store in much more upscale fashion. This 1927 promotional postcard reads, "Kempner's is known by reputation throughout the whole country as the most up-to-date and most beautiful shoe store in the South." The card, mailed to a prospective customer in Flippin, Arkansas, went on to promote the store's mail-order business.

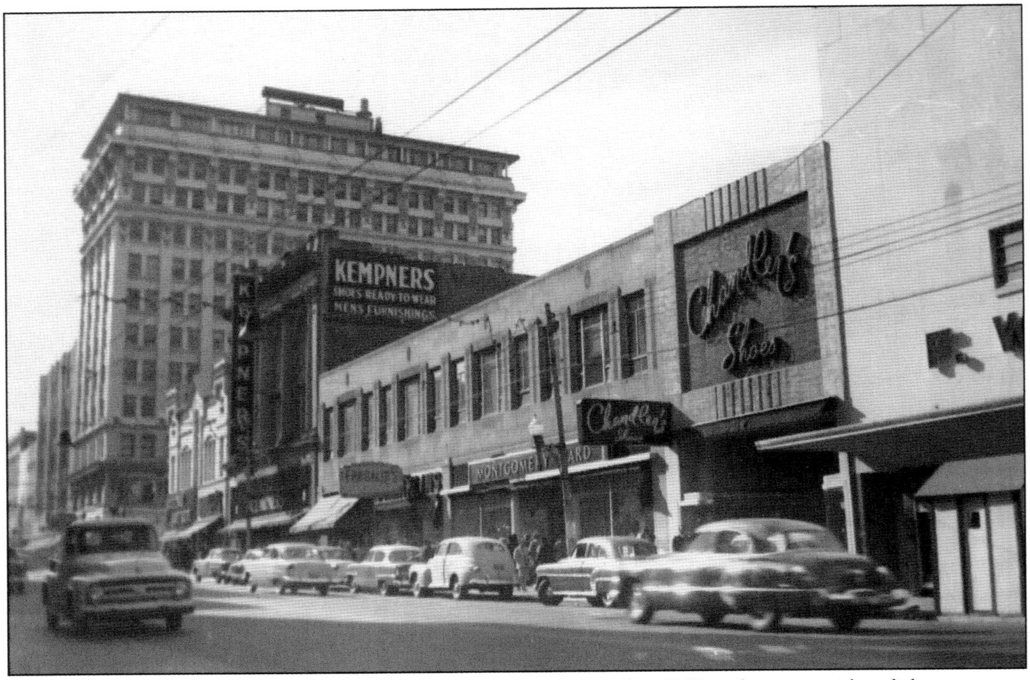

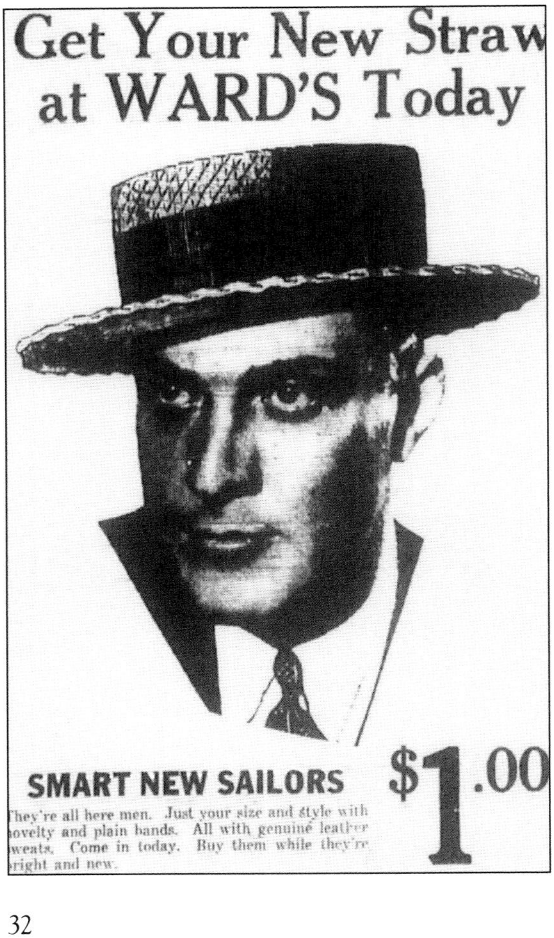

By the 1950s, the west side of the 400 block of Main Street found Kempner's competing for customers with Montgomery Ward and Chandler's Shoes. Franklin Paint & Wallpaper stood between Kempner's and Wards. F.W. Woolworth's is seen to the far right. The once-thriving center of commerce is a block-long parking lot today.

During the Depression, stores in downtown Little Rock had to offer attractive sales to lure shoppers. In a 1933 newspaper advertisement, Montgomery Ward promised "Smart New Sailors," or men's straw hats, for $1—"all with genuine leather sweats." Today, Montgomery Ward has disappeared into retail history, and the Little Rock block it once occupied is a parking lot.

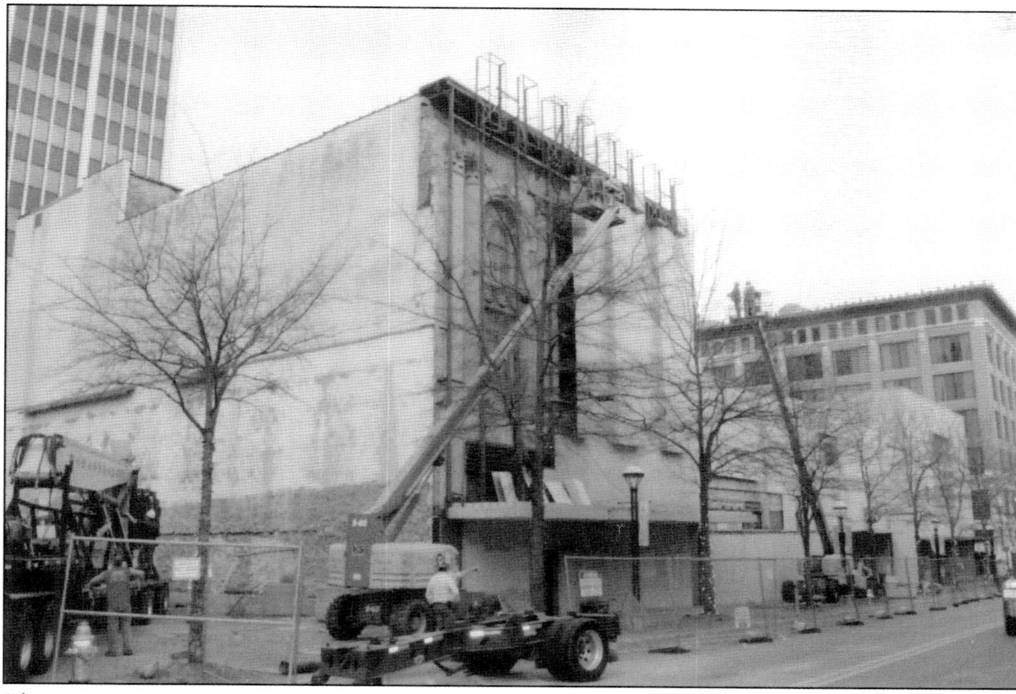

The "new" Kempner's store, rising from the ashes of its 1916 predecessor, had been shuttered for years when workmen began to remove the 1960s facade that had obscured its distinctive architecture. Sadly, the work in 2009 was not to restore a symbol of Little Rock's retailing heritage but to begin to raze the entire block, leaving behind a parking lot. (Photograph by Ray Hanley.)

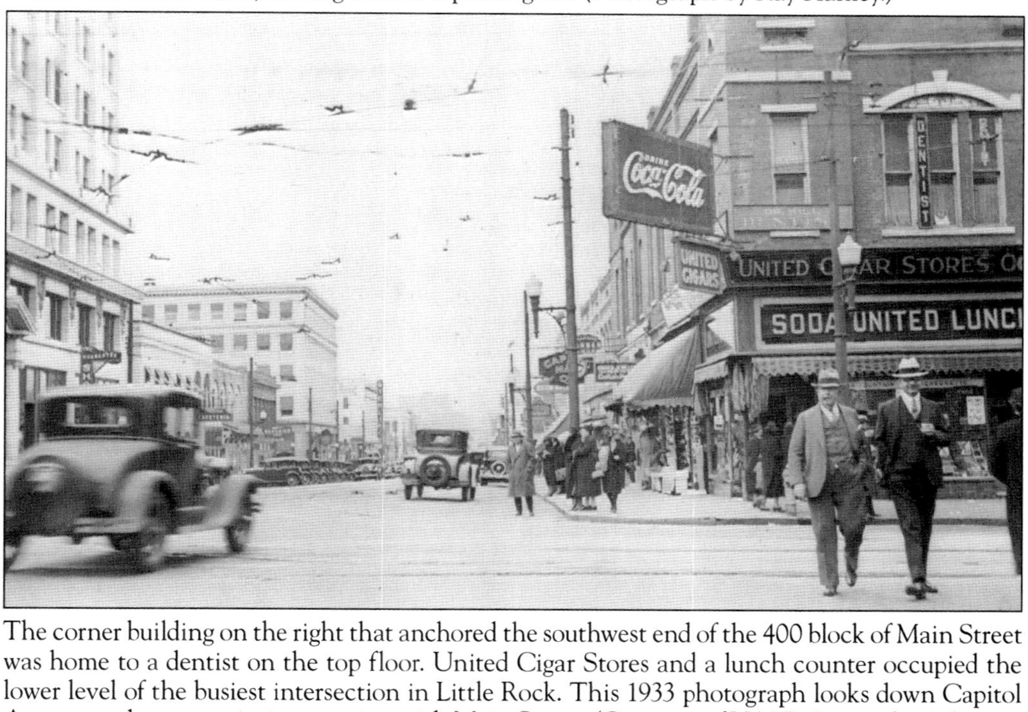

The corner building on the right that anchored the southwest end of the 400 block of Main Street was home to a dentist on the top floor. United Cigar Stores and a lunch counter occupied the lower level of the busiest intersection in Little Rock. This 1933 photograph looks down Capitol Avenue to the west at its intersection with Main Street. (Courtesy of UALR Center for Arkansas History & Culture.)

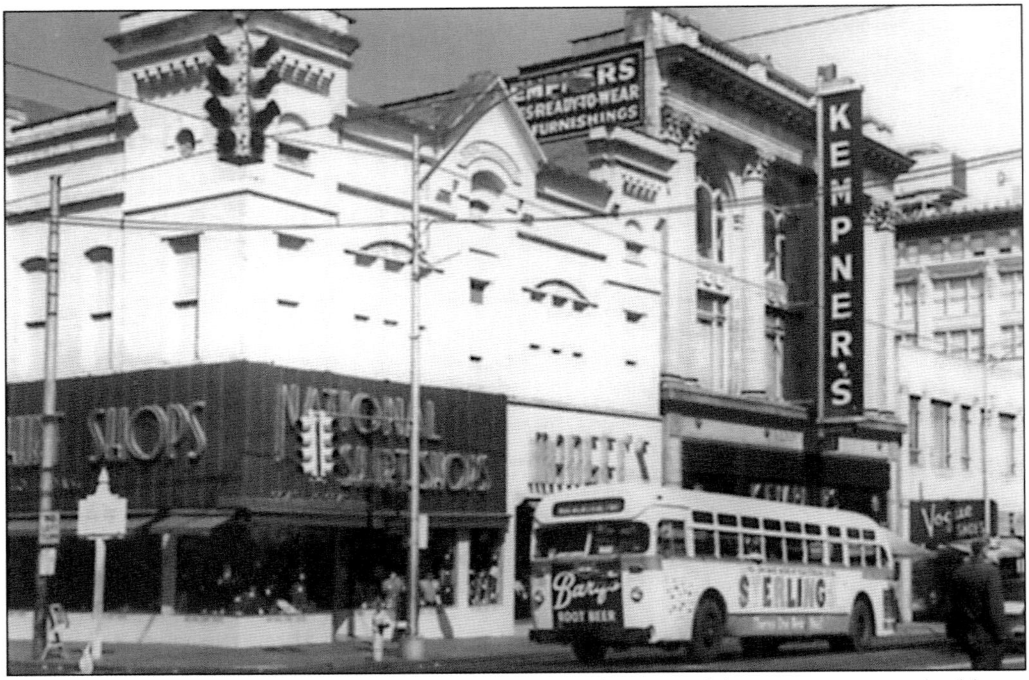

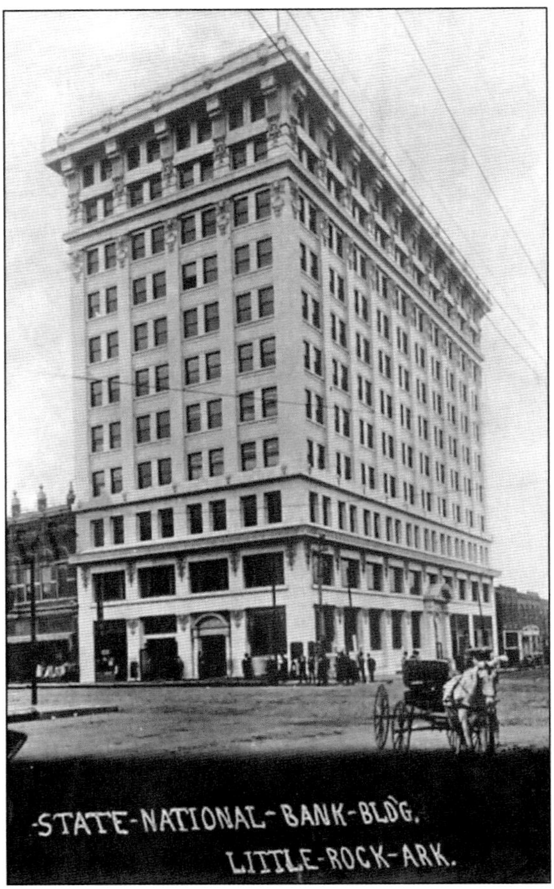

The turn-of-the-century corner building shown in the previous 1933 photograph is seen here around 1960, still intact, but now home to National Shirt Shops. The second-floor windows had been closed and painted over with the same white paint applied to the rest of the building. In the late 1970s, the building was razed and replaced by a McDonald's. Today, the entire block is a parking lot. (Courtesy of UALR Center for Arkansas History & Culture.)

The State National Bank building, seen here in 1911, was designed by architect George Mann. It was built in 1909 at 501 Main Street at its intersection with Fifth Street. The bank was gone by the 1930s, and the structure became the Boyle Building, housing retailers and offices. A rare success story in preservation, the structure today is being converted into an upscale Aloft Hotel.

Two

MAIN STREET FROM CAPITOL AVENUE SOUTH

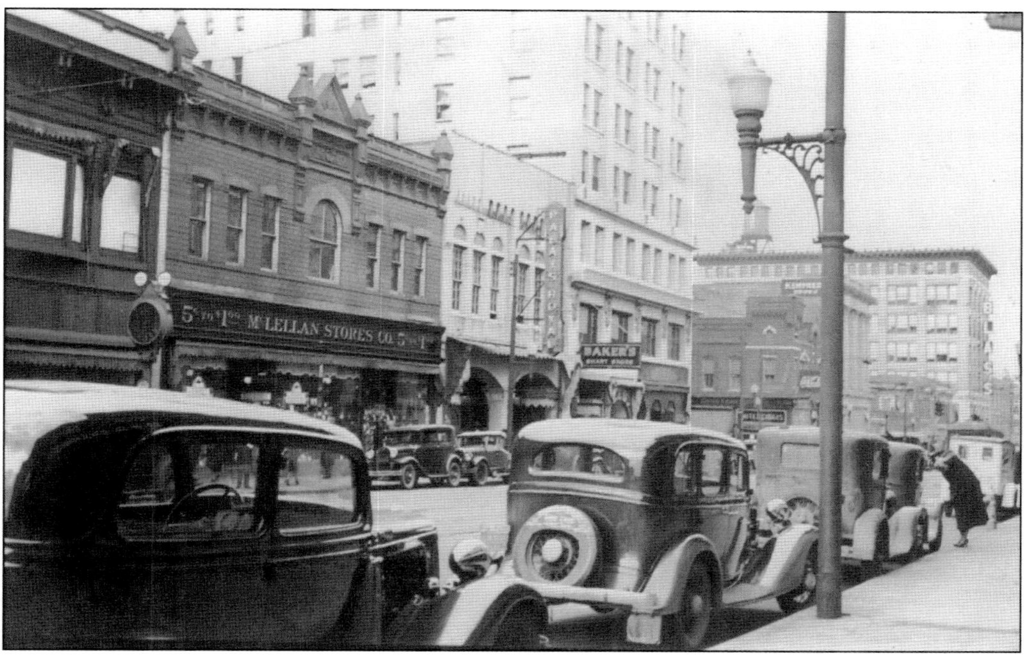

Main Street south of Capitol Avenue developed slowly and with small-scale retailers from World War I into the 1940s. In this 1933 photograph of the west side of Main Street's 500 block are, from left to right, the Gans Building, McLellan Stores ("5 cents to $1.00"), Palais Royale Women's Wear and Millinery, and Baker's Shoes, which was a footwear icon on Main Street for decades. (Courtesy of UALR Center for Arkansas History & Culture.)

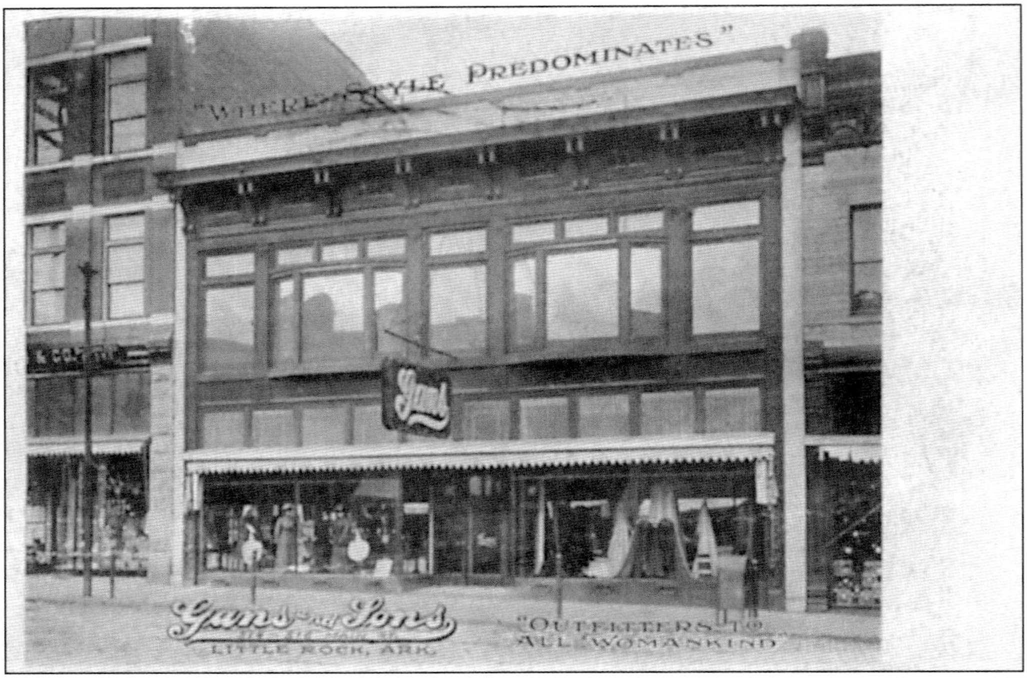

This 1910 photograph shows the impressive storefront of Gans and Sons, "Outfitters to All Womankind," which did business at 514–516 Main Street, three doors down from the State National Bank. Gans would fade away into retail history, but the building, with its architectural features removed or covered over, would survive to serve the adjoining Pfiefer's Department Store.

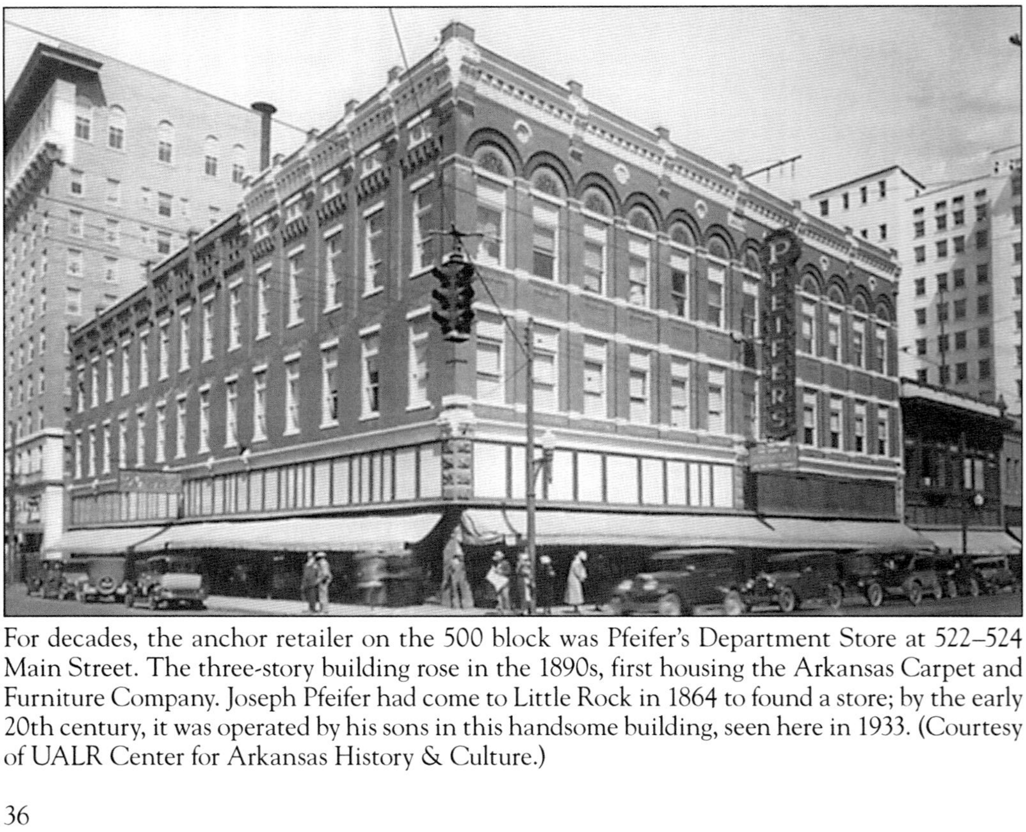

For decades, the anchor retailer on the 500 block was Pfeifer's Department Store at 522–524 Main Street. The three-story building rose in the 1890s, first housing the Arkansas Carpet and Furniture Company. Joseph Pfeifer had come to Little Rock in 1864 to found a store; by the early 20th century, it was operated by his sons in this handsome building, seen here in 1933. (Courtesy of UALR Center for Arkansas History & Culture.)

Like other retailers during the Great Depression, Pfeifer's worked hard to lure shoppers into the Main Street store. The big sale advertised in the summer of 1933 was for suits at $14.95; shirts were on sale for 29¢ each or four for $1. Ties could be had for 44¢, and men's pajamas cost only 89¢. Surviving the Depression, the store flourished for many years until being sold to Dillard's in 1963.

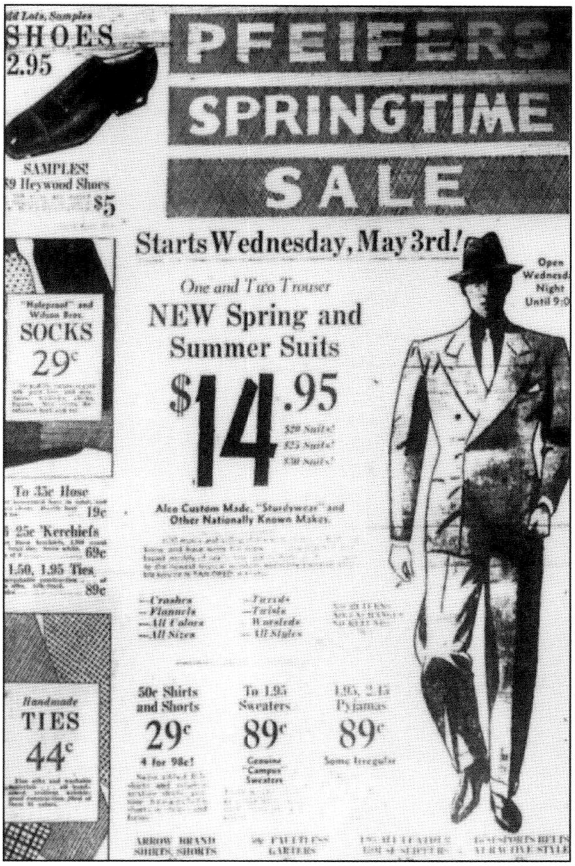

Closed up and under threat of becoming yet another parking lot, the historic Pfeifer Building was rescued. In 2014, a major renovation was in process. With plans to become loft apartments, with office or dining space on the street level, the effort is one of several positive rehabilitation projects on Main Street made possible by private investors with a vision of life returning to downtown. (Photograph by the author.)

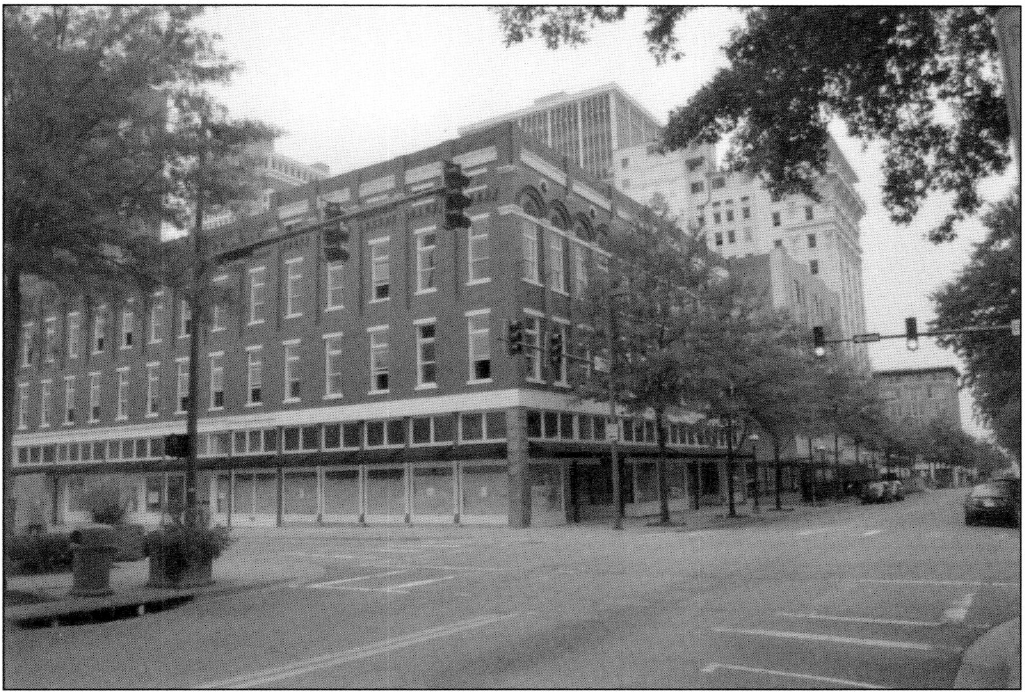

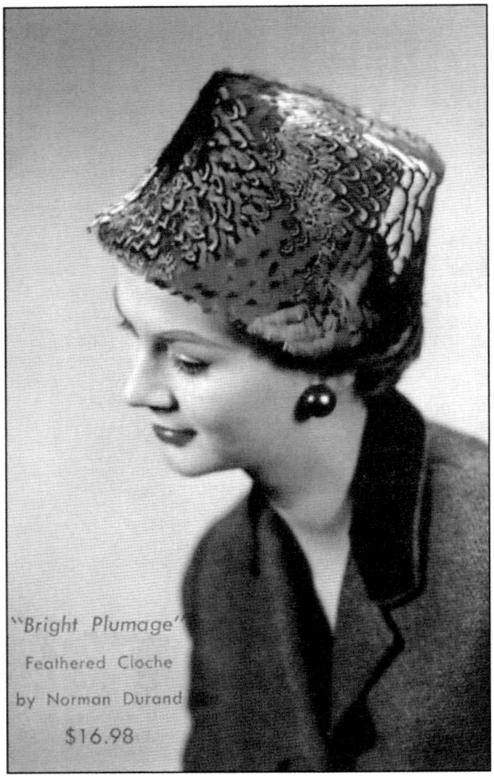

In 1958, the millinery buyer at Pfeifer's announced, "The New Fall Hats from New York are Breathtaking." A few years later, Pfeifer's was sold to Dillard's and then merged with Blass Department Store. At some point, the building's facade was covered with metal siding. After the store closed, the building stood vacant for a number of years. Today, it is being restored to house apartments as the memories of its iconic retail heritage fade.

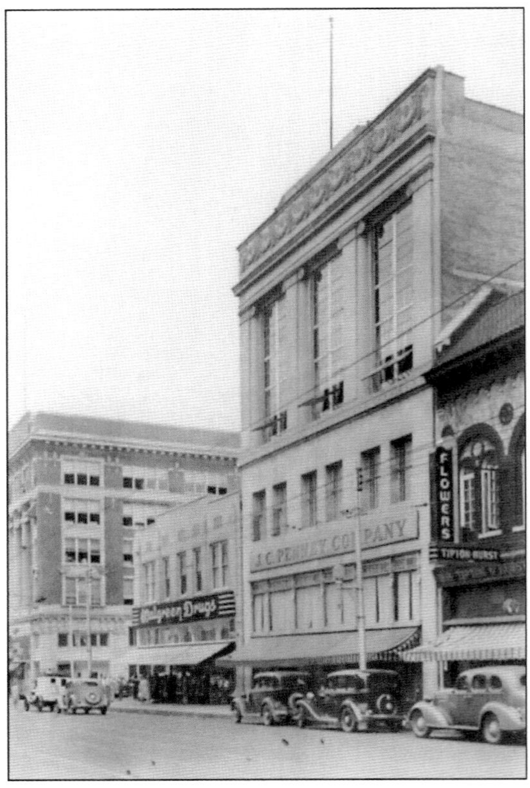

In 1940, the 500 block of Main Street was anchored on the east by Walgreen Drugs, next to the J.C. Penney building and the ornately designed Tipton & Hurst florist shop. The entire block was remade in the 1980s, when the disparate buildings were connected with a new facade to form a downtown mall. The mall failed, and the block-long complex is now home to state and private offices. (Courtesy of Butler Center for Arkansas Studies.)

Across the street from J.C. Penney was Arkansas's best-known retailer until the rise of Wal-Mart. Mark M. Cohn had founded his first store in the 1870s on the 100 block of Main Street, later moving it to the 300 block. In 1940, the Cohn family broke ground for a new flagship MM Cohn store adjacent to the Boyle Building on the site of what had been the Palais Royale and McClellan's stores.

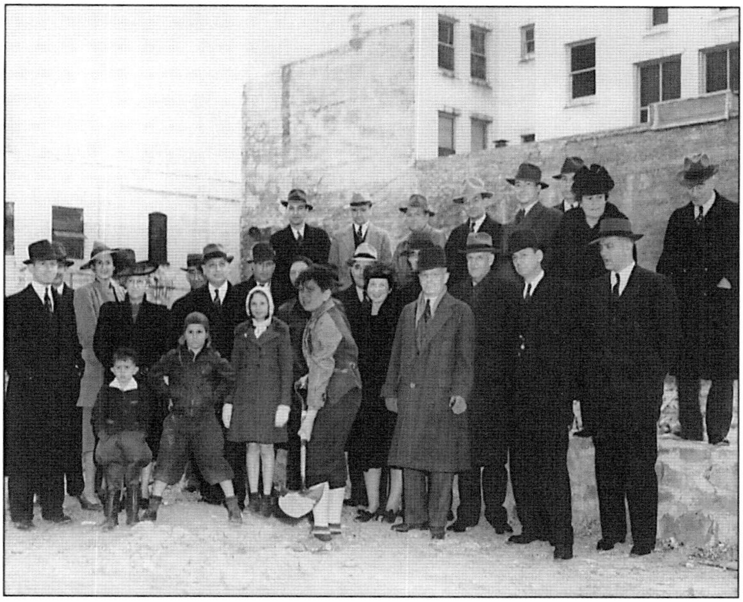

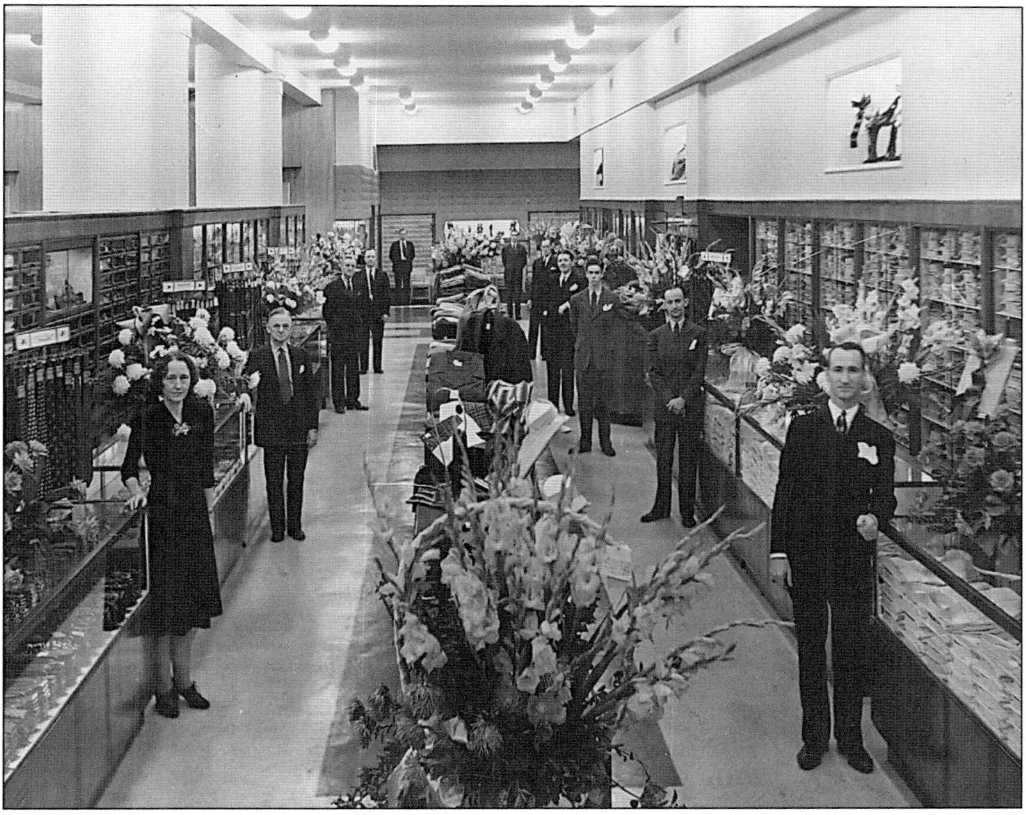

Opening day at the 75,000-square-foot MM Cohn's store found an impeccably dressed staff ready to assist new customers. Business flourished; the store eventually had a dozen locations and took over five floors of the adjacent Boyle Building in 1960. The Dunlap Company bought MM Cohn's in 1989 but operated under its name. Today, the store is vacant, with retail fleeing Main Street. The long-shuttered building is being renovated for loft apartments.

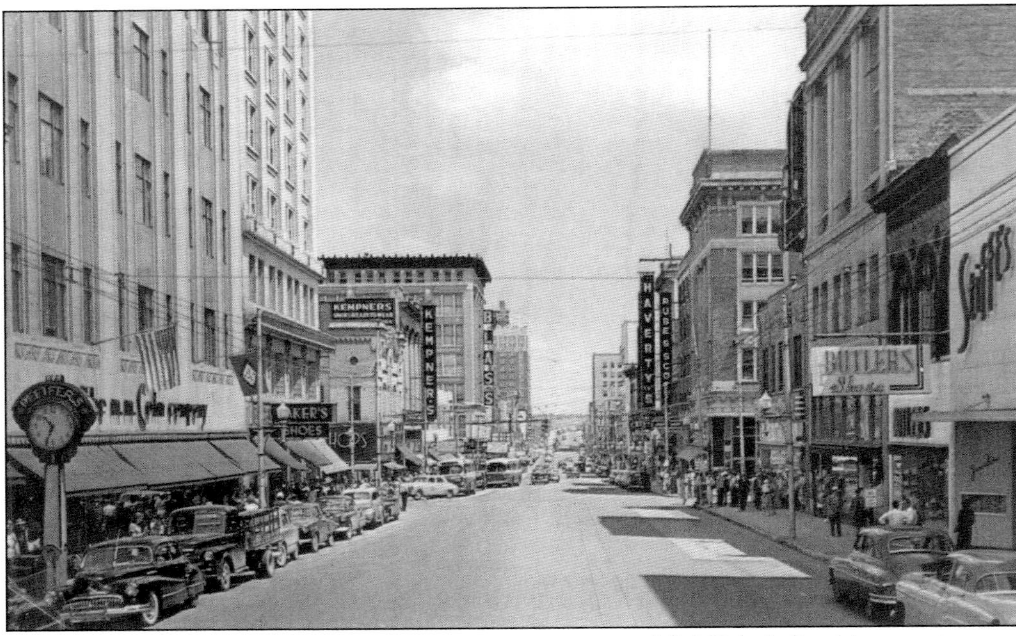

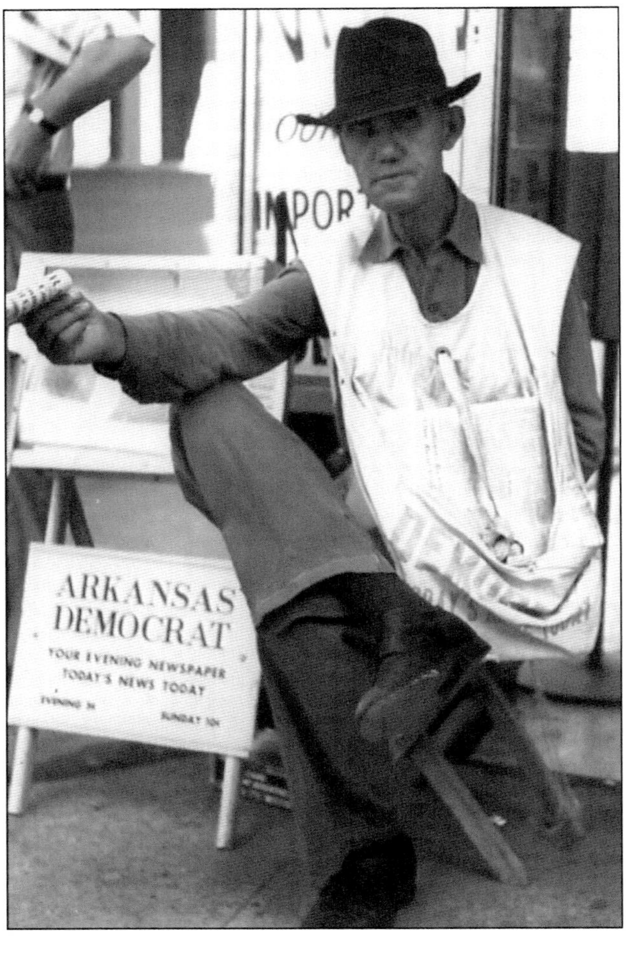

MM Cohn's flagship store is seen in this 1952 north-facing photograph of the 500 block of Main Street. Baker's Shoes is on the ground floor of the Boyle Building, with Butler's shoes across the street in the former Tipton & Hurst Florist location, next to Stifft's Jewelers. The numerous retailers seen in this expansive view are all gone today, with only Haverty's surviving in far west Little Rock. (Courtesy of UALR Center for Arkansas History & Culture.)

Walgreen's busy corner at the intersection of Main Street and Capitol Avenue made a prime spot in 1960 for an unidentified blind newspaper vendor for the *Arkansas Democrat*. At that time, the daily paper cost a nickel and came out every afternoon; the Sunday edition cost a dime. The *Democrat* competed with the city's morning paper, the *Arkansas Gazette*. (Courtesy of UALR Center for Arkansas History & Culture.)

The newspaper vendor seen in the previous photograph walks through the Walgreen's Store using his white cane to navigate. He was perhaps seeking a seat at the lunch counter, where a sirloin strip steak or a fried chicken dinner could be purchased for $1.09, while a chocolate soda cost 30¢. (Courtesy of UALR Center for Arkansas History & Culture.)

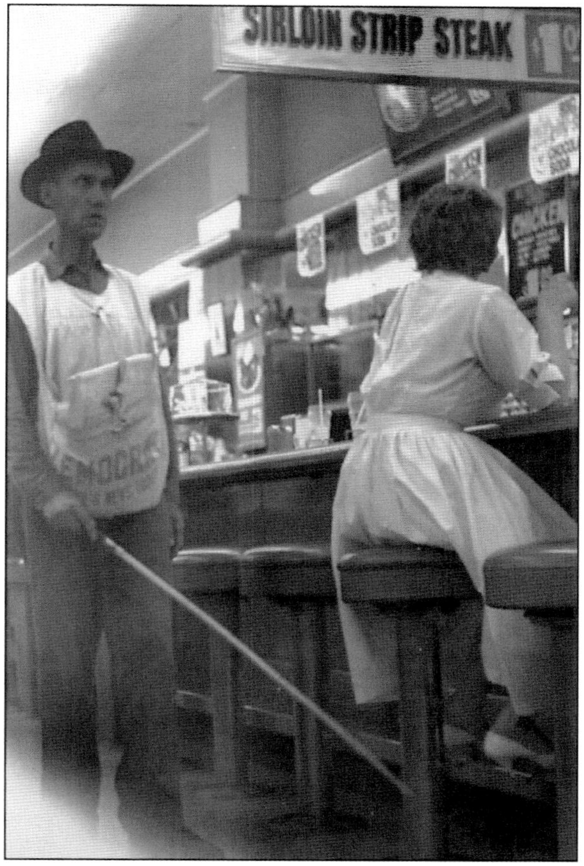

The photographer stood on the 600 block of Main Street, looking north to the 500 block with Pfeifer's department store on the left, in this 1930 photograph. Opposite Pfeifer's was a corner bank building dating from 1886, which had become a cigar shop. The taller building housed Bracy Brothers Hardware, with Haverty's Furniture just beyond. The western side of the 600 block was anchored by the Capitol Theater, which is today a vacant lot.

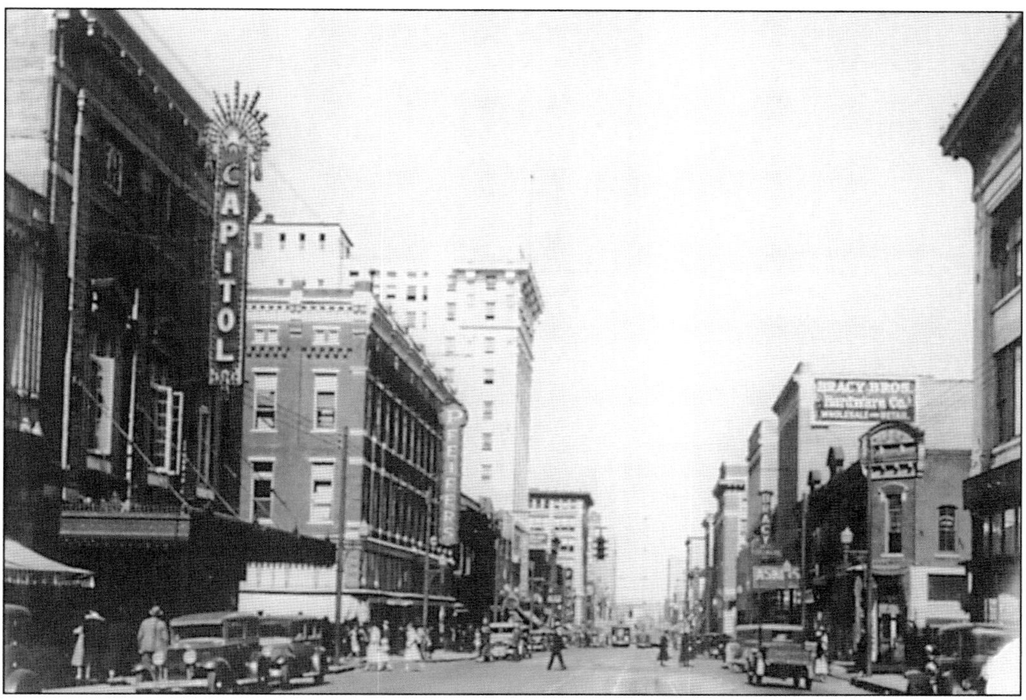

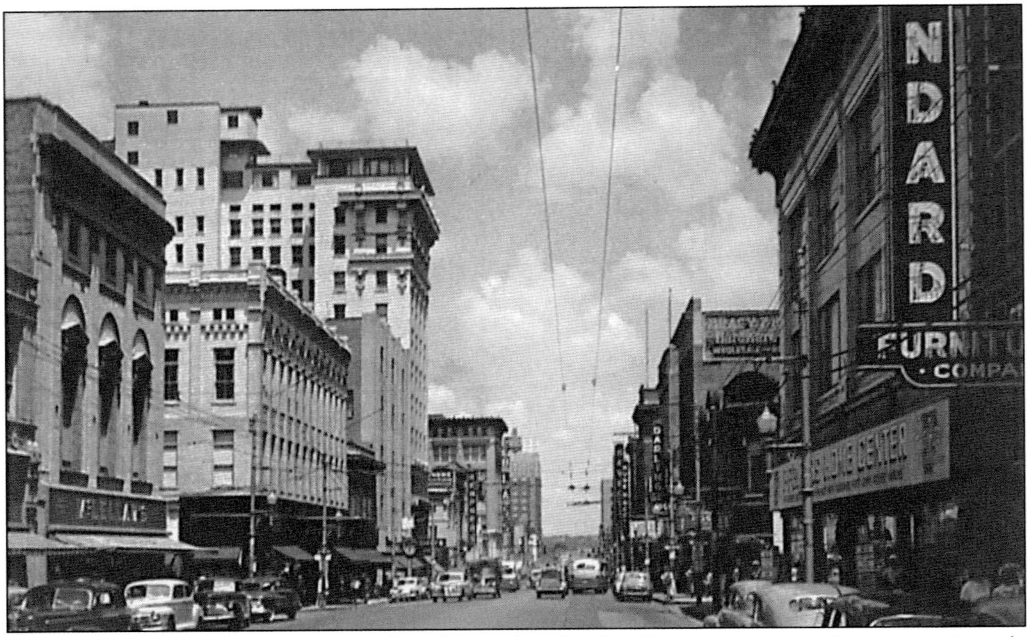

This 1940 postcard photograph was taken about a decade after the previous image from approximately the same vantage point. The Capitol Theater had been converted to McClellans' bargain store, and the Pfeifer building had been painted white. Across the street, on the eastern corner of the 600 block, was the Standard Furniture Company, which today has been nicely converted to become the home of the Arkansas Repertory Theater.

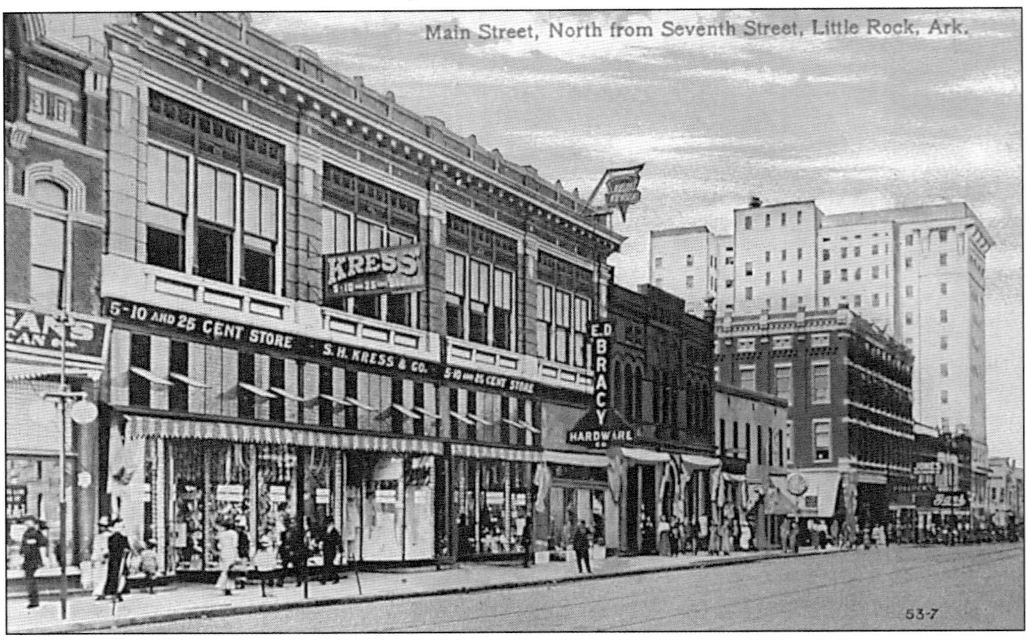

S.H. Kress and Company operated a chain of hundreds of "5–10 and 25 Cent Stores" that did business from 1896 until 1981. One of these was at 612 Main Street in Little Rock, seen here in 1917 with several fashionably dressed citizens moving along the broad sidewalk. At the time, the Kress store was flanked by Gans Store on the south and Bracy's Hardware on the north. The building serves today as a Montessori school.

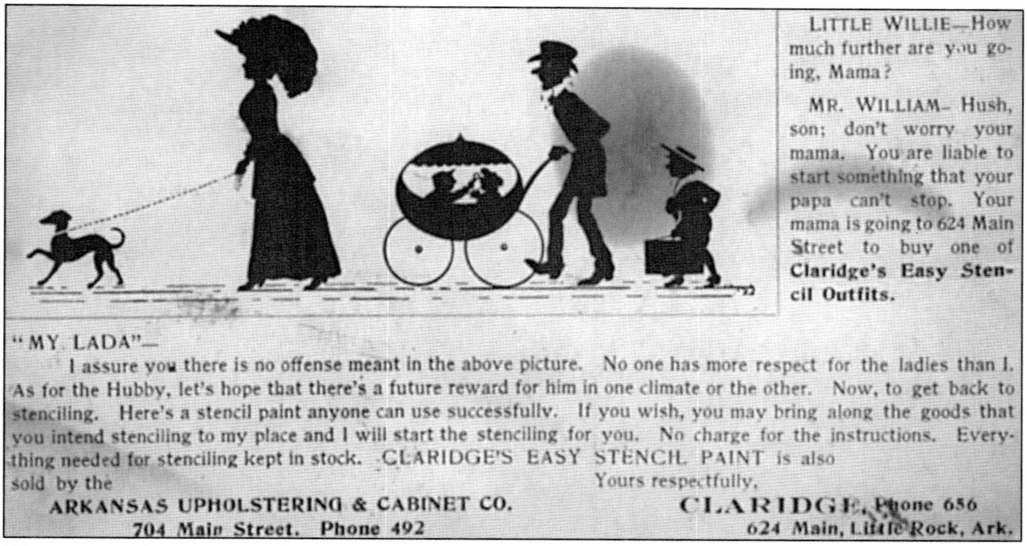

Shoppers with an artistic flare in 1910 might have been drawn to Claridge's, at 624 Main Street, reachable at phone no. 656. Claridge's furnished supplies for the trendy craft of stenciling, including its own "Never Crawls" paint. The business also gave instruction in stenciling, a sample of which illustrates the postcard. Arkansas Upholstering & Cabinet, perhaps sharing ownership with Claridge's, was listed on the card, with an address a block south.

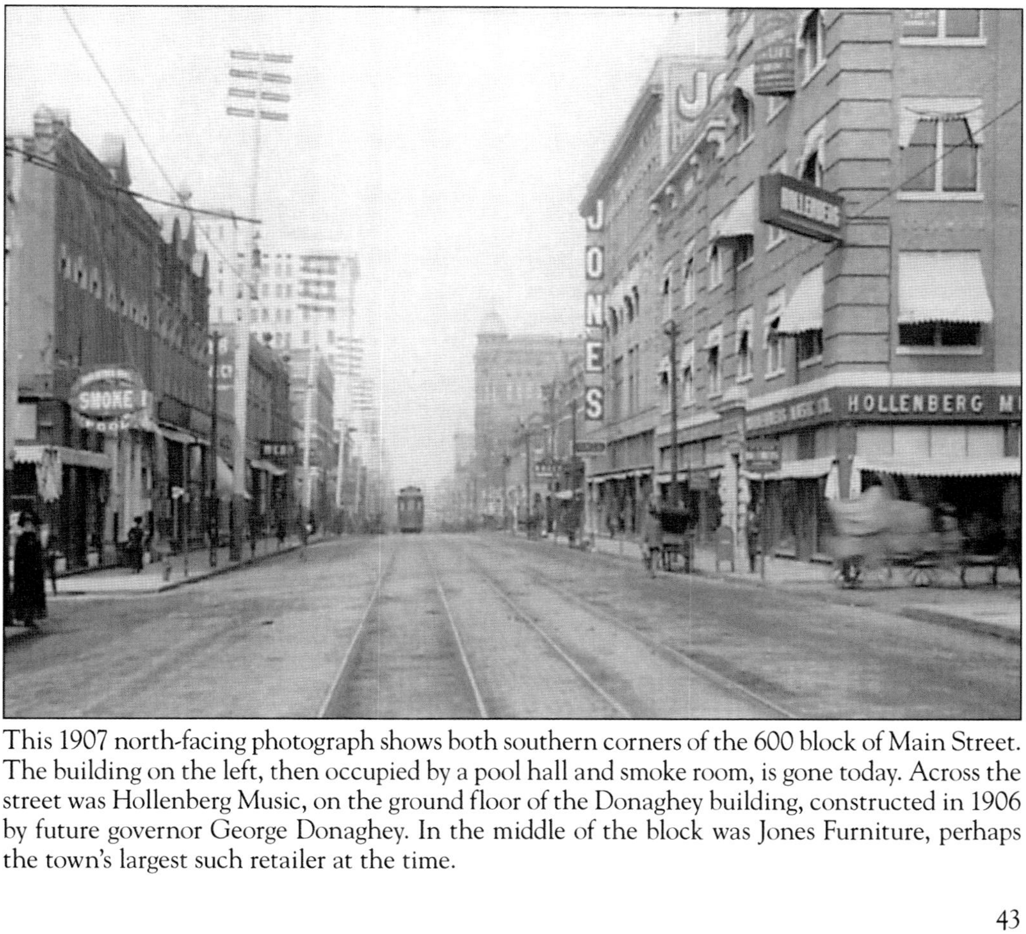

This 1907 north-facing photograph shows both southern corners of the 600 block of Main Street. The building on the left, then occupied by a pool hall and smoke room, is gone today. Across the street was Hollenberg Music, on the ground floor of the Donaghey building, constructed in 1906 by future governor George Donaghey. In the middle of the block was Jones Furniture, perhaps the town's largest such retailer at the time.

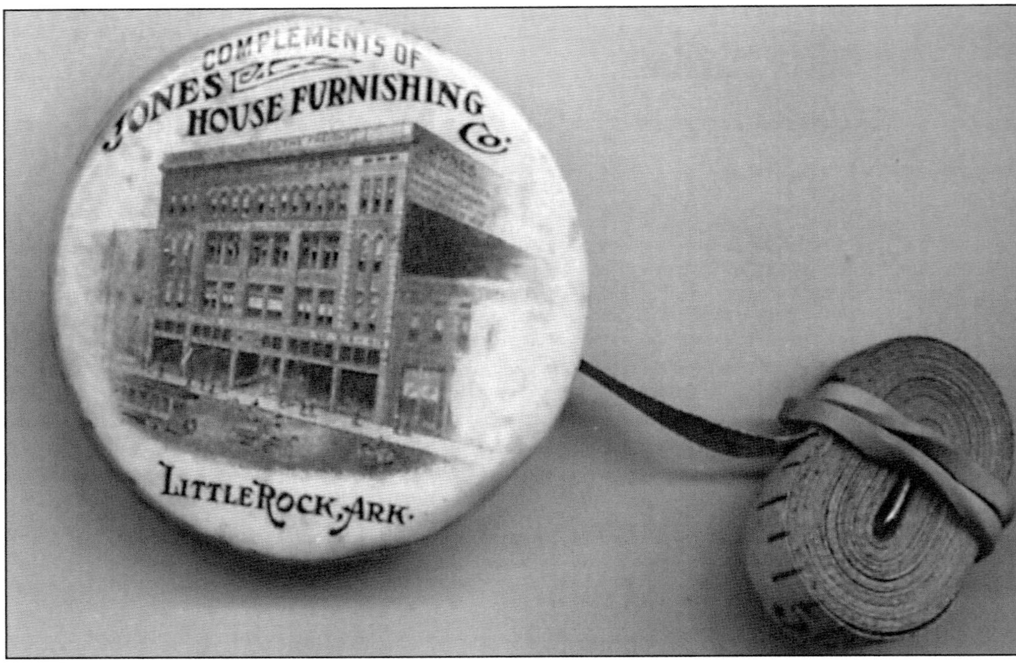

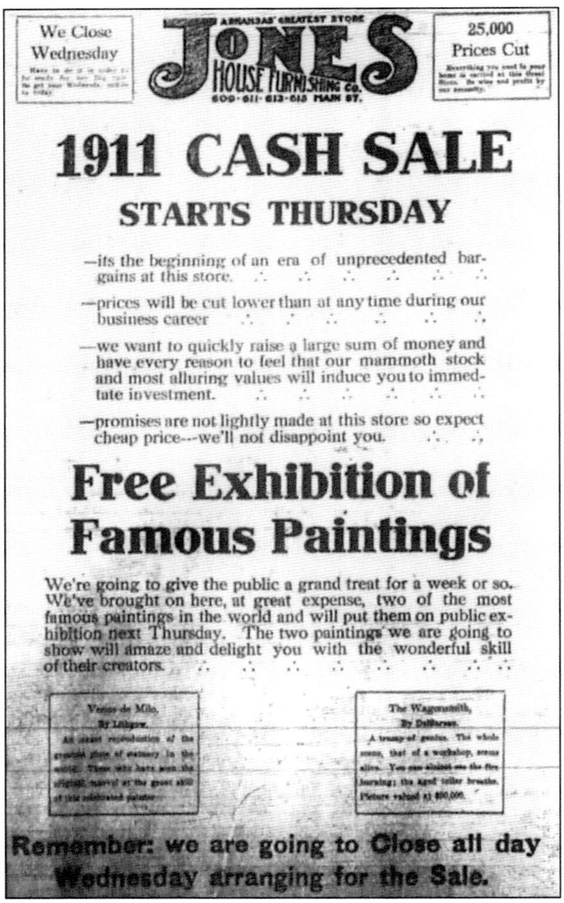

In 1910, Jones Furniture, on the 600 block of Main Street, offered an inducement for ladies to come into their four-story center of home furnishings. The tape measure spooled out of a metal reel bearing an image of the store. Regardless of a spelling error on the label, the printed image is highly detailed for the time.

During the first weekend of January 1911, Jones Furniture ran this newspaper advertisement promoting a huge sale scheduled for the following Thursday. As an inducement for store traffic, there was a promised showing of two famous works of art, reproductions of the paintings *Venus de Milo* by Lithgow and *The Wagonsmith*, reportedly valued at $50,000. Sadly, the store was destroyed by fire before the advertised sale and showing could get under way.

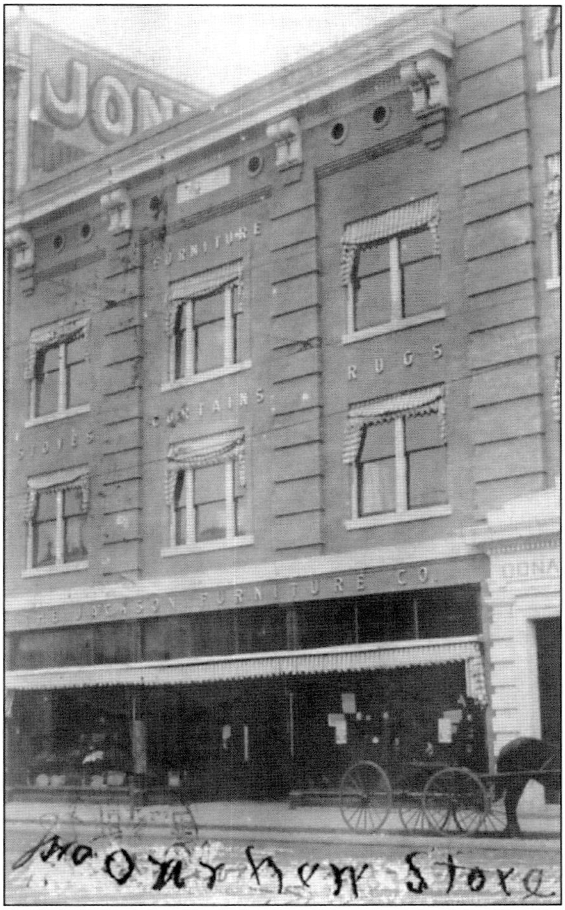

This 1907 postcard shows how the Jackson Furniture Company was sandwiched between Jones Furniture on the north and the Donaghey Building at the southern corner of Seventh and Main Streets. Mounted words on the upper levels of the building listed some of the things the store sold, including stoves, furniture, rugs, and curtains. A nimble horse and carriage awaits its owner, likely shopping within.

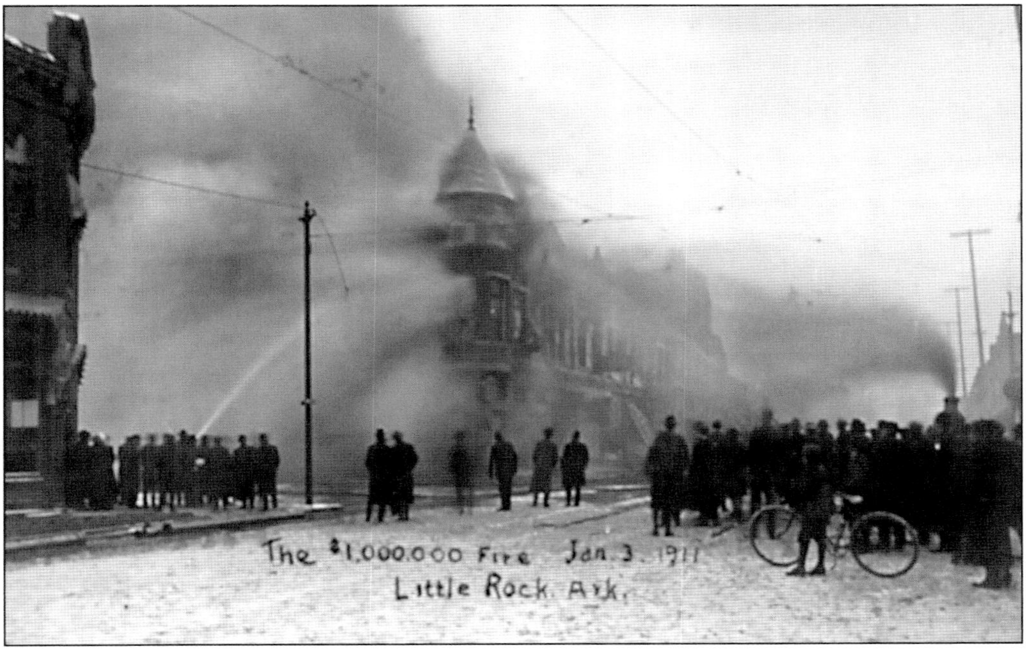

On a cold January 3, 1911, three teenage boys were cleaning the Hollenberg Music store at Seventh and Main Streets late at night, and they took a break to smoke. One boy reportedly dropped a cigarette butt, which went unnoticed as it slowly smoldered through the night. Fire erupted, which eventually took the entire eastern side of the 600 block of Main Street, burning through to the west side of Scott Street one block over.

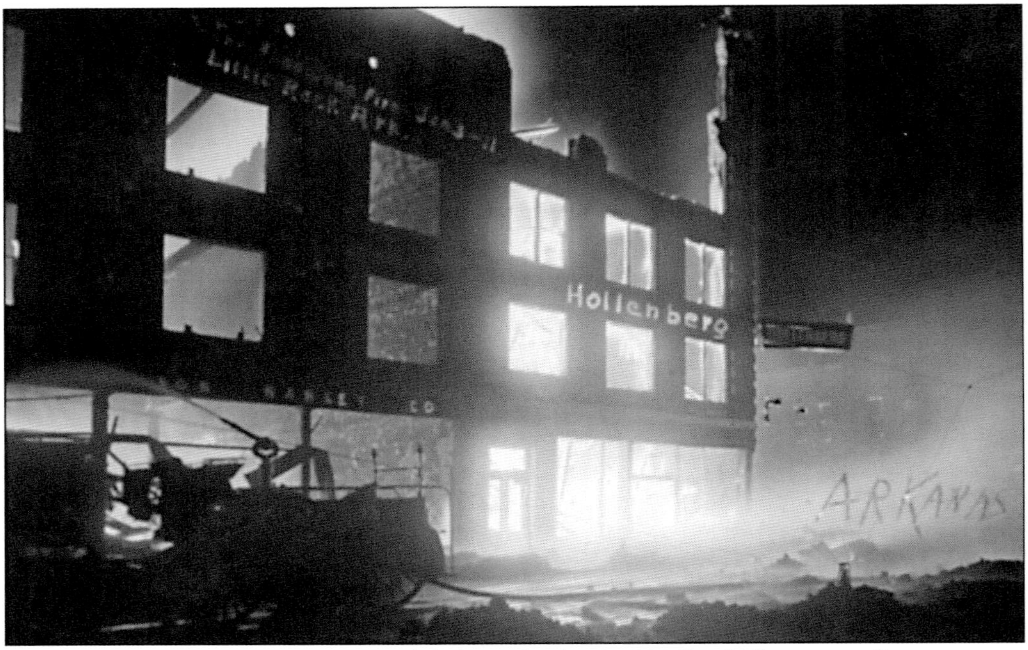

A postcard made of the 1911 disaster labels it "the $1,000,000 Fire." The raging flames gutting Hollenberg Music and the Jackson-Hanley Furniture store served to illuminate the scene for the photographer, who captured the valiant efforts of the Little Rock Fire Department to fight the blaze. The inadequate pumper truck is shown sending a stream of water into the furniture store.

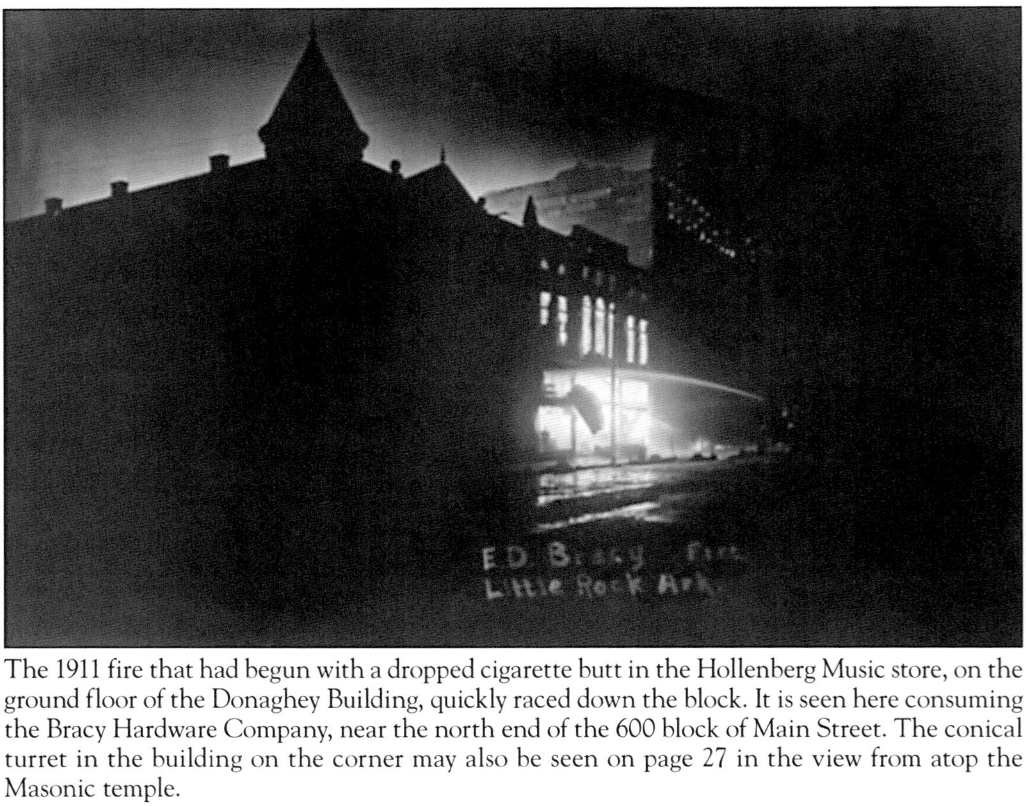

The 1911 fire that had begun with a dropped cigarette butt in the Hollenberg Music store, on the ground floor of the Donaghey Building, quickly raced down the block. It is seen here consuming the Bracy Hardware Company, near the north end of the 600 block of Main Street. The conical turret in the building on the corner may also be seen on page 27 in the view from atop the Masonic temple.

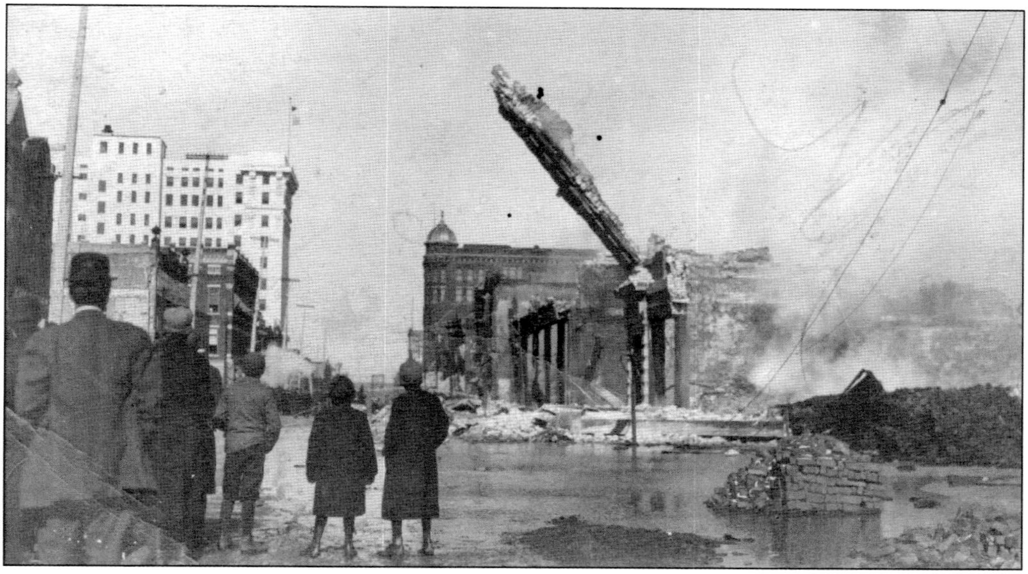

This 1911 postcard, mailed two weeks after the January 3 fire, captures the morning after the blaze with the ruins still emitting smoke. Amid the gutted ruins of the Donaghey Building, the last tall piece tumbled onto Main Street. The notation on the back reads, "Hollenberg corner falling." The entire block would be quickly leveled and rebuilt, including the Donaghey Building, where the blaze had begun.

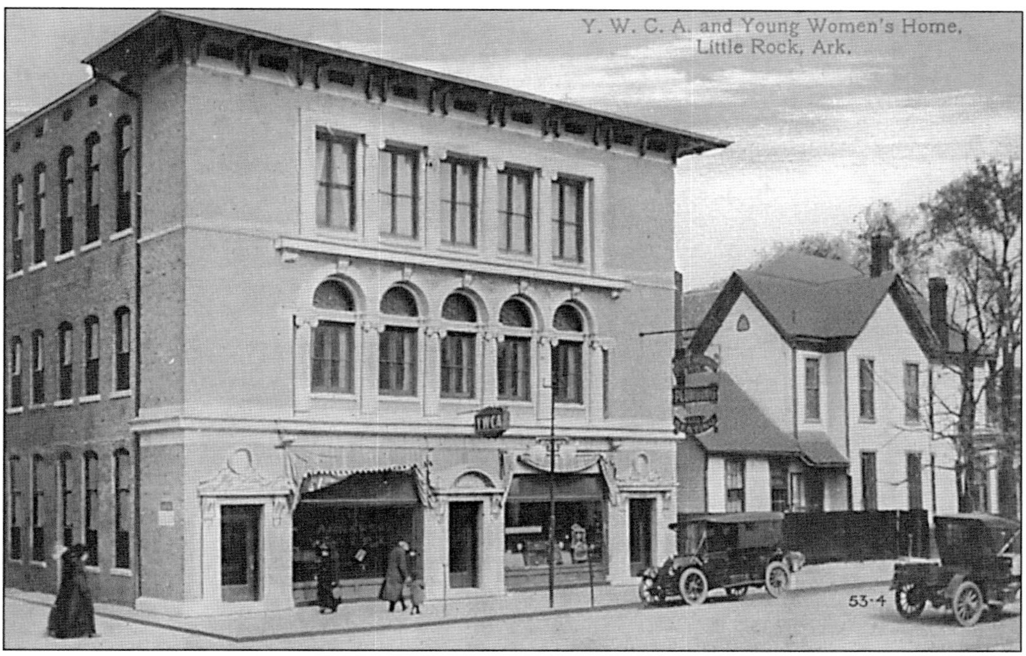

In terms of property loss, the most devastating fire in Little Rock's history had begun on Main Street, but it did not end there. Leaping the back alley, flames consumed neighboring businesses facing Scott Street. Also devastated was the north side of Seventh Street, seen here in 1909. The YWCA, at 114 East Seventh Street, was in a structure around the corner from the Donaghey Building.

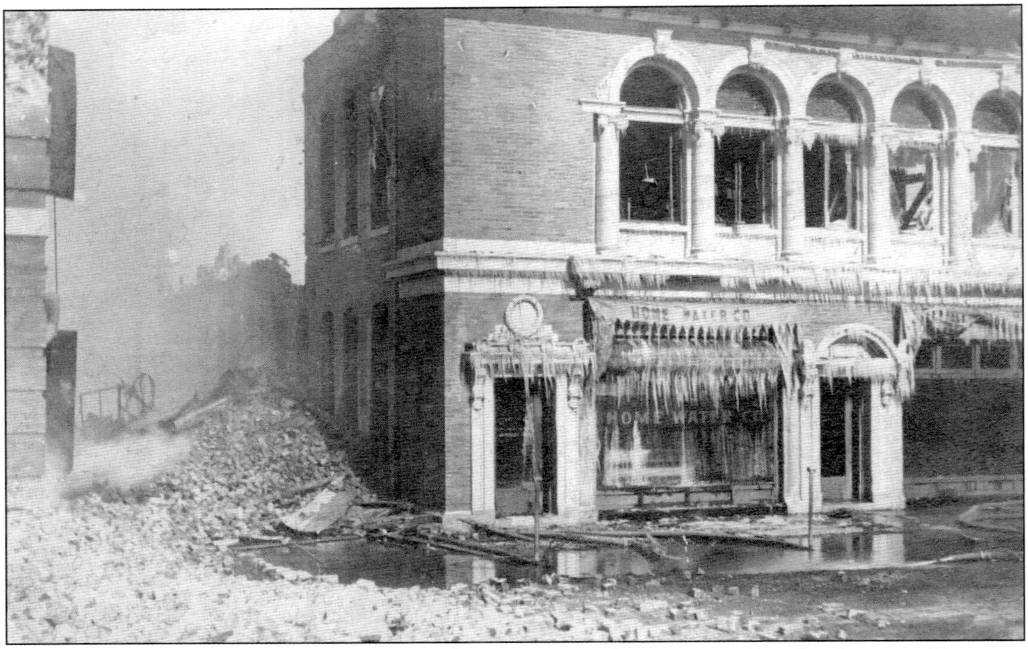

The YWCA building also housed the Arkansas Water Company and a plumbing and heating firm. The entire structure was a burned-out shell on the morning after the fire, adorned with large frozen icicles formed by the spray of the firemen's hoses. The corner of the ruined Donaghey Building is seen to the left, across a back alley filled with crumbled bricks.

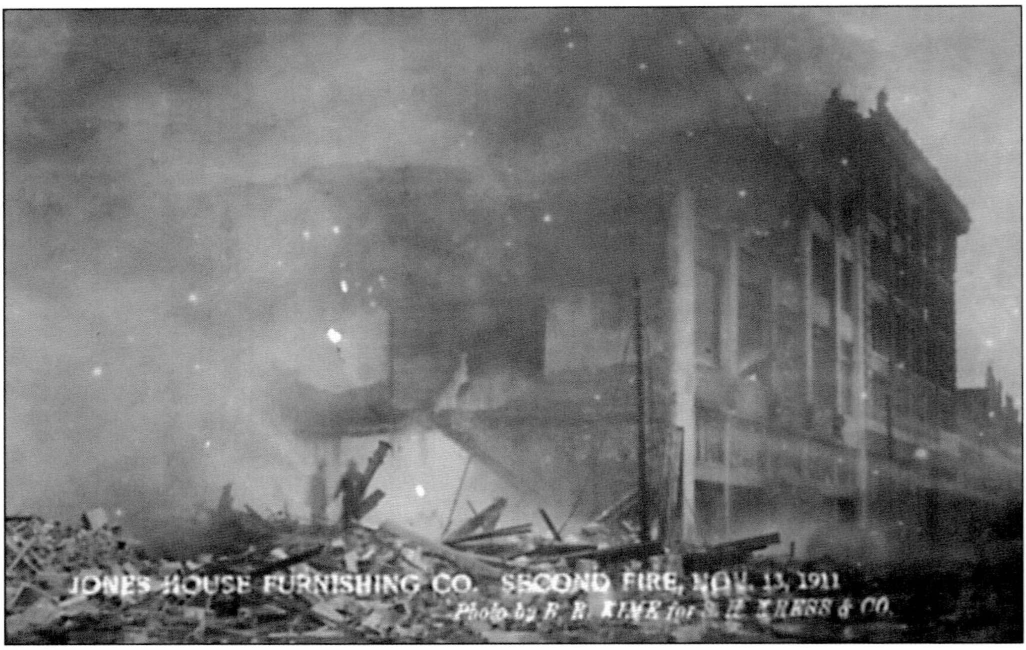

The Jones Furniture Company quickly rebuilt after the January 1911 fire, completing a new building by November of the same year. Its renewed hopes were short lived, however, as noted by the sender of this postcard on November 23, 1911: "This is the block that burned a year ago and rebuilt and burned again the day it was completed this year. They just got started and it burned again on 13th."

The location of Jones Furniture, destroyed in the double fires of 1911, was rebuilt and became home to the *Arkansas Democrat* and Haverty's Furniture, seen here in 1930. Those businesses have moved, but the buildings remain, now housing a Subway sandwich shop and RAO Video Store. For decades, the front of the building was covered in ceramic siding that hid its arched windows. In 2014, the siding was removed to reveal the interesting facade and the business names.

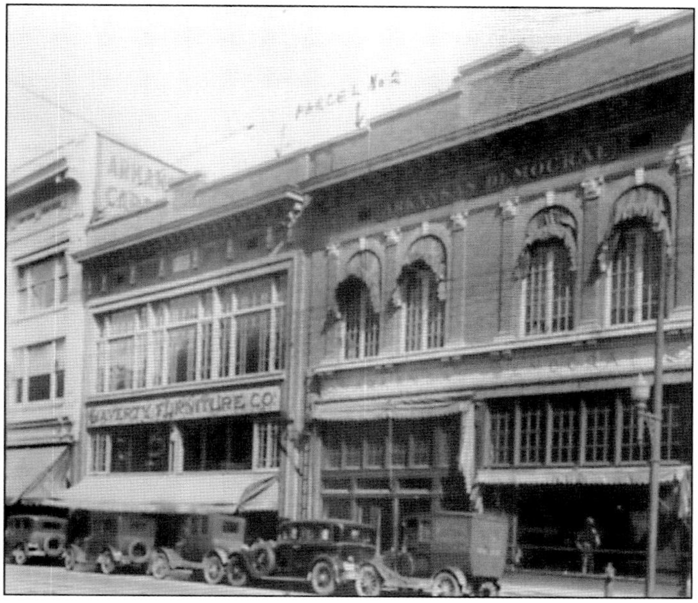

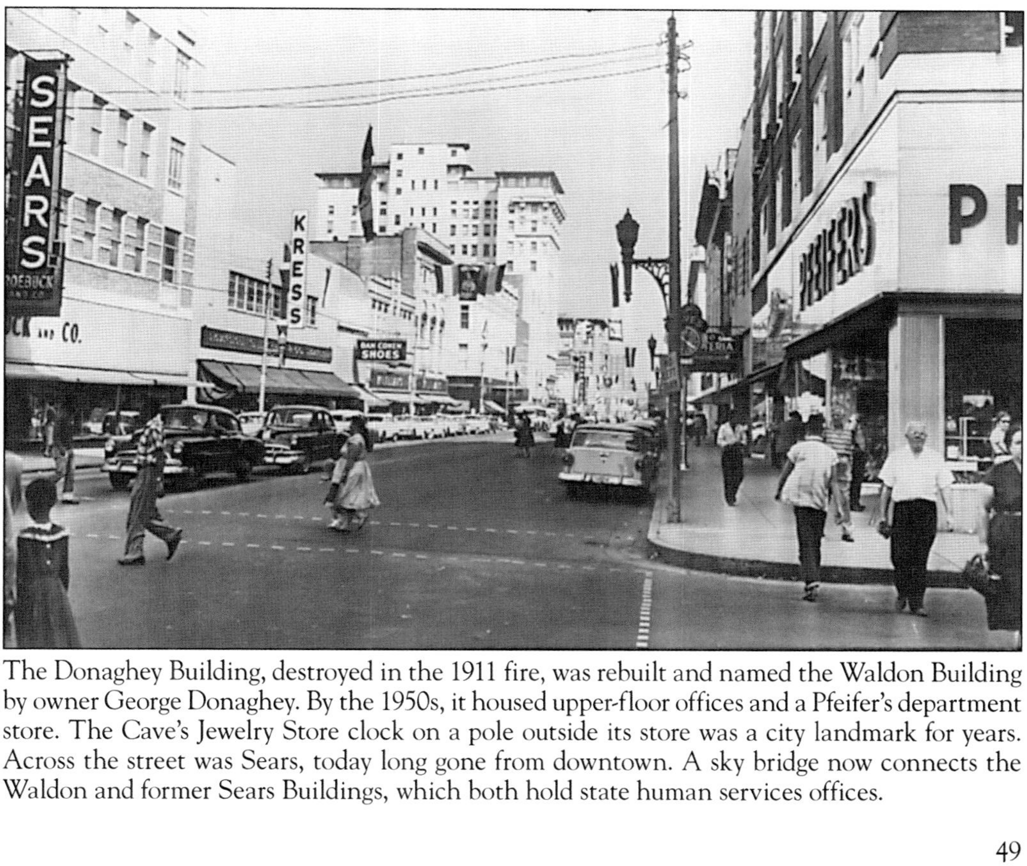

The Donaghey Building, destroyed in the 1911 fire, was rebuilt and named the Waldon Building by owner George Donaghey. By the 1950s, it housed upper-floor offices and a Pfeifer's department store. The Cave's Jewelry Store clock on a pole outside its store was a city landmark for years. Across the street was Sears, today long gone from downtown. A sky bridge now connects the Waldon and former Sears Buildings, which both hold state human services offices.

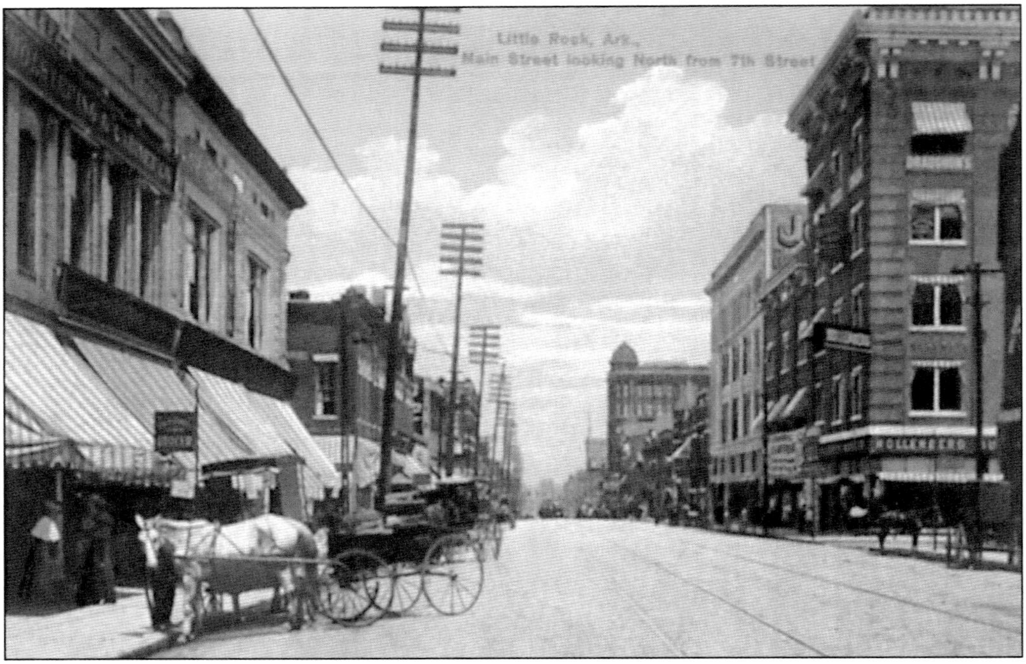

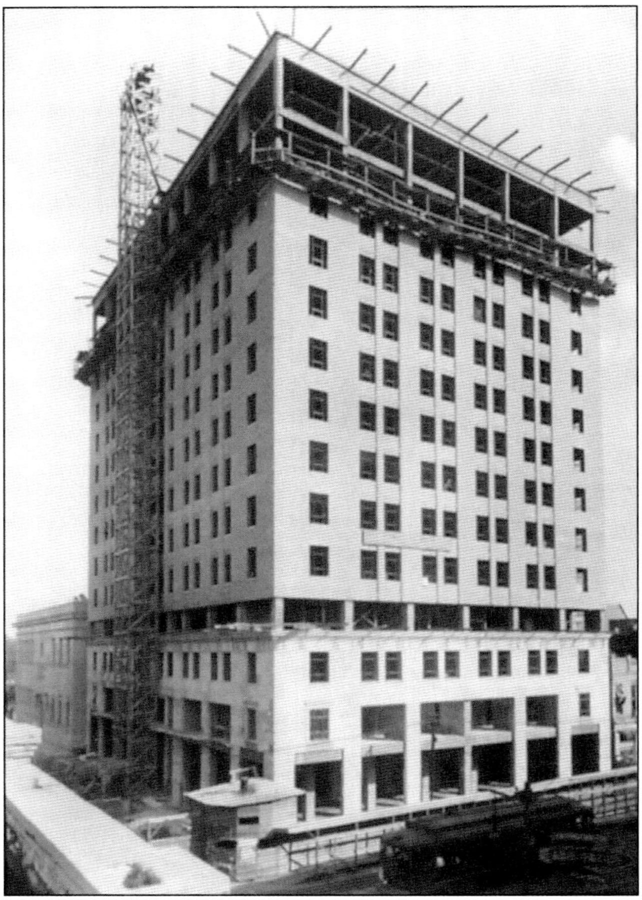

This 1910 photograph shows the northwest end of the 700 block of Main looking north across Seventh Street. A horse and buggy are parked at the corner grocery on the left at what is today the entrance to the Arkansas Department of Human Services building, erected in the late 1990s. Across the street is the Donaghey Building, with Hollenberg Music. The structure would be destroyed in the 1911 fire.

Former governor George Donaghey erected the 14-story Donaghey Building in 1926 at the southeast corner of Seventh and Main Streets. For 30 years, the building was Little Rock's tallest structure. Today, it is almost entirely vacant after the Arkansas Department of Human Services (DHS) moved across the street to a new structure erected by the Donaghey Foundation. After sitting empty for a decade, the fate of the historic building hangs in the balance.

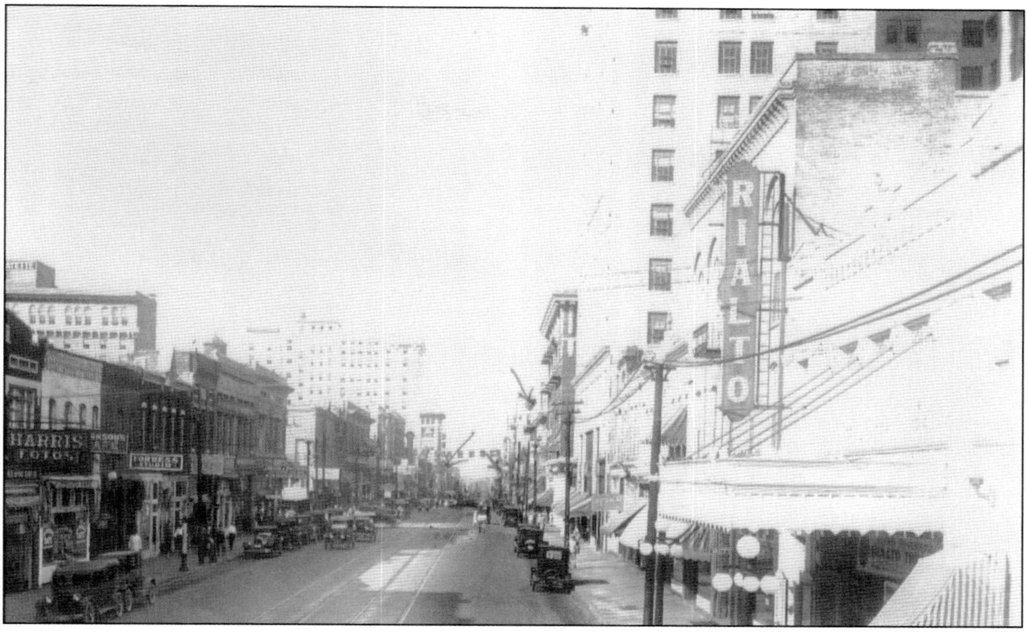

This 1930 photograph looks north up the length of the 700 block of Main Street, where the Donaghey Building towers on the right. Across the street stretches a block of turn-of-the-century buildings housing two photography studios, a café, and a men's clothier. The entire block on the left is gone today, replaced by a new Arkansas DHS building. On the right, the Rialto Theater and several other buildings have been replaced by a parking deck. (Courtesy of Butler Center for Arkansas Studies.)

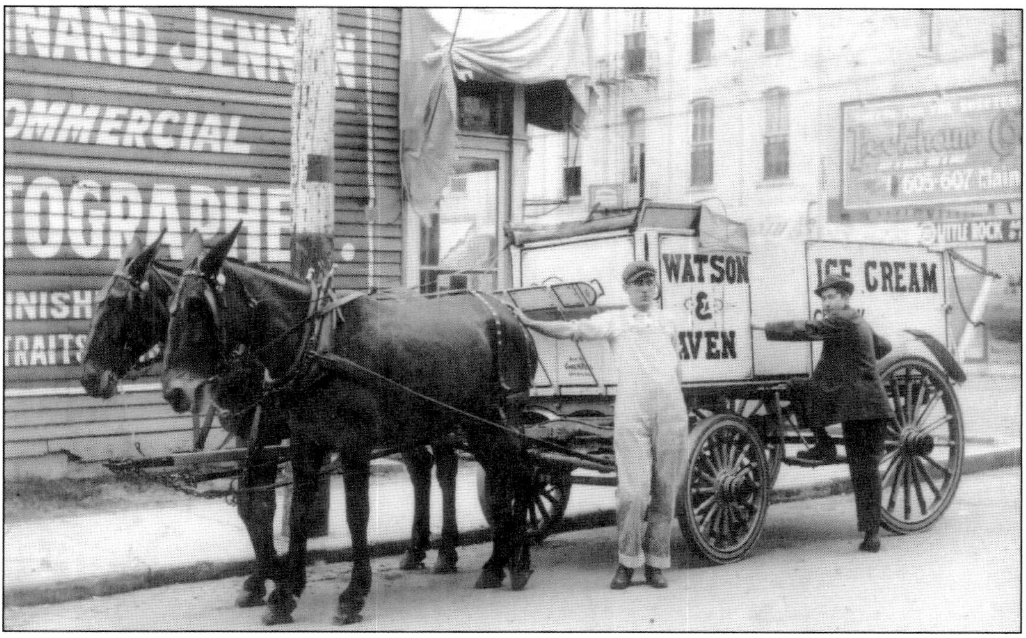

A mule-drawn ice cream wagon is parked at the southwest corner of Seventh and Main Streets in front of a photographer's studio. The site today is at the southern end of the block-long Arkansas DHS headquarters building. Across Main Street today, where this Peckham Candy sign hung in 1910, stands a modern parking deck.

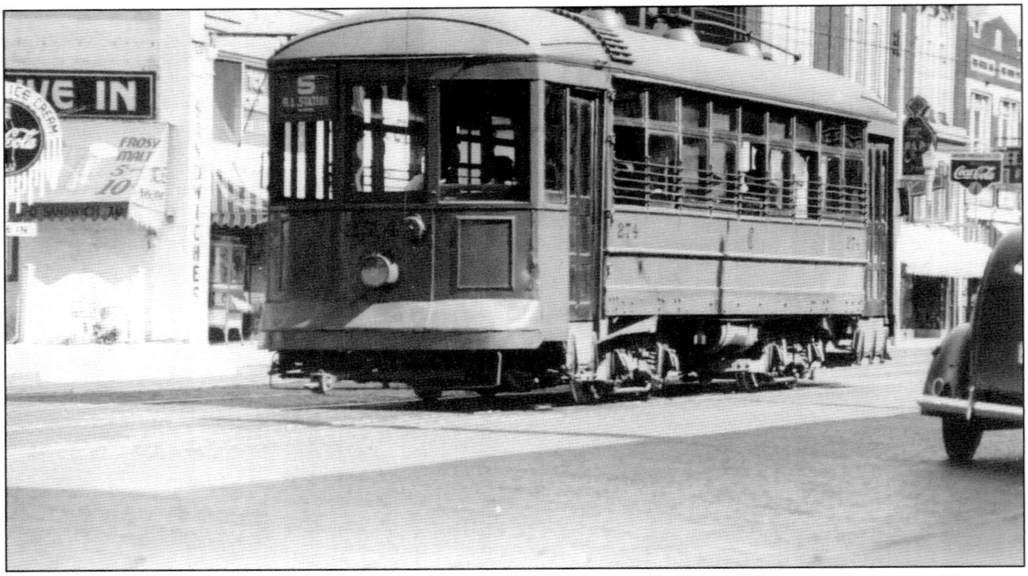

The corner seen in the previous photograph is shown here in 1940, with a streetcar rumbling by a café where a frosty malt could be enjoyed for 10¢. Streetcars disappeared from the city by 1947, but a few returned in 2005 to the River Market area some seven blocks north. The drive-in café and other businesses at the intersection are long gone, replaced by the DHS building.

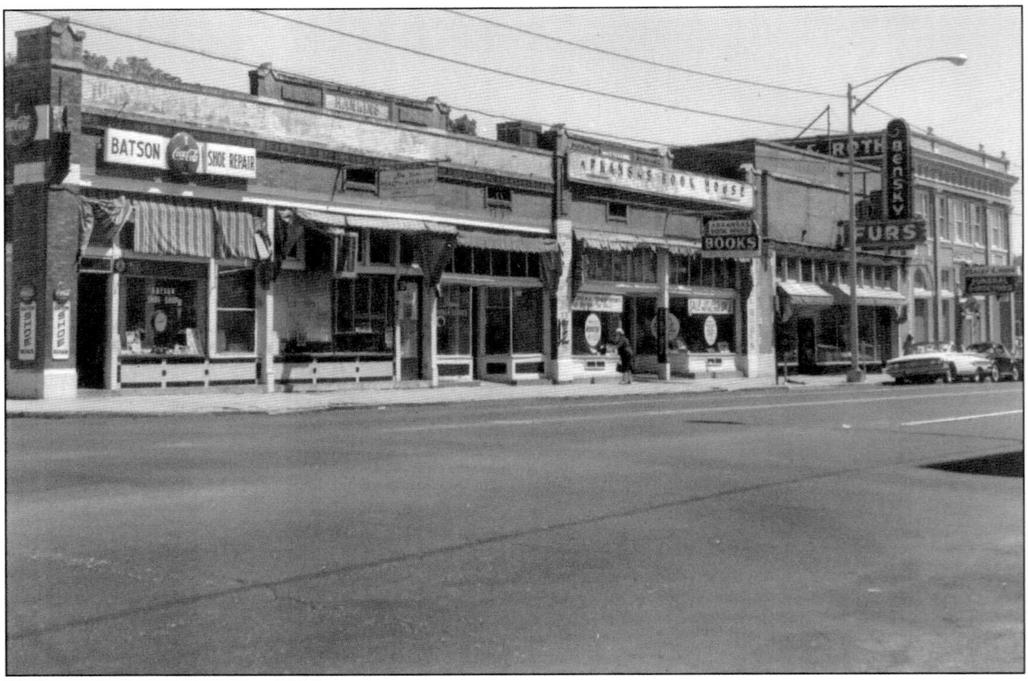

The east side of the 800 block of Main Street is seen here in 1965. The businesses include Batson Shoe Repair in the Hankins Building, as well as the Arkansas Book House, Bensky Furs, and the Healy & Roth funeral home. Today, a parking deck occupies the space up to the former Bensky building, which is still present but standing vacant, as is the former funeral home. (Courtesy of Butler Center for Arkansas Studies.)

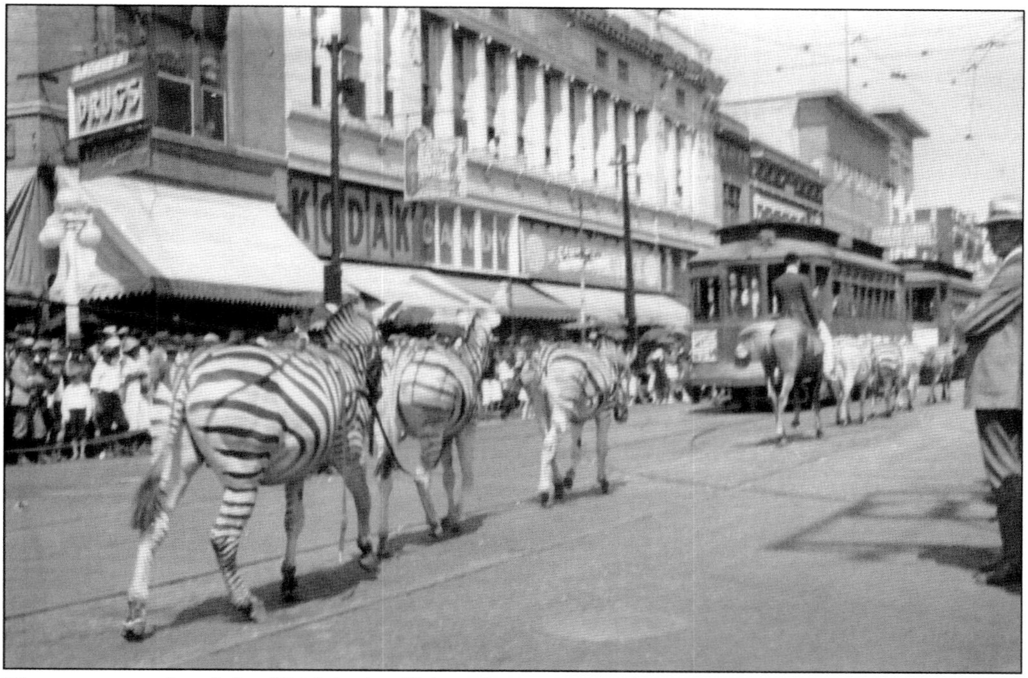

The western side of the 800 block of Main Street is seen here in 1920. A circus parade heads north, giving the crowd an unlikely view of zebras sharing the way with streetcars. Businesses include a corner drugstore, a photography shop, and a sweet shop. The entire block, leveled by the 1960s, is today a parking lot.

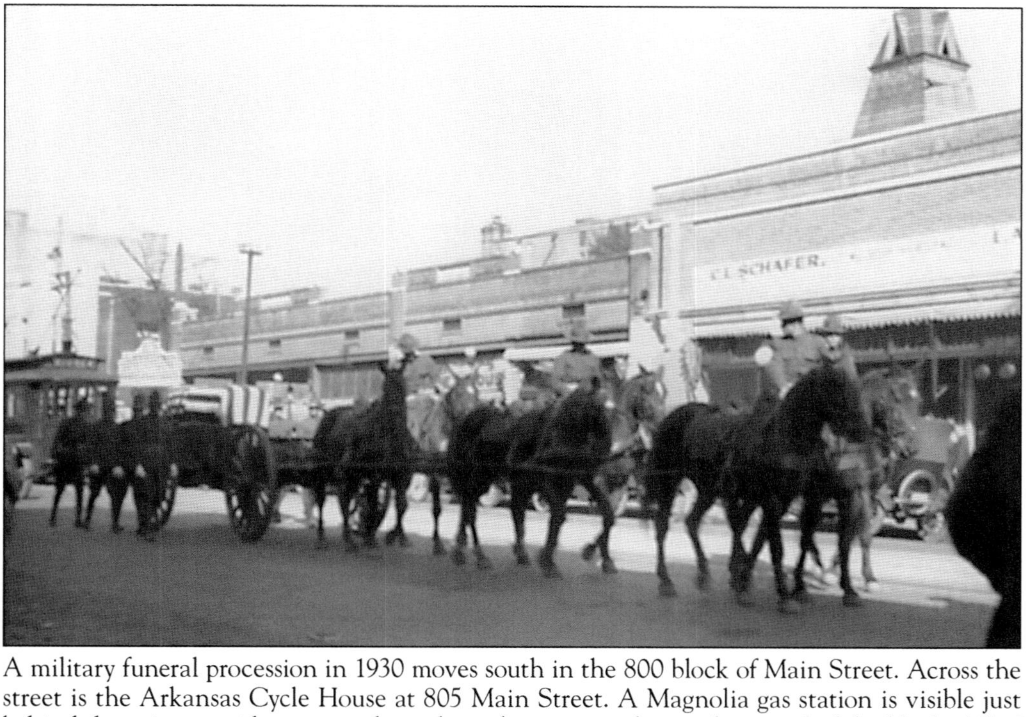

A military funeral procession in 1930 moves south in the 800 block of Main Street. Across the street is the Arkansas Cycle House at 805 Main Street. A Magnolia gas station is visible just behind the caisson, with an open drive-through corner at the northern end of the block. All of these buildings are gone today.

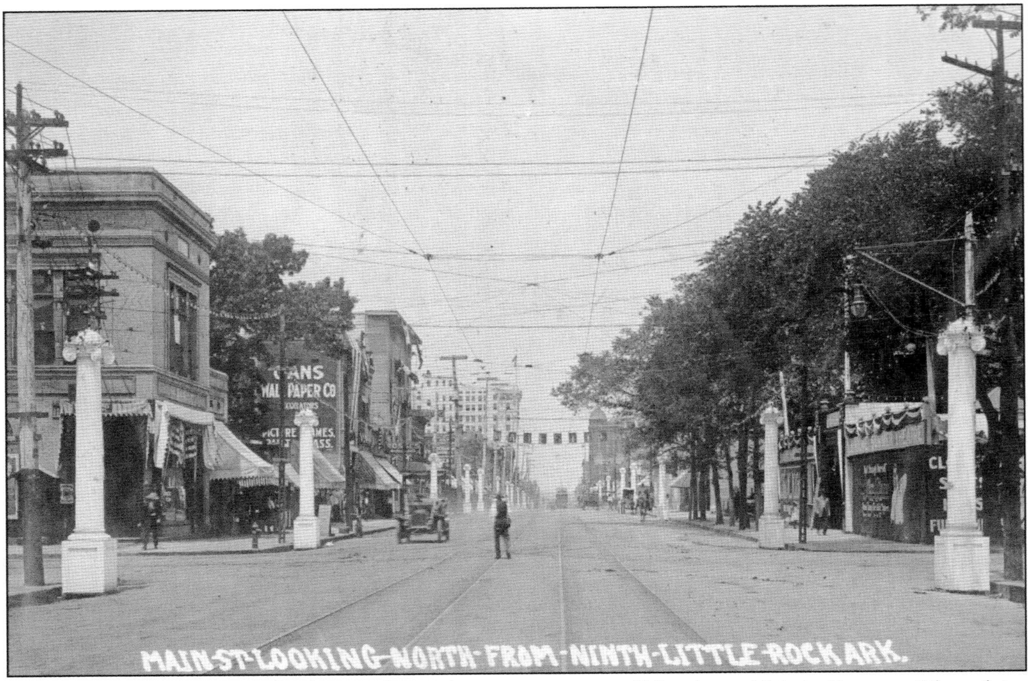

This early postcard view looks north up the intersection of Ninth and Main Streets. The white columns are temporary plaster decorations marking the United Confederate Veterans' reunion, which Little Rock hosted in May 1911. To the right is the Airdome, an open-air summer theater behind a wooden fence. Across the street are Gans Wallpaper Co. and Rossi's Majestic Café. Everything on the 800 block seen here is gone today.

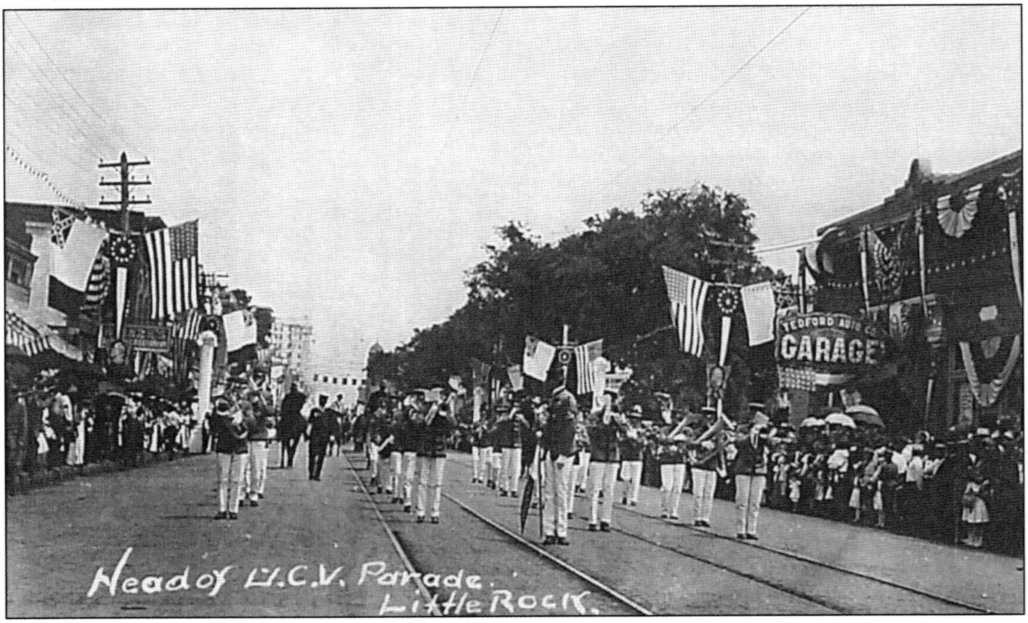

On the third and final day of the 1911 United Confederate Veterans' reunion, the 900 block of Main Street was on the route of a grand parade. On that hot May day, some in the well-dressed crowd used umbrellas for shade. Spectators stand on the sidewalk in front of Tedford Auto Co. Garage (right) at 910 South Main Street.

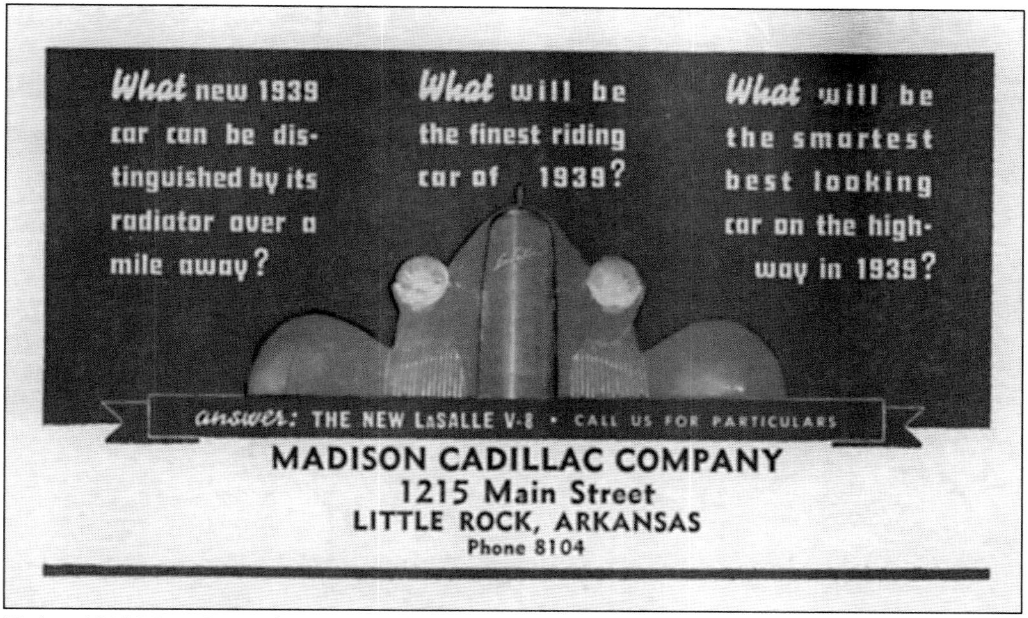

Today, 1215 Main Street lies just south of where Interstate 630 passes beneath the Main Street overpass. In 1939, long before the coming of modern highways, prosperous Little Rock citizens could purchase a luxury car at Madison Cadillac Company. The dealership was replaced decades ago by other commercial endeavors.

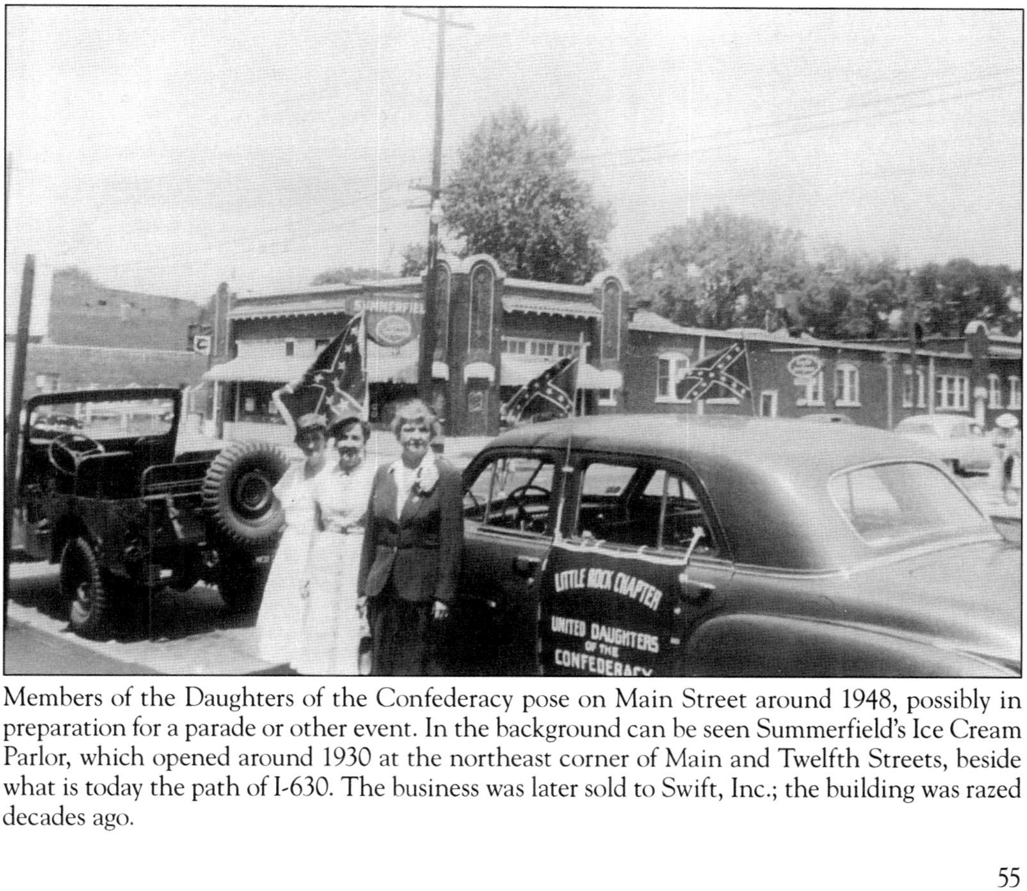

Members of the Daughters of the Confederacy pose on Main Street around 1948, possibly in preparation for a parade or other event. In the background can be seen Summerfield's Ice Cream Parlor, which opened around 1930 at the northeast corner of Main and Twelfth Streets, beside what is today the path of I-630. The business was later sold to Swift, Inc.; the building was razed decades ago.

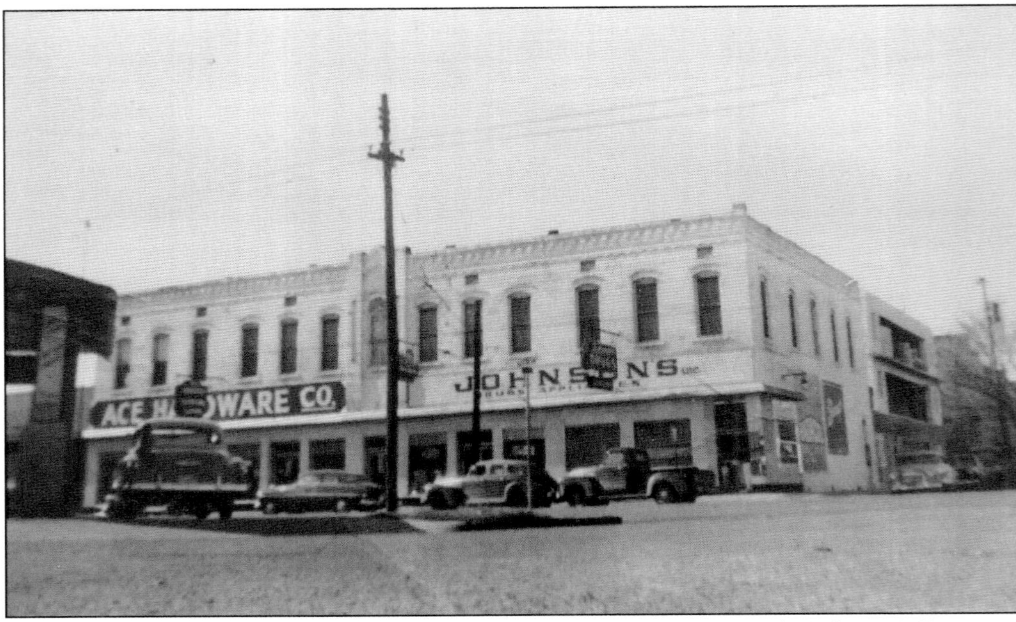

The west side of the 1200 block of Main Street was anchored in 1950 by Johnson's Drug and Appliance store and its next-door neighbor, Ace Hardware. The building today is fully restored. The space used formerly by Johnson's is now home to Community Bakery, one of the most popular meeting spots in Little Rock. (Courtesy of Joe Fox of Community Bakery.)

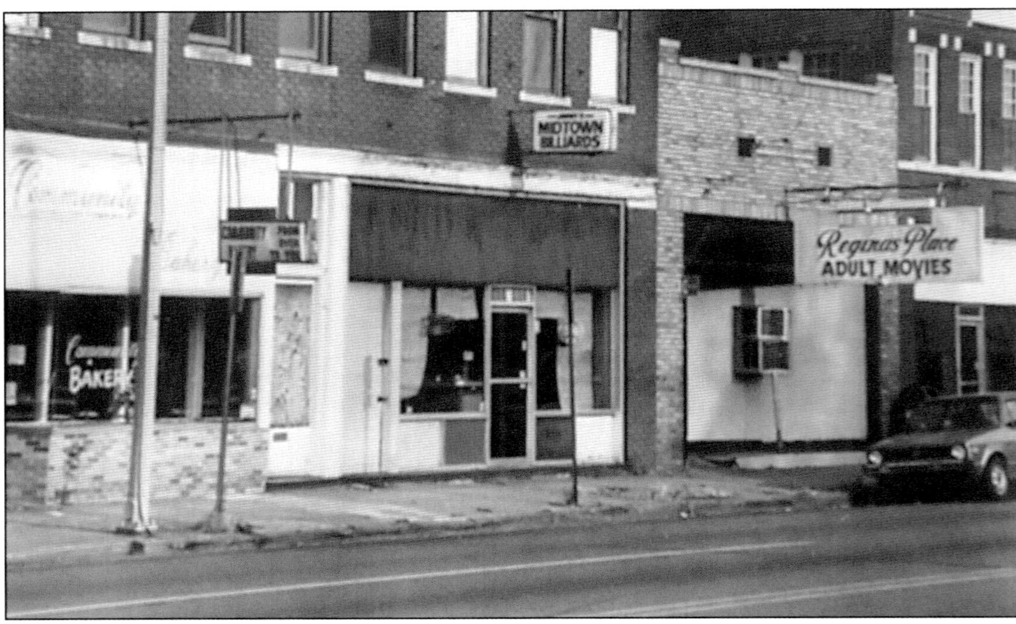

Community Bakery, seen here in 1983, began in the Rose City area of North Little Rock in 1947, and in 1952 it moved to 1318 Main Street in Little Rock. In 1983, it was purchased by current owner Joe Fox, who moved it to the 1200 block. It now thrives in the restored space formerly occupied by Johnson's Appliance. Midtown Billiards (center) still operates as well. Regina's Place (right) no longer exists. (Courtesy of Joe Fox of Community Bakery.)

Visiting motorists would often do a double take and make a U-turn to look at the giant Viking that stood watch atop Brown's Carpet Warehouse, seen here in 1980. The business, at the southwest corner of Fourteenth and Main Streets, is gone today, and the site is home to another business. The fate or whereabouts of the Viking statue is unknown. (Courtesy of Joe Fox of Community Bakery.)

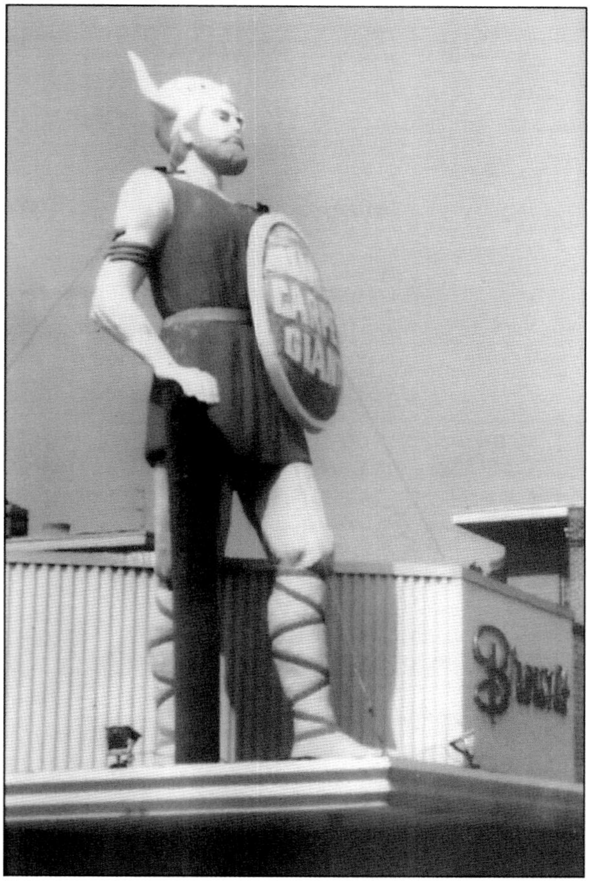

A success story in restoration is the Lincoln Building, at the southeast corner of Fifteenth and Main Streets. Built in the neoclassical style by C.J. Lincoln in 1905, it is seen here in 1970, languishing somewhat but still housing two businesses: a drugstore and a bar. Following its restoration (inset), it was added to the National Register of Historic Places in 1994. (Courtesy of Encyclopedia of Arkansas.)

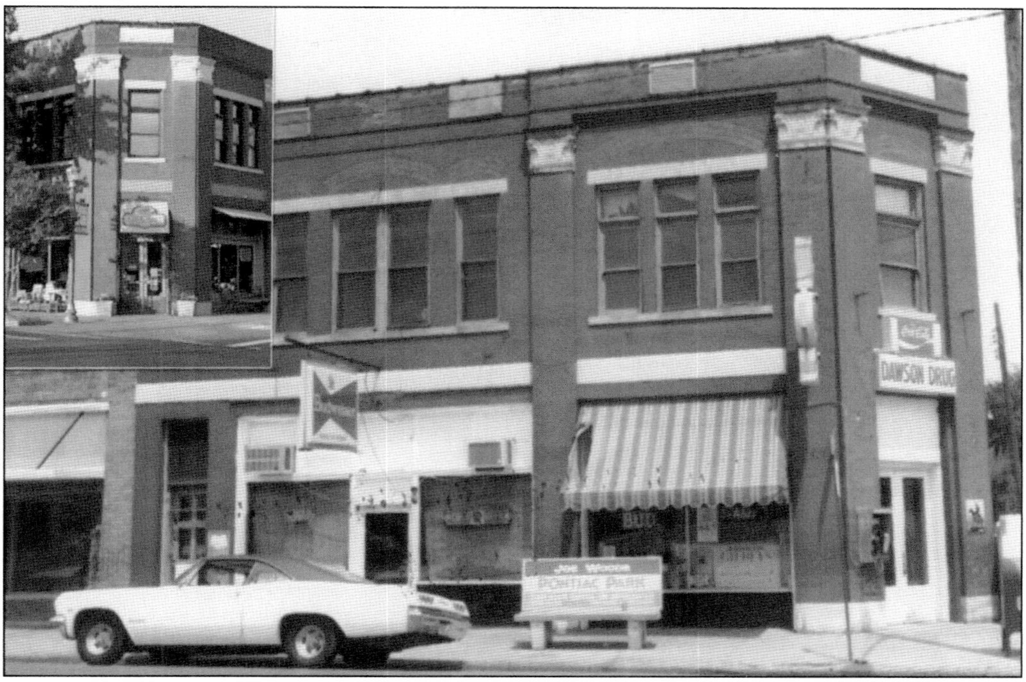

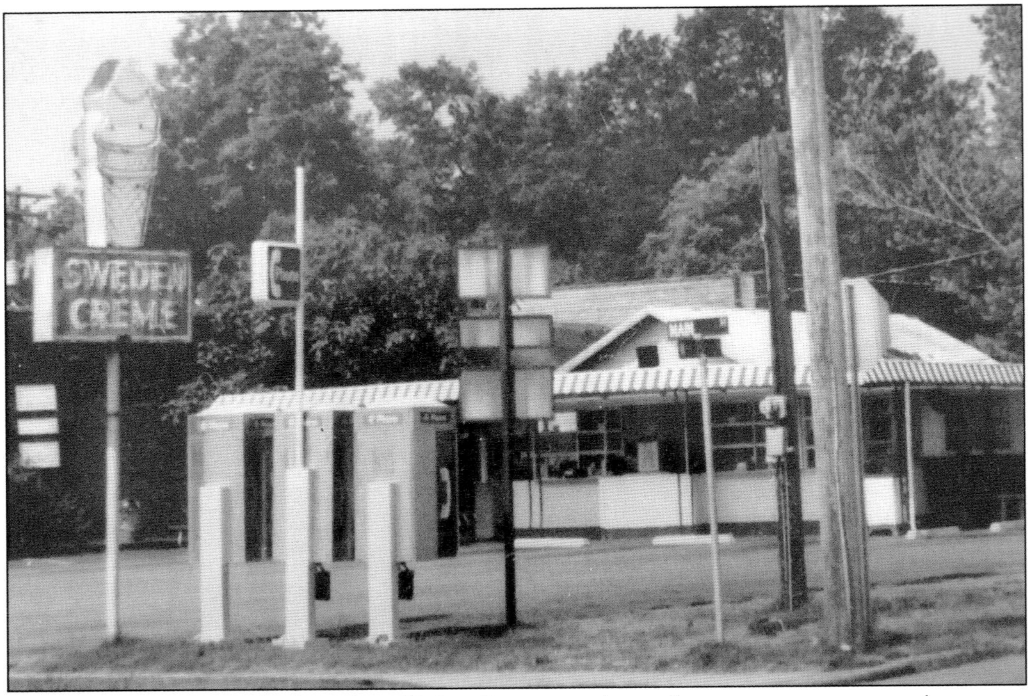

The southwest corner of Fifteenth and Main Streets was home for many years to a popular eatery, the Sweden Creme Drive-In, seen here around 1980. The business is long gone, as are the once-common pay phones by the street; however, the building is restored and now houses the popular Root Café, providing one more testimony to the rebirth of South Main Street. (Courtesy of Joe Fox of Community Bakery.)

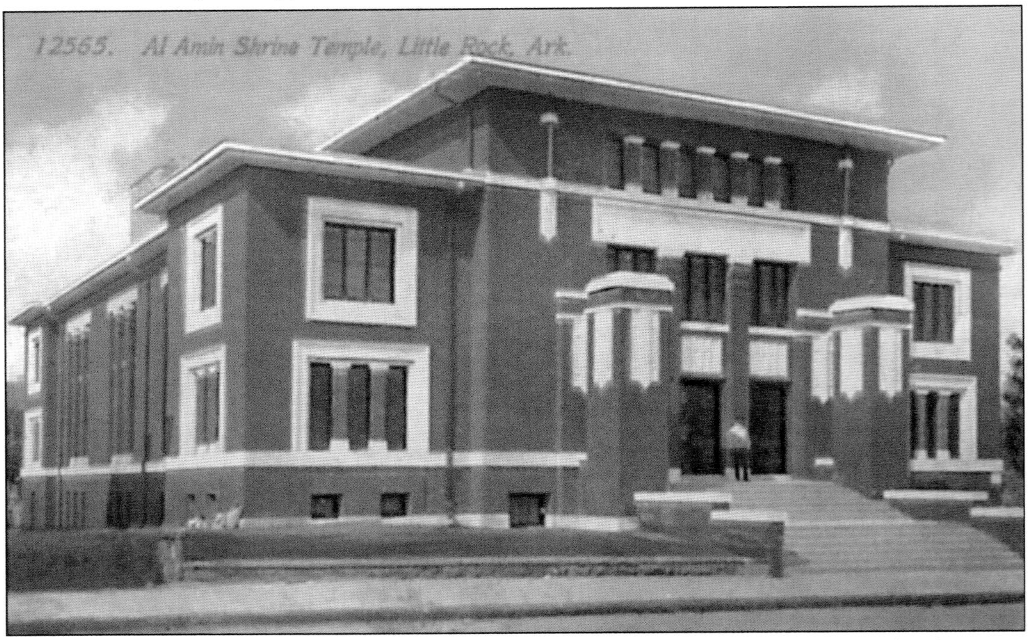

The Al Amin Shrine Temple was built in 1912 at the corner of 2100 Main Street as the headquarters of the local Masonic lodge. The building was destroyed by an arson fire in 1985, and the site today is home to a church.

Three

Markham Street

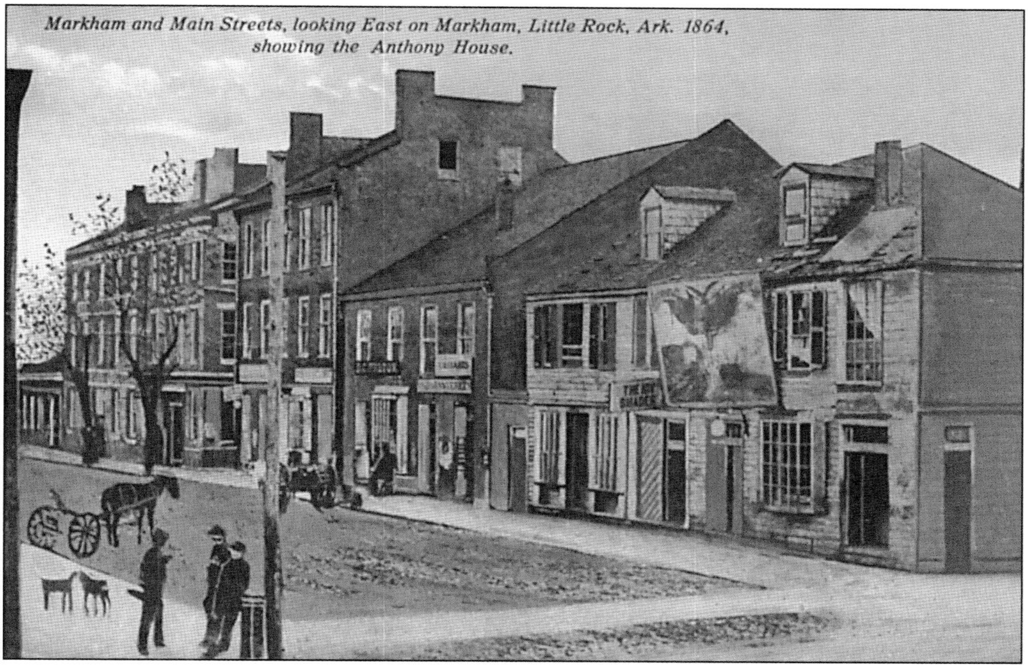

By the time of the Civil War, Markham Street was Little Rock's major commercial district. This 1864 illustration, made during the Union occupation of the city, looks east from the intersection of Markham and Main Streets. The Anthony House, the town's hotel, is seen in the center of the block. None of the structures depicted here survived into the next century.

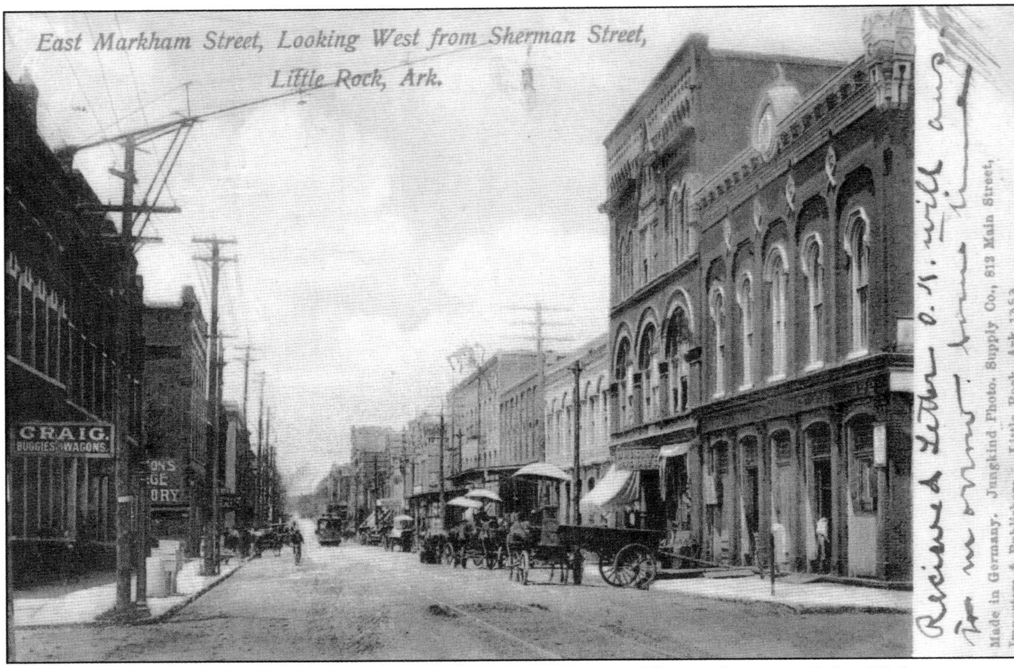

The early part of the 20th century found East Markham Street well developed, with livery stables, warehouses, and wholesale outlets that served retailers a few blocks west on Main Street. This 1907 postcard photograph looks west from the intersection of Sherman and East Markham Streets. Today, these buildings are gone, replaced by a new Marriott Courtyard hotel on the left and the Museum of Discovery and River Market on the right.

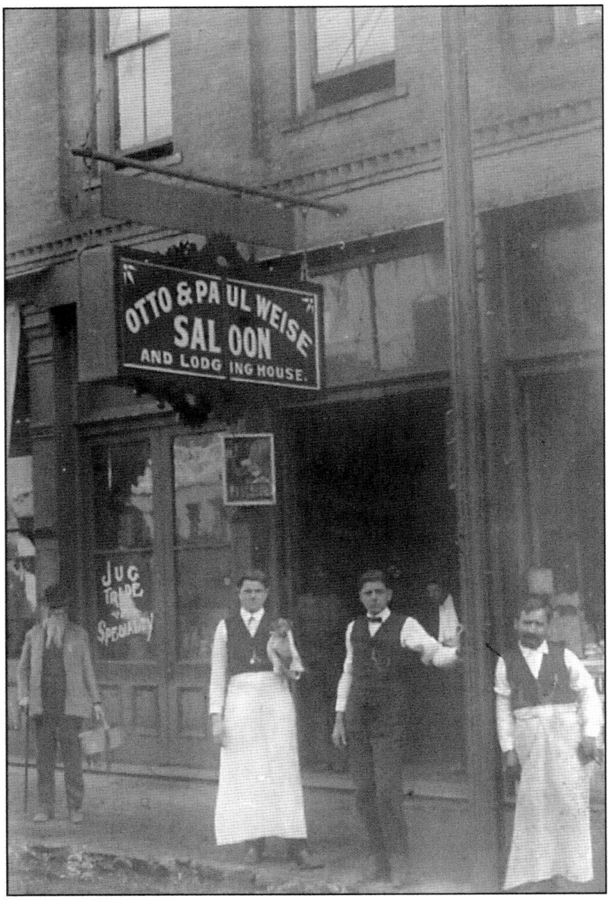

Otto and Paul Weise's saloon and lodging house was located at 330 East Markham Street, just three blocks off the Main Street business district. The brothers proclaim in one of the windows, "Jug Trade Our Specialty." Seen here around 1900, the brothers appear to be identical twins; one is holding a small puppy. An employee poses at right, and an elderly customer looks on. The building is long gone. (Courtesy of Butler Center for Arkansas Studies.)

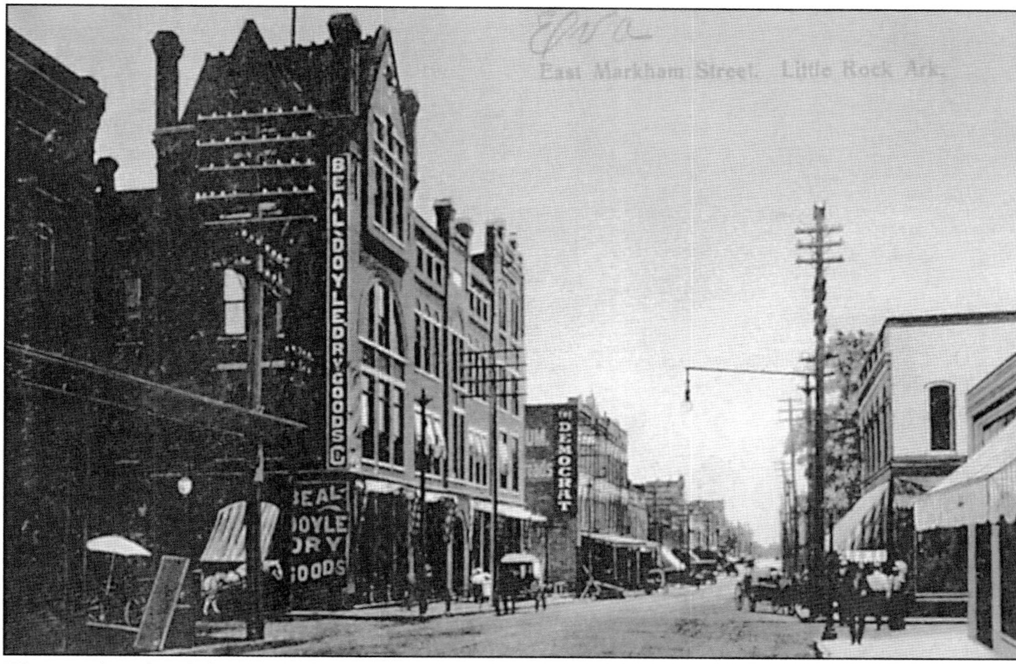

The north side of the 200 block of East Markham Street was home to the striking building of the Beal-Doyle Dry Goods business, seen here in 1910. Today, all the buildings in this postcard scene are gone. The Little Rock Regional Chamber of Commerce occupies the former Beal-Doyle block.

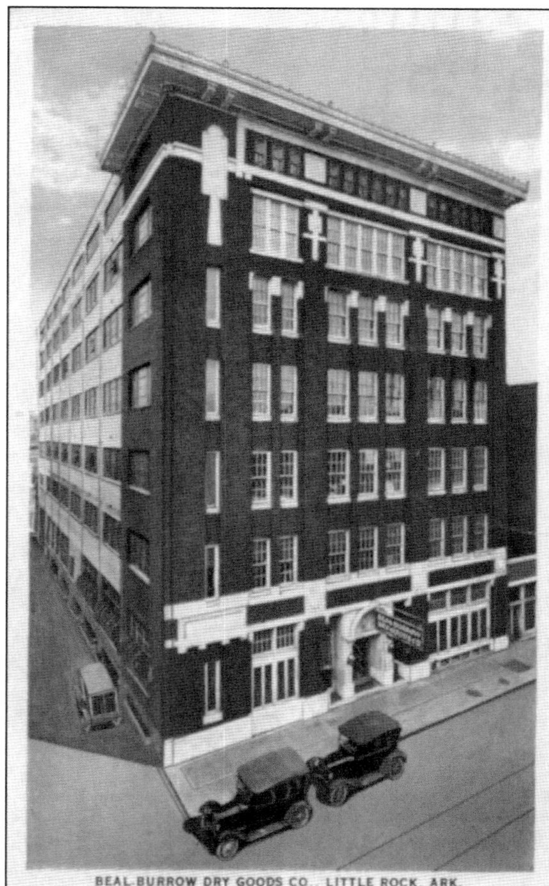

Mr. Beal apparently ended his partnership with Doyle and teamed with Mr. Burrow in the dry goods business. The firm's new home in 1920 was a seven-story building designed in a modified Prairie School style by well-known local architect Charles Thompson. Later serving as home to Archer Drug Company, the structure is mostly empty today, but it is nicely restored and has been added to the National Register of Historic Places.

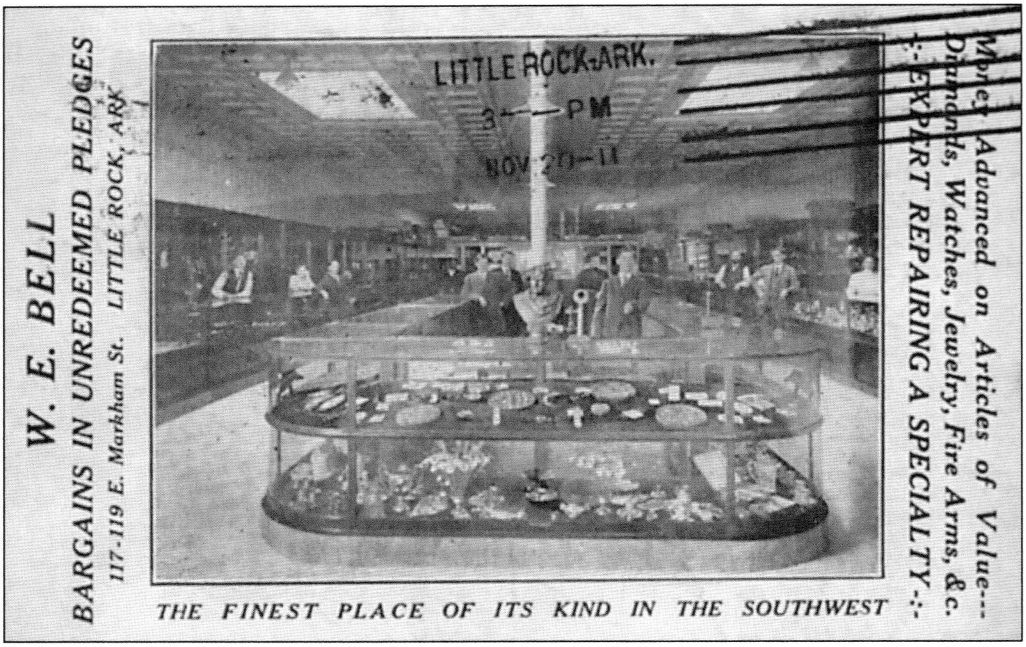

W.E. Bell operated a pawnshop at 117–119 East Markham Street, using the adage "W.E. Bell Rings for You." He loaned money on diamonds, watches, jewelry, and guns and also advertised a repair service. The interior of Bell's business is seen in this 1911 advertising card. Many lovely items fill the glass cases, and a large staff stands at the ready. Today, the site of the business is part of the Little Rock Convention Center complex.

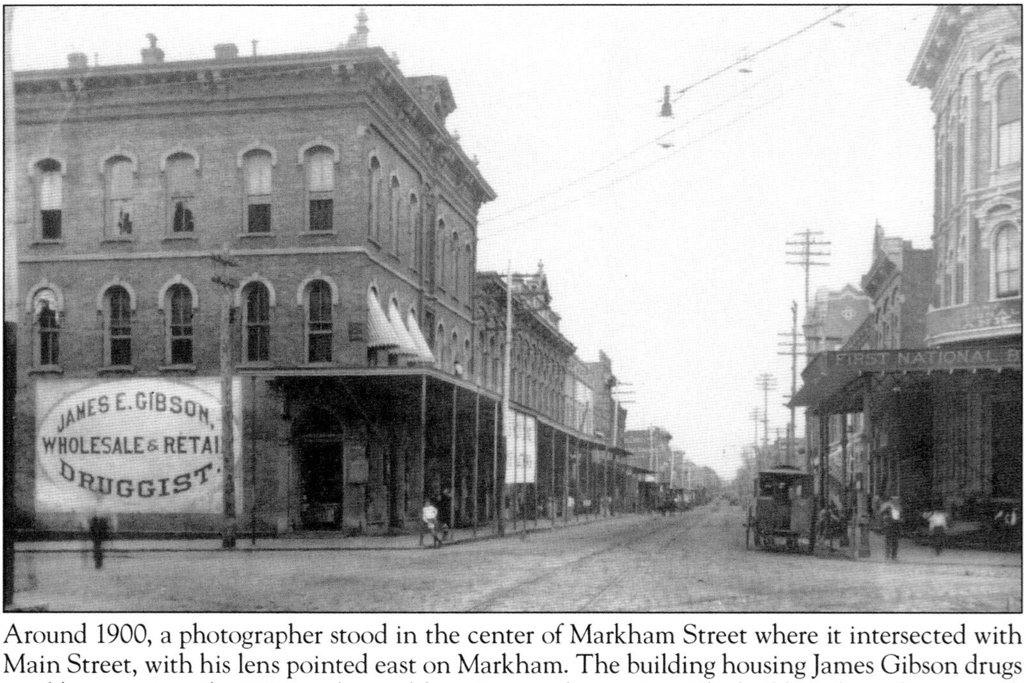

Around 1900, a photographer stood in the center of Markham Street where it intersected with Main Street, with his lens pointed east on Markham. The building housing James Gibson drugs would survive into the 1970s and served for a time as a bus station. The buildings have disappeared, and the Little Rock Convention Center now fills the block.

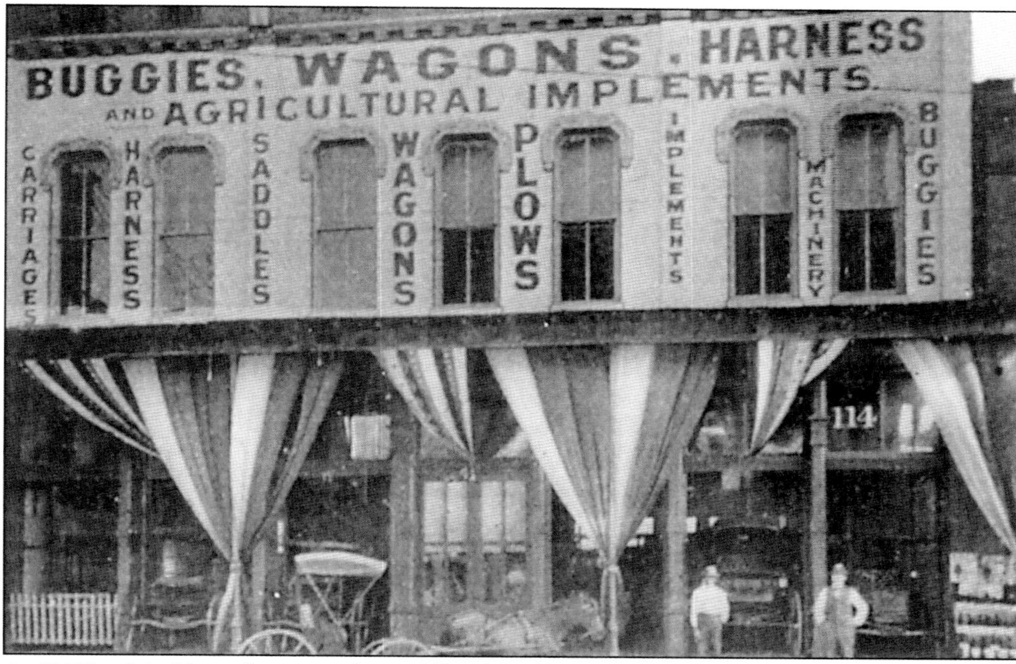

At 114 East Markham Street, in the middle of the block, was a thriving livery business, seen here around 1900. Lettering on the building proclaims a specialty in "Buggies, Wagons, Harness and Agricultural Implements." On this day, the building is decked out in patriotic bunting, perhaps for an Independence Day celebration. In front of the building are two employees and a horse and carriage.

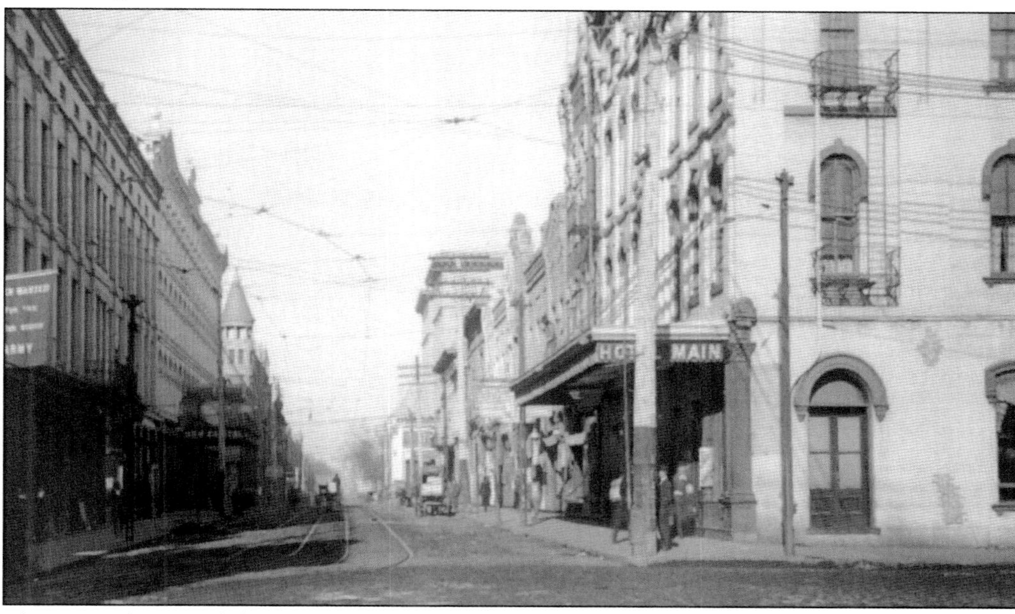

This 1907 photograph looks west down the streetcar tracks on West Markham Street. On the left, a sign solicits Army recruits, with the cast-iron facade of the Capital Hotel just beyond. On the right, the Hotel Main anchors a block of commercial buildings stretching to the Hotel Marion. Everything on the right has been replaced by the Little Rock Convention Center and the Marriott Hotel; on the left are now a parking lot and the restored Capital Hotel.

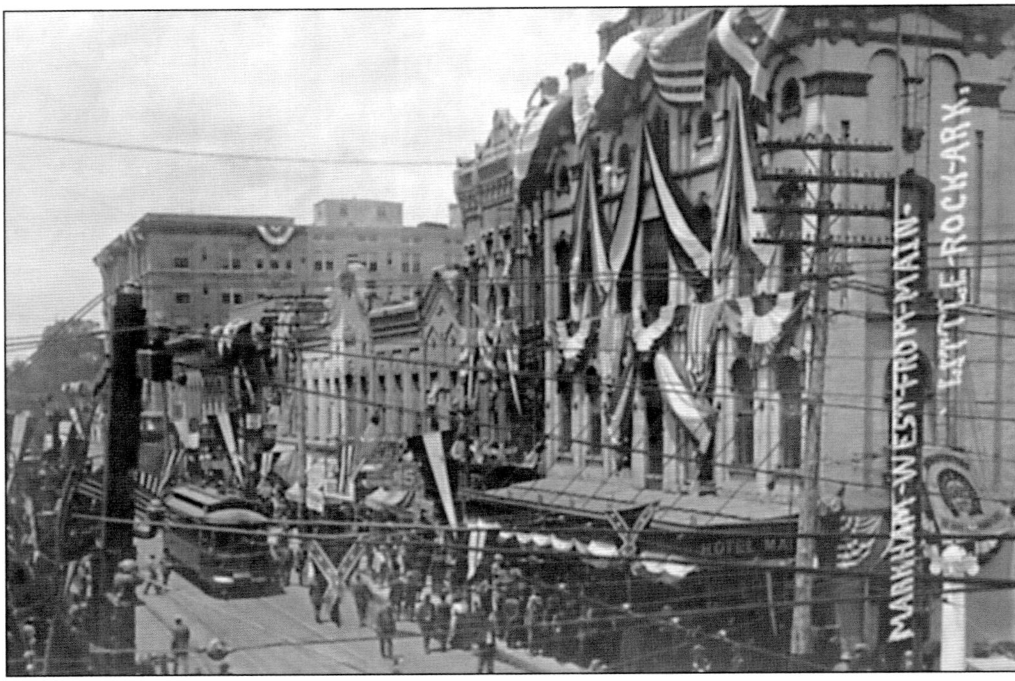

This photograph offers a similar perspective as the previous image. The north side of the 100 block of West Markham Street is decorated for the annual meeting of the United Confederate Veterans, hosted by Little Rock in May 1911, fifty years after the Civil War began. At the intersection with Main Street, the view encompasses the Hotel Main, as well as the Marion Hotel rising in the distance.

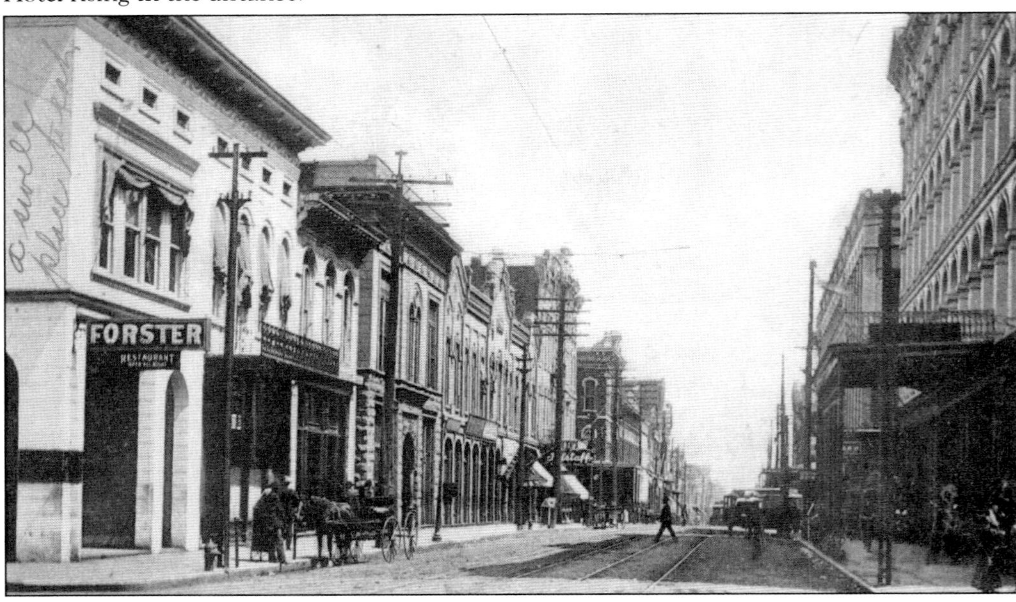

This 1907 photograph looks east from Louisiana Street toward the intersection of Main and Markham Streets. The end of the 100 block was anchored by Forster's Restaurant, "Open all night." The long line of handsome brick and stone buildings gradually gave way over the next few decades; they are all gone. The proudly restored five-star Capital Hotel, on the immediate right, preserves the memories of days past.

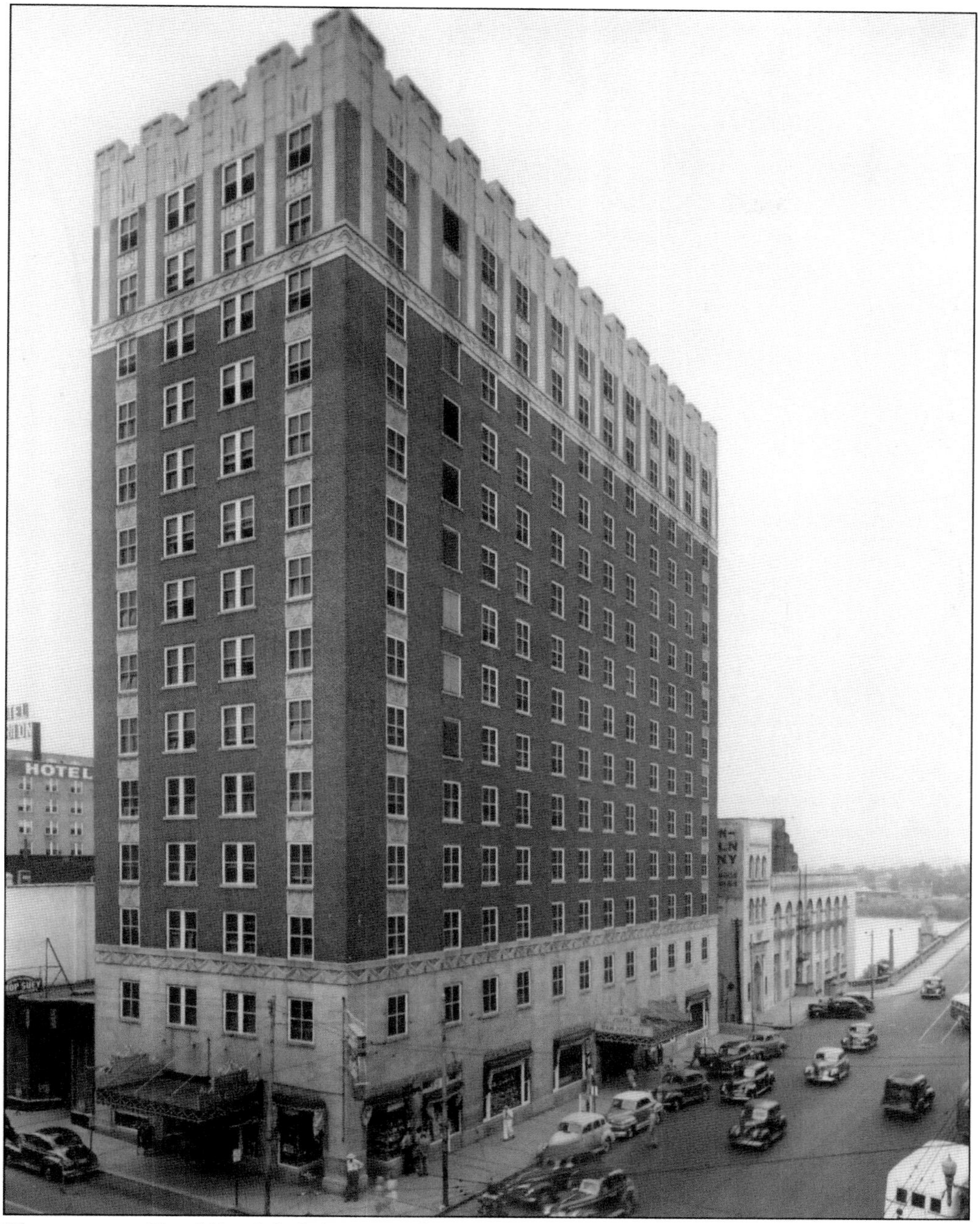

The towering Hotel Ben McGehee, seen here around 1940, stood at the foot of the Main Street Bridge. At 14 stories, the Ben McGehee was the tallest hotel in Little Rock when it was built in the 1930s in the Beaux-Arts style. (Courtesy of Butler Center for Arkansas Studies.)

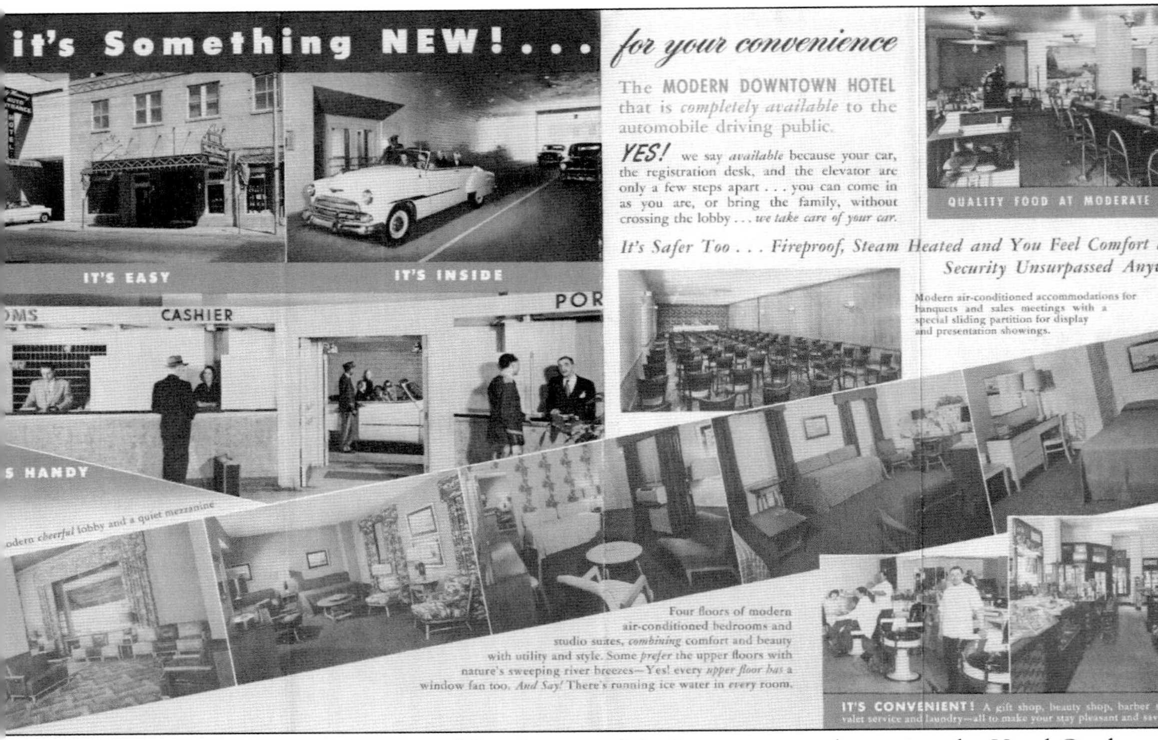

The Hotel Ben McGehee was sold and renamed for its new owner, becoming the Hotel Grady Manning. Its 1950 brochure advertised a "Modern 300 Room Air Conditioned Downtown Hotel that is Completely Available to the Automobile Driving Public." The ability to park within feet of the registration desk was a feature designed to counter the growing popularity of tourist courts and motels spreading to the edges of the city.

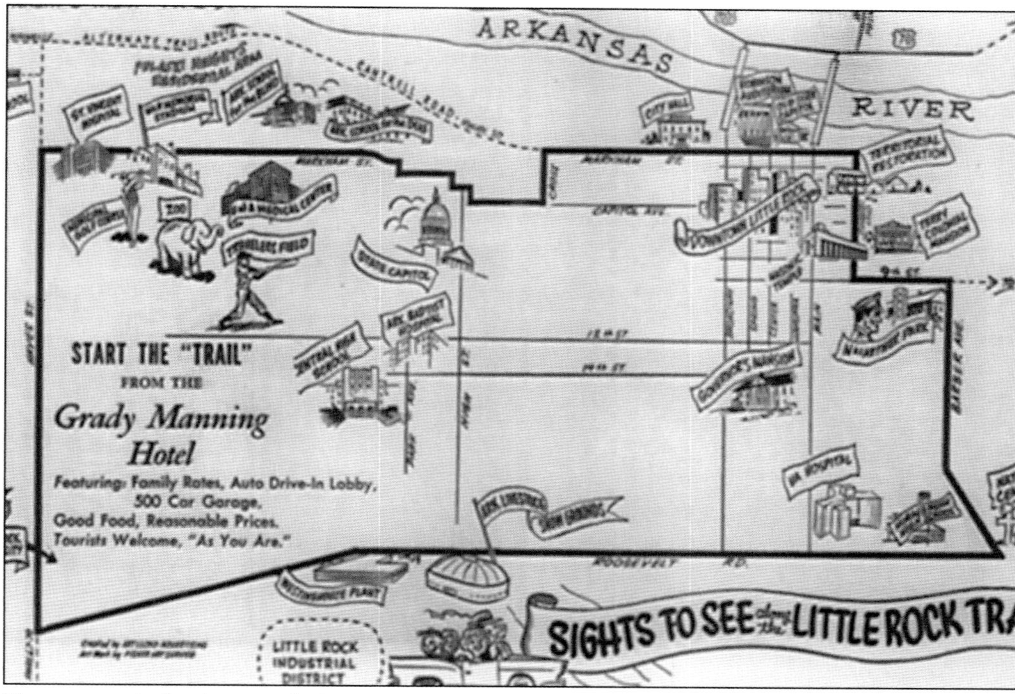

To promote its business and city, the owners of the Grady Manning helped sponsor "the Little Rock Trail," beginning, of course, at the hotel. Sights promoted included MacArthur Park, the VA Hospital, Central High, the Baptist Hospital, the schools for the Deaf and Blind, and two new hospitals farther west on Markham Street, the University Hospital and St. Vincent's. (Courtesy of Butler Center for Arkansas Studies.)

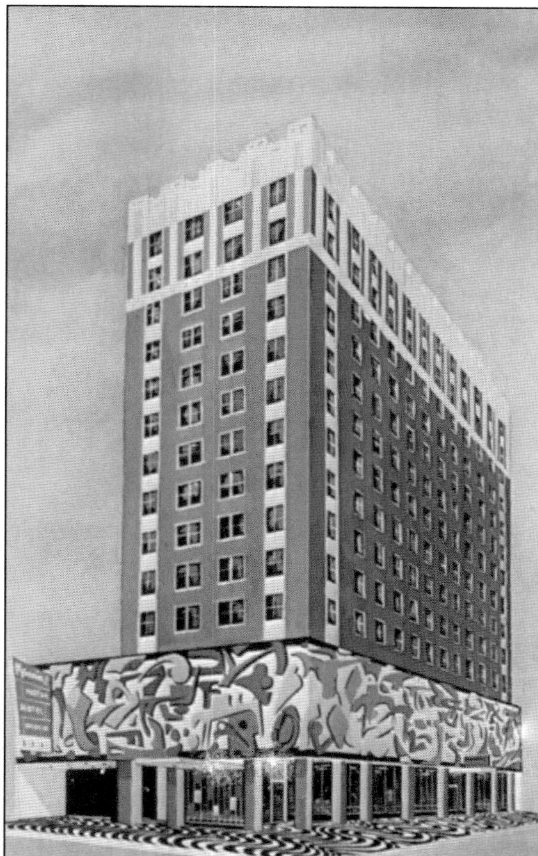

The Grady Manning was renamed the Manning Motor Hotel by the 1960s, "Featuring the new décor 'Colorama.' " The colorful abstract panels were wrapped around the lower portion of the building at the second-floor level. The establishment at that time offered "special privileges" for travelling salesmen. It ceased operations and stood boarded up for years. The hotel was imploded in 1980 to make way for a new convention center.

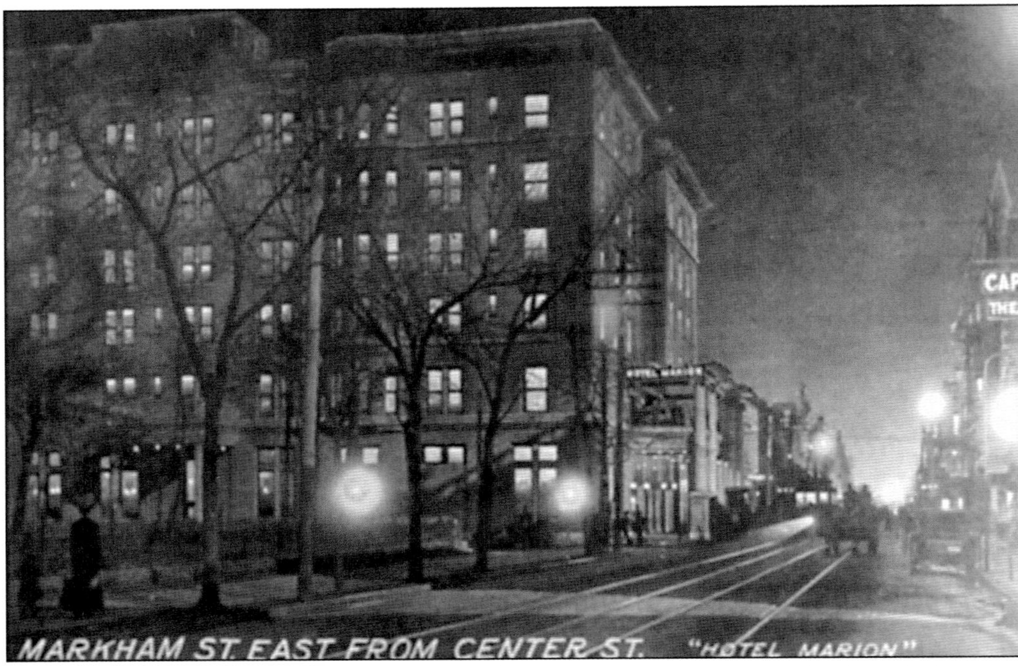

The Hotel Marion, illuminated in this c. 1920 postcard image, was erected in 1907 by Herman Kahn as designed by architect George Mann. The hotel, named for Kahn's wife, anchored much of the 200 block of West Markham Street. Over the years, its celebrated guests included Theodore Roosevelt, Harry Truman, Douglas MacArthur, Helen Keller, and Charles Lindbergh.

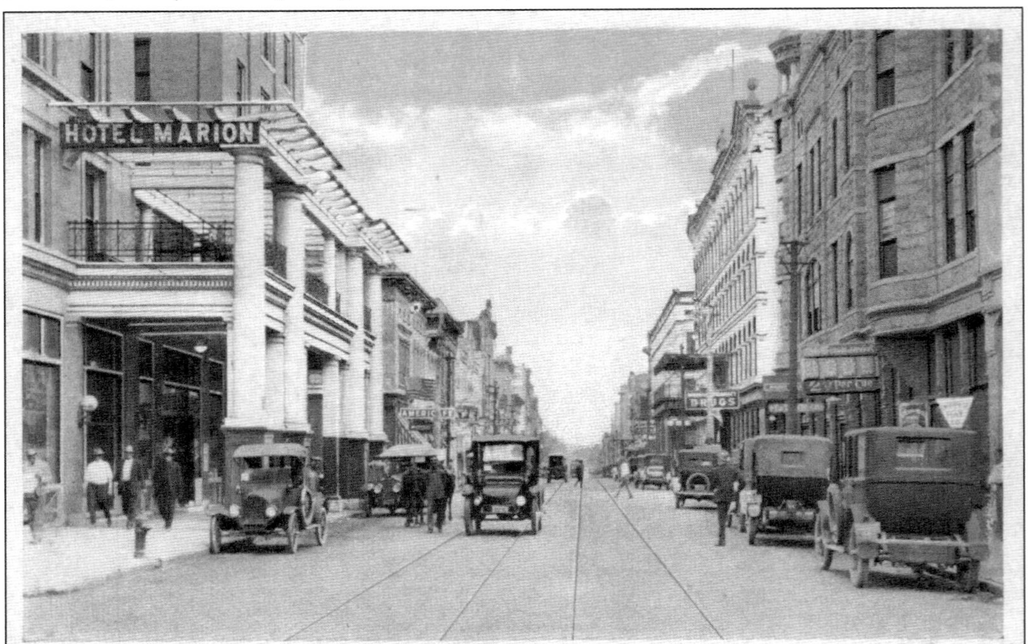

The Hotel Marion, seen here in 1920, was located in perhaps the busiest section of Little Rock, competing with the Capital Hotel just up the street on the right. Other neighboring businesses included a pool hall, a hat shop, and the Americafe, an eatery that advertised itself as "run by ladies." All of the structures seen here, except the Capital Hotel, have disappeared.

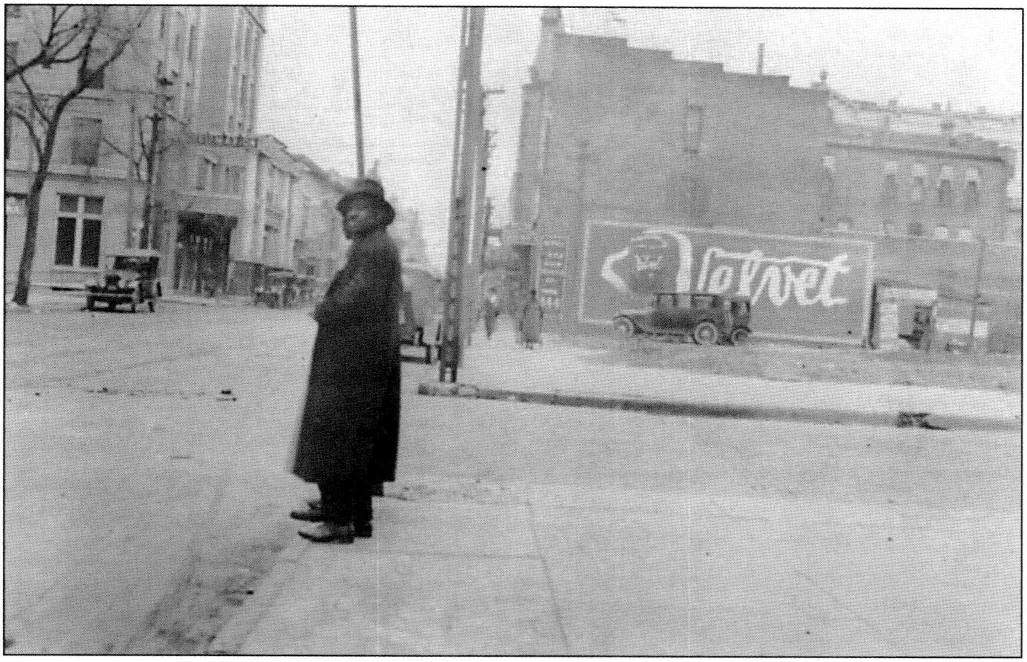

Some of the turn-of-the-century buildings that had stood across from the Marion were gone by the time of this 1930 photograph of two gentlemen waiting to cross the street. Everything seen here was gone by 1980, including the offices of the Little Rock Taxicab Co., which sported a large painted advertisement for Velvet smoking tobacco. (Courtesy of Butler Center for Arkansas Studies.)

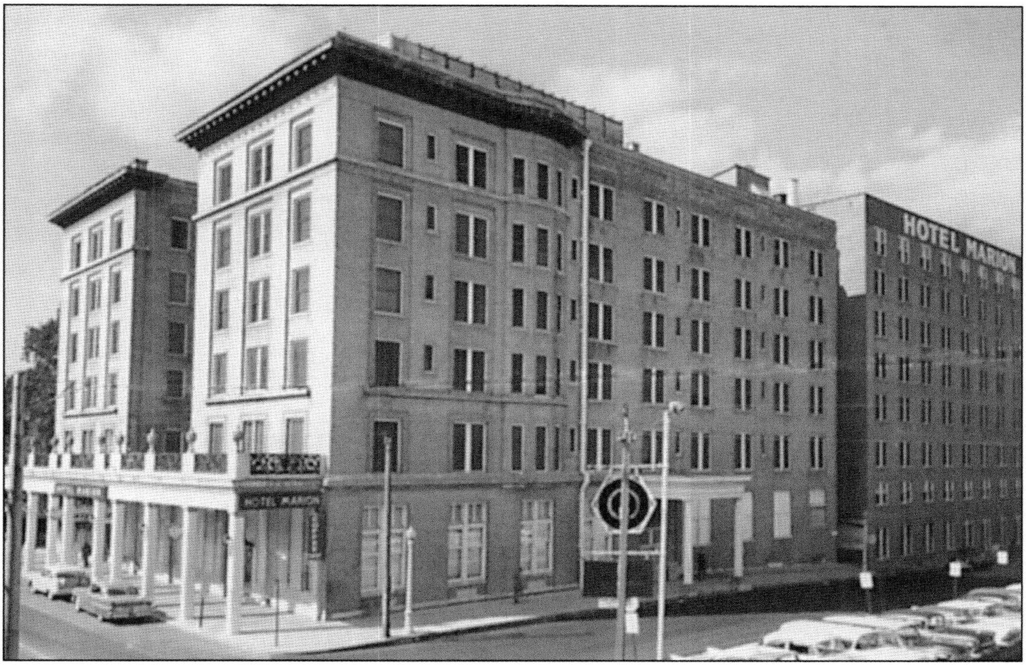

The Hotel Marion had expanded over the years to include an annex behind the original structure, giving it a capacity of 500 rooms. This 1957 advertising card proclaims, " 'Meet me at the Marion in Little Rock'—a familiar expression coast to coast." The postcard also promoted the Gar Hole bar, a 24-hour coffee shop, two parking garages, and family rates.

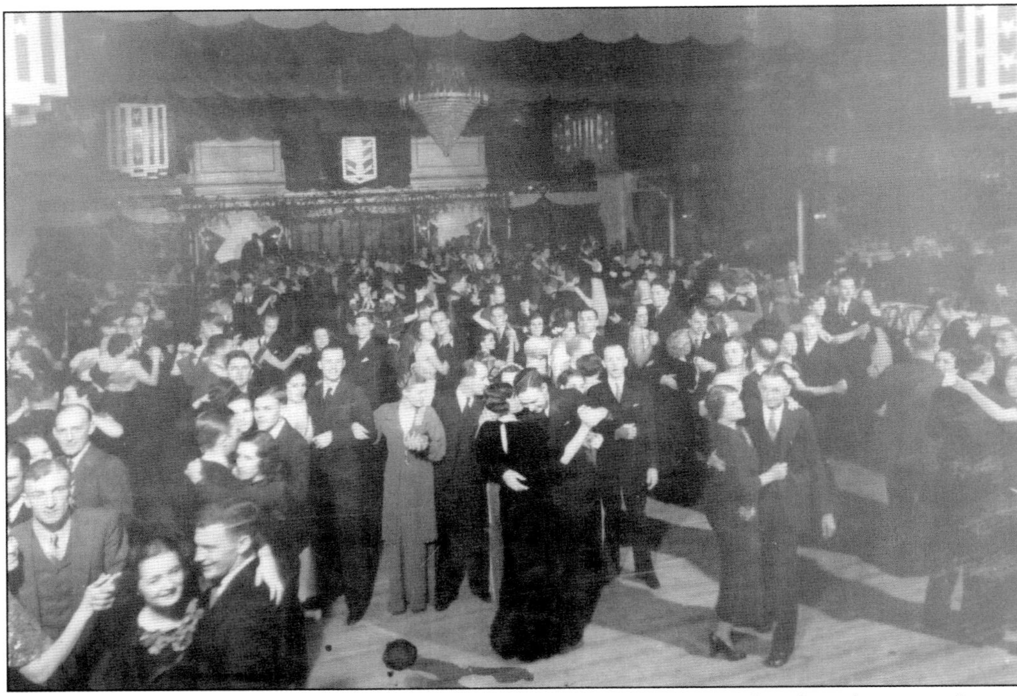

The ballroom of the Hotel Marion hosted many gala events over its decades of service. At one such occasion around 1930, well-dressed couples twirl on the dance floor. The photograph was apparently taken from the bandstand. A likely witness to many such events was American author Richard Ford, who claimed the Marion Hotel as home. He spent the summers of his youth living with his grandparents, who managed the hotel.

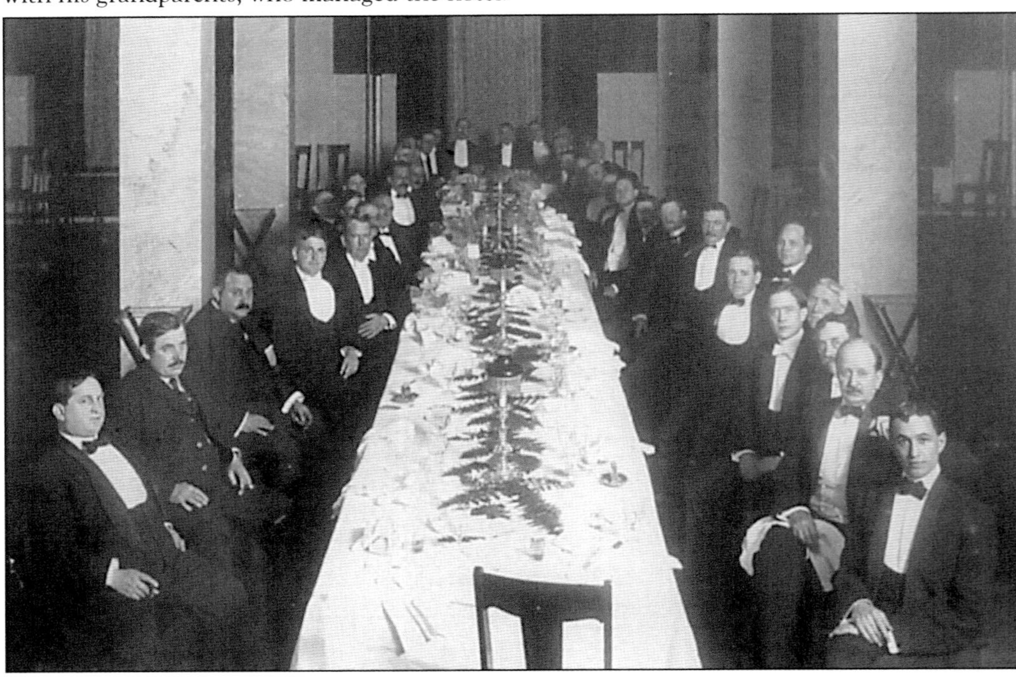

The Marion was for decades Little Rock's leading convention hotel. The tuxedo-clad men finishing dinner in this 1907 photograph were attending a convention at the new hotel.

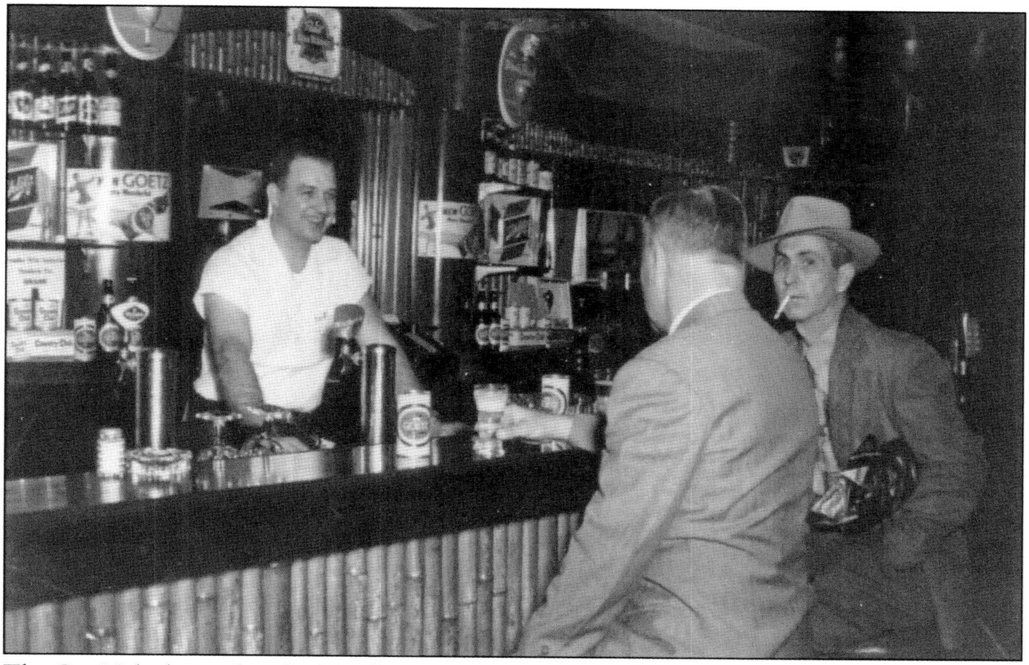

The Gar Hole, located in the Hotel Marion, was likely the best-known bar in Arkansas for many years. It was quite popular with politicians and those who sought to influence them. Pictured behind the bamboo-fronted bar in 1960 is owner George Morgan, serving Goetz Beer to his suited customers. (Courtesy of Butler Center for Arkansas Studies.)

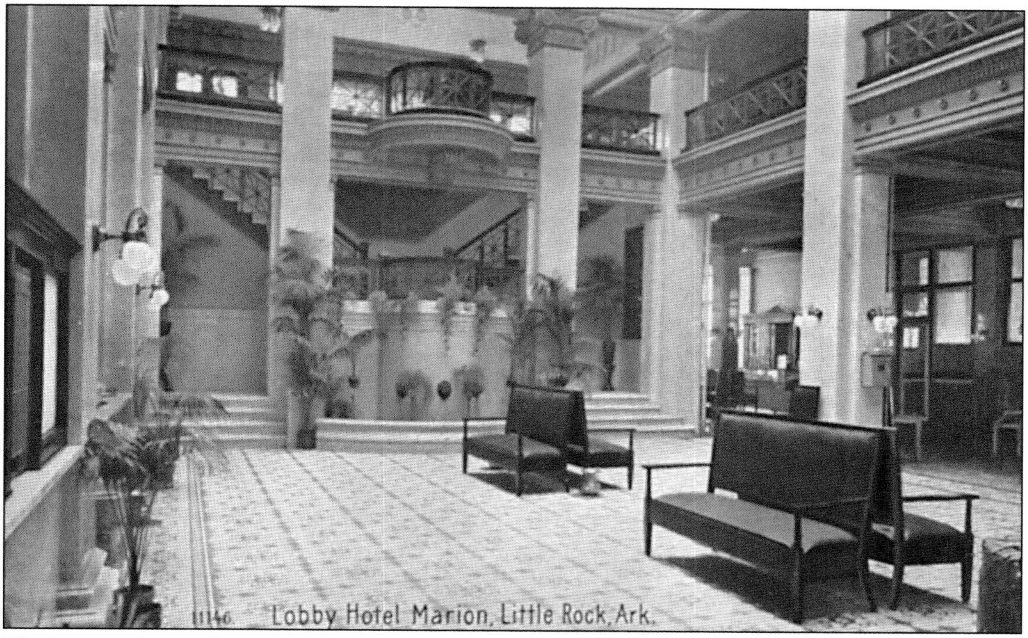

The Marion boasted a spacious, well-appointed lobby, seen here in 1910, a few years after opening. The lobby saw thousands of people pass through its halls, from famous celebrities to businesspeople, conventioneers, and tourists. The Marion Hotel was boarded up for a number of years after the business closed; this center of history was imploded in 1980 to make way for a new hotel and convention center.

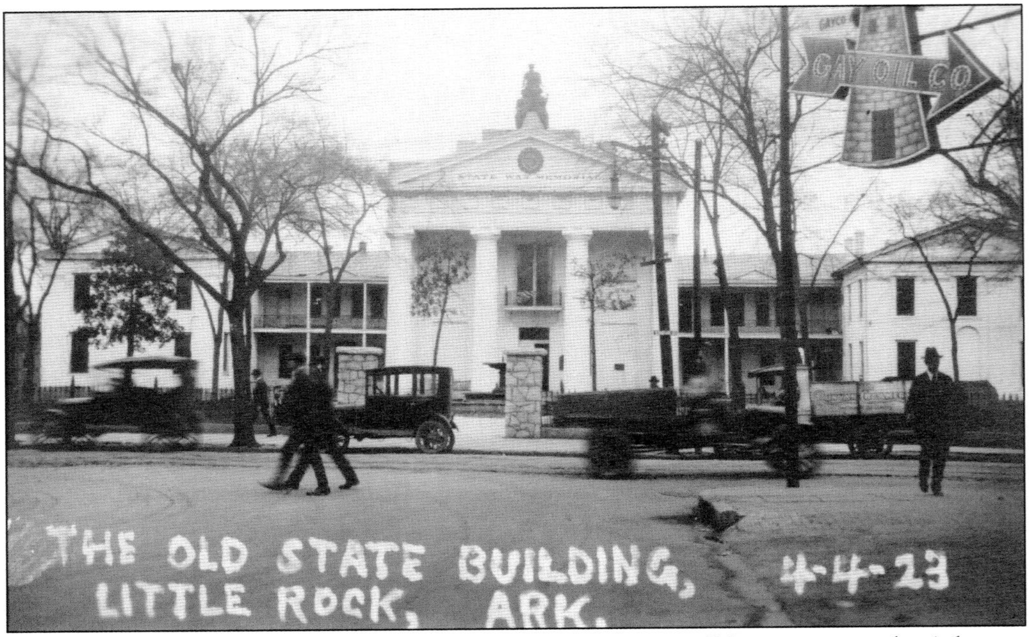

When the Marion opened in 1907, its neighbor to the west was still functioning as the Arkansas State Capitol. A short time later, however, a new capitol building was completed a few blocks away. In 1921, right before this photograph was taken, the building was renamed the Arkansas War Memorial and was used for meetings and events. The statues visible atop the building were removed by a local ladies club in the 1920s, which considered them in poor taste.

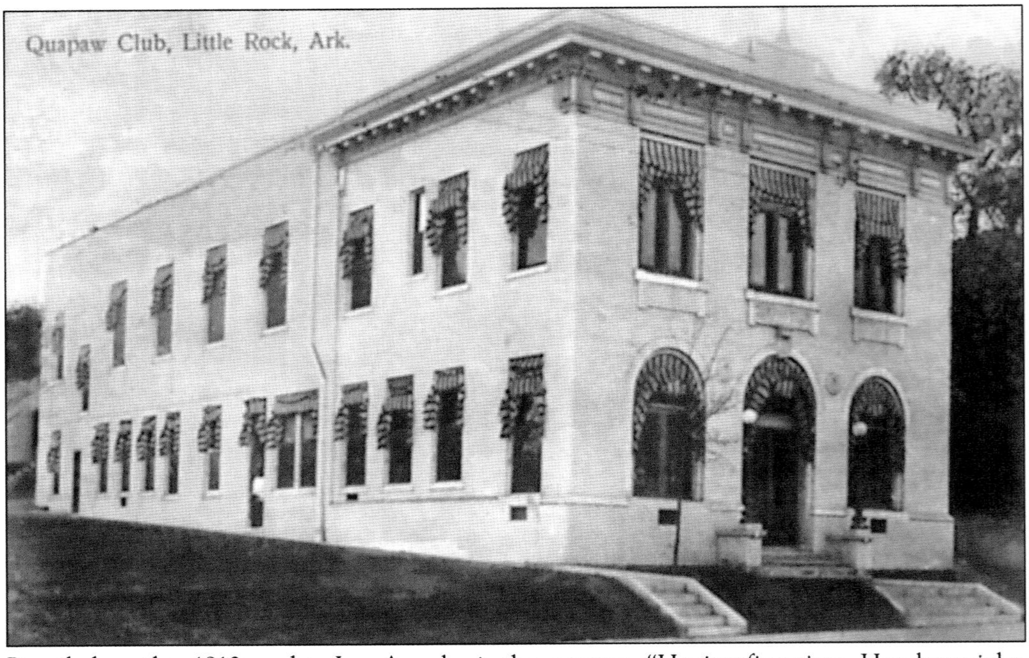

Penciled on this 1910 card to Los Angeles is the message, "Having fine time. Hop last night, Snooker to-night. Hot Springs Friday." The postcard image is of the Quapaw Club, a prestigious men's club in Little Rock society. The building stood on West Markham Street between Spring Street and Broadway.

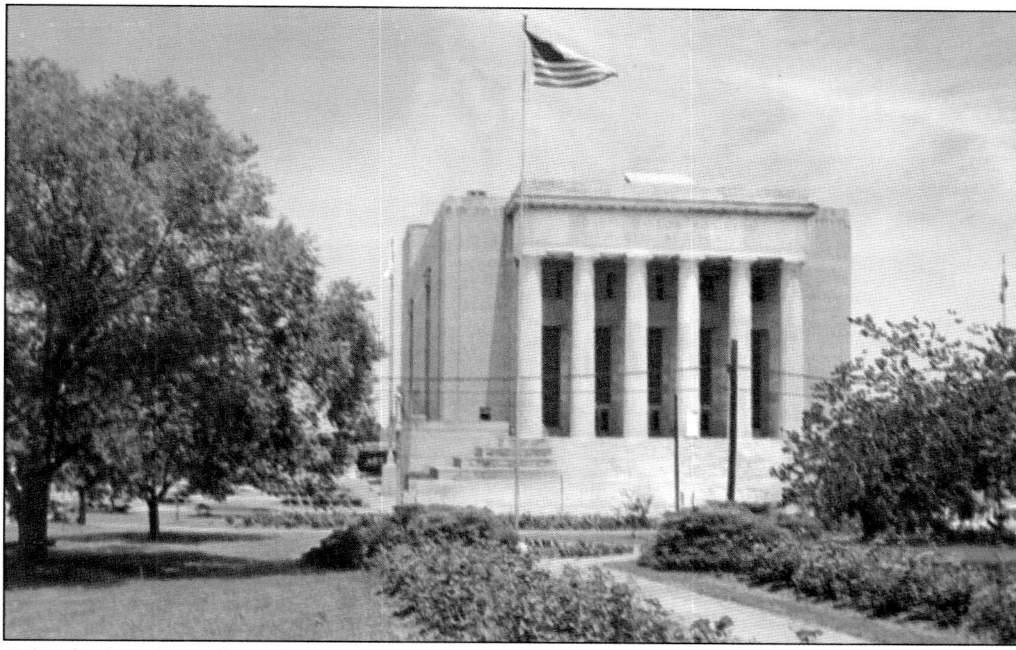

A bit farther down from the Old State House, also on the north side of East Markham Street, stands the Robinson Auditorium, completed in 1940. Named for the late Arkansas senator Joe T. Robinson, the building boasted a 3,000-seat music hall. Though freestanding in this 1950 photograph, today the empty space to the right is filled with a DoubleTree Hotel. Robinson Auditorium closed in 2014 to undergo a multiyear, $70-million renovation.

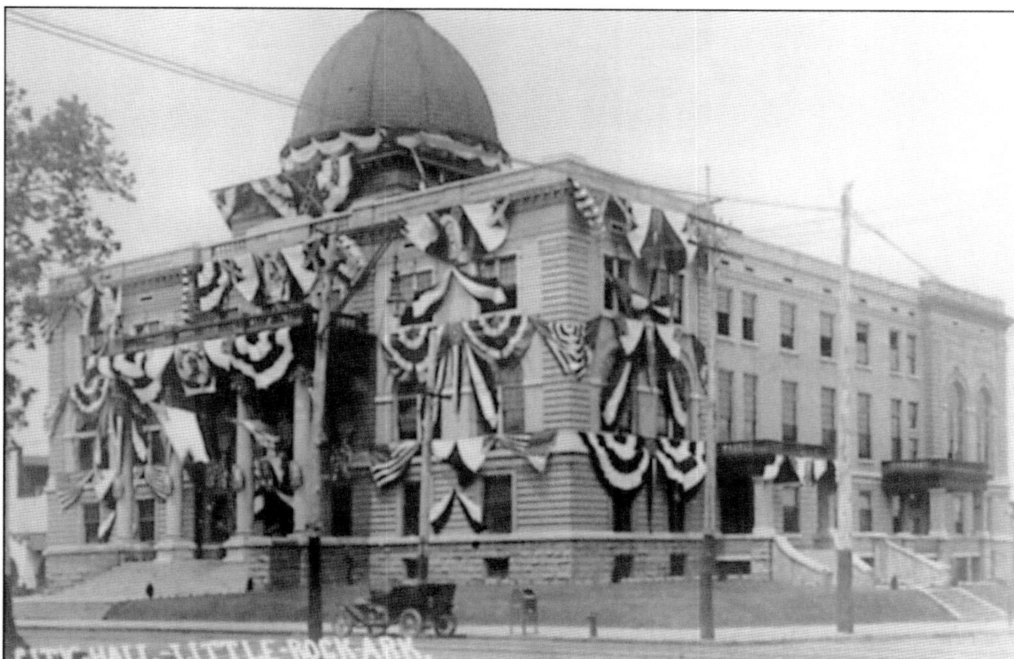

Little Rock City Hall, seen here decorated for the 1911 Confederate Veterans' reunion, was located across Broadway from the future home of Robinson Auditorium. Erected in 1906, the building still stands, minus its dome, which was removed in the 1950s.

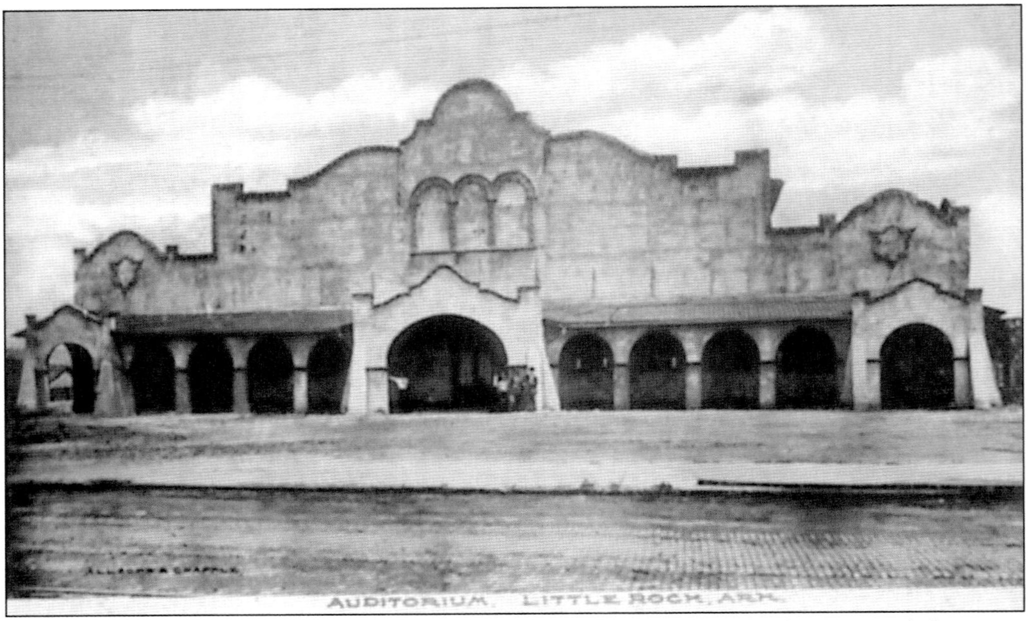

The first Little Rock city auditorium, built in a Southwest Mission style, occupied the space next to city hall. Among the many events it hosted over the years was the Confederate Ball for the 1911 Confederate Veterans' reunion. The building was gone by 1920 to make way for a fire station. Little Rock was without a large performance hall until the completion of Robinson Auditorium in 1940.

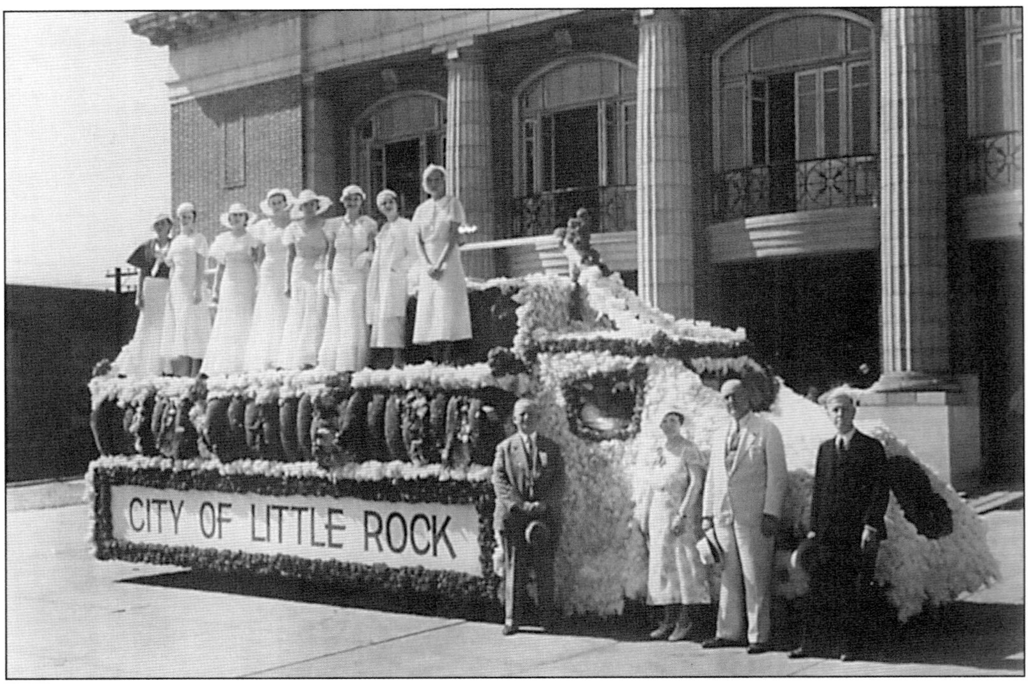

The Central Fire Station, which replaced the old city auditorium, was the backdrop for a 1930 parade promoting the city of Little Rock. The handsome building is no longer a fire station, as its pillars were unable to accommodate the newer, larger fire trucks. It has been converted to office space and adjoins city hall, but it retains its original facade.

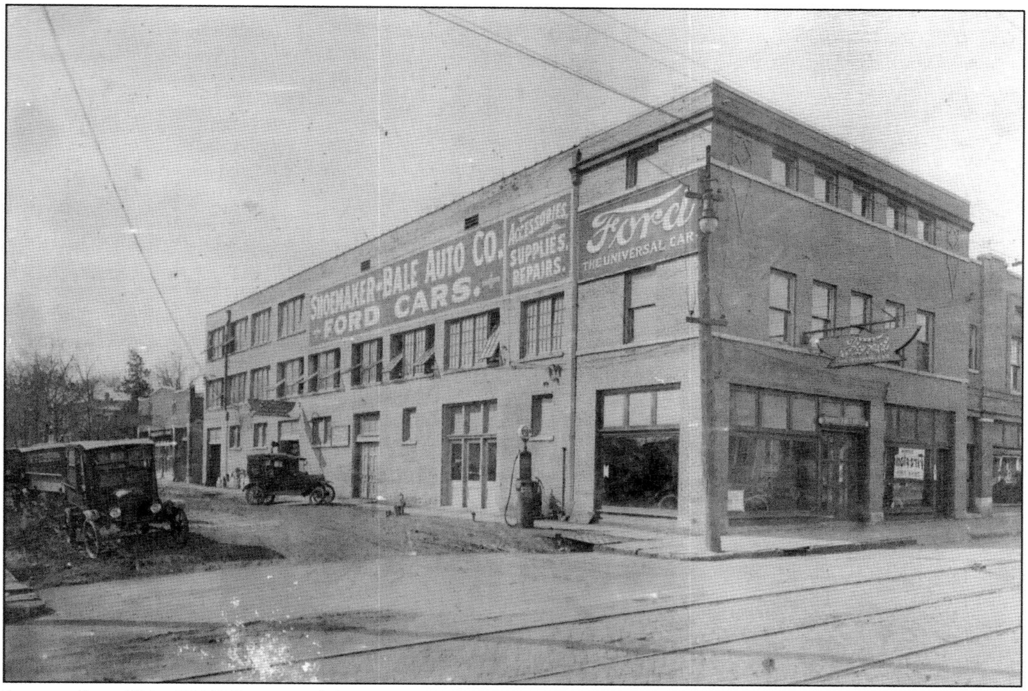

Located at 601–603 West Markham Street was the Shoemaker-Bale Auto Company, selling Ford, "the universal car," according to the sign. In the photograph above, taken in 1915, a banner in the front window advertises Firestone tires. The Bale name would be well known in Little Rock car sales for decades to come, to the present day. The photograph below shows the interior of the dealership's service department, where these mechanics are studying a stripped-down model under repair.

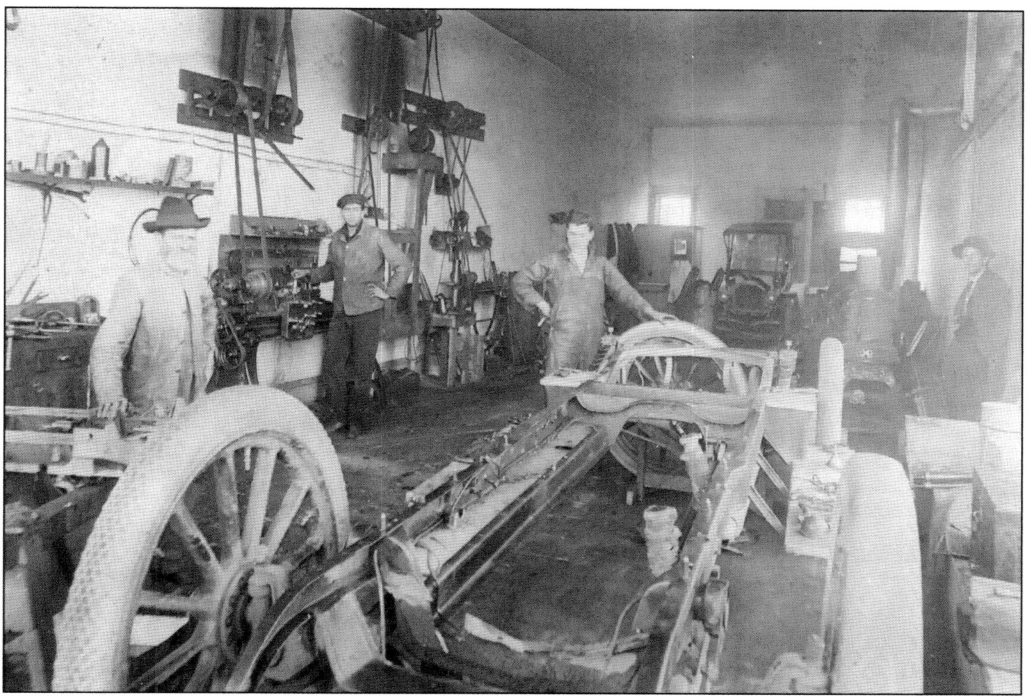

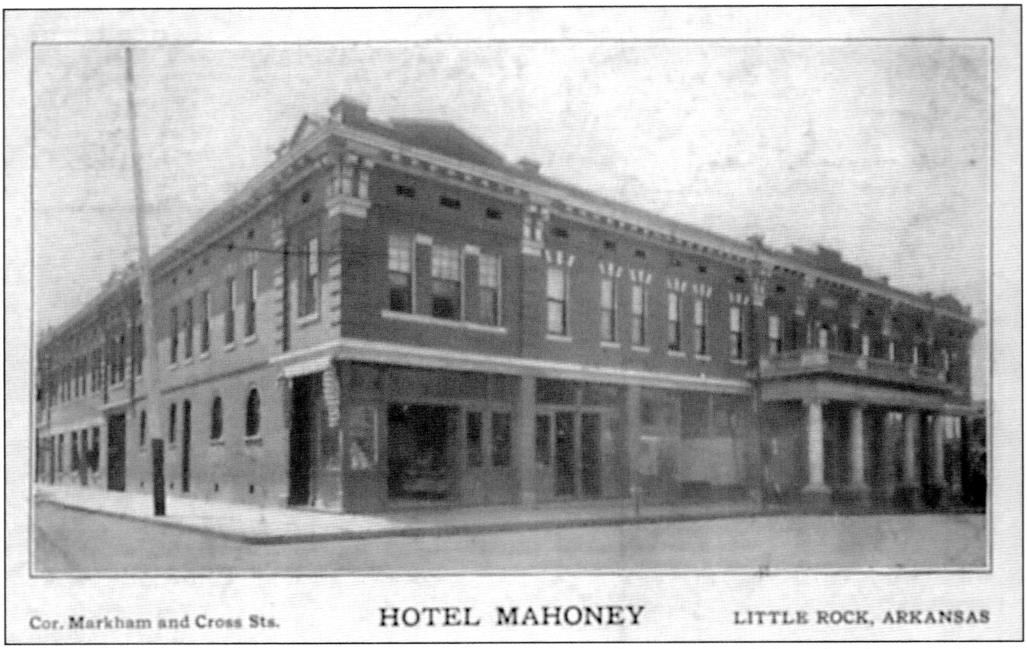

As Markham Street neared the train station, budget hotels were established for the use of those arriving in town but unable or unwilling to pay to stay at the Hotel Marion or Capital Hotel. One such was Hotel Mahoney, at the corner of Markham and Cross Streets, seen here around 1915. The hotel is gone, replaced by the facilities of the Salvation Army.

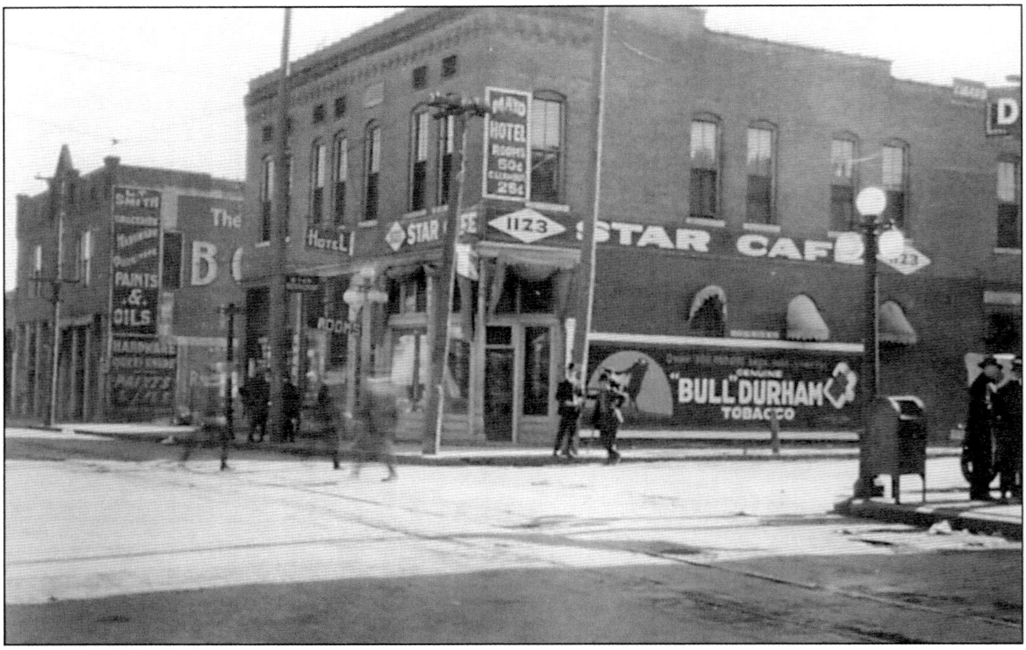

The Star Café, on the corner at 1123 West Markham Street, shared a building with the Mayo Hotel, which advertised rooms for 50¢, though another option was "clean beds 25 cents." Nearby, across a vacant lot, stands the store of L.T. Smith, who advertised hardware, queens ware dishes, paints, and oils. Both buildings have disappeared, and the site is home to lodgings of the Salvation Army. This photograph was taken in 1910. (Courtesy of Butler Center for Arkansas Studies.)

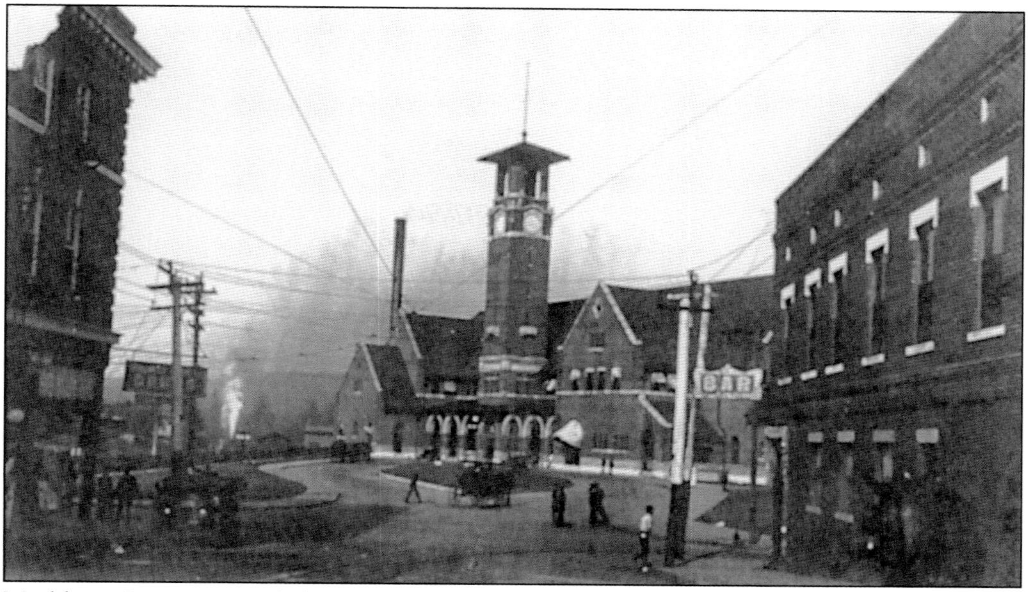

Markham Street proceeded downhill to meet the St. Louis & Iron Mountain train station. The depot burned down in 1922, but it was quickly rebuilt, in an era when trains were still the way people traveled. The building seen on the left in this 1910 photograph housed a drugstore, barbershop, and hotel. It survives today for other uses. The building on the right with the "Bar" sign is gone.

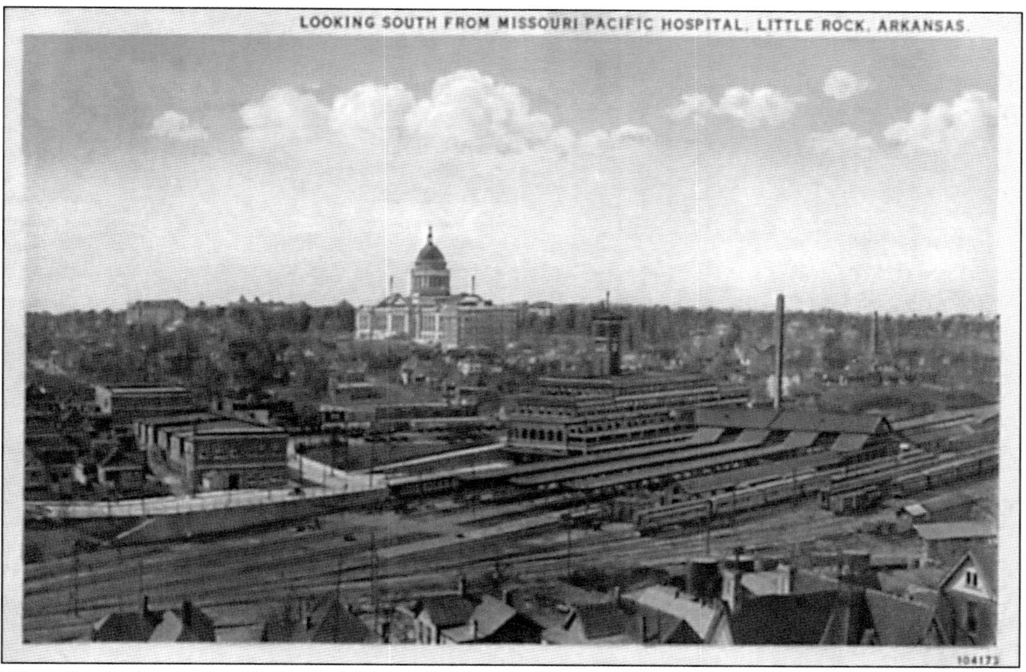

The rebuilt depot, seen here in 1925, had a flat roof but retained its distinctive square bell tower. This photograph, taken from atop the Missouri Pacific Hospital, features the extensive covered passenger loading areas spread over four spur tracks. The depot still stands today, used for office space and as the Amtrak train station. The covered loading platforms are long gone, with only two tracks in use.

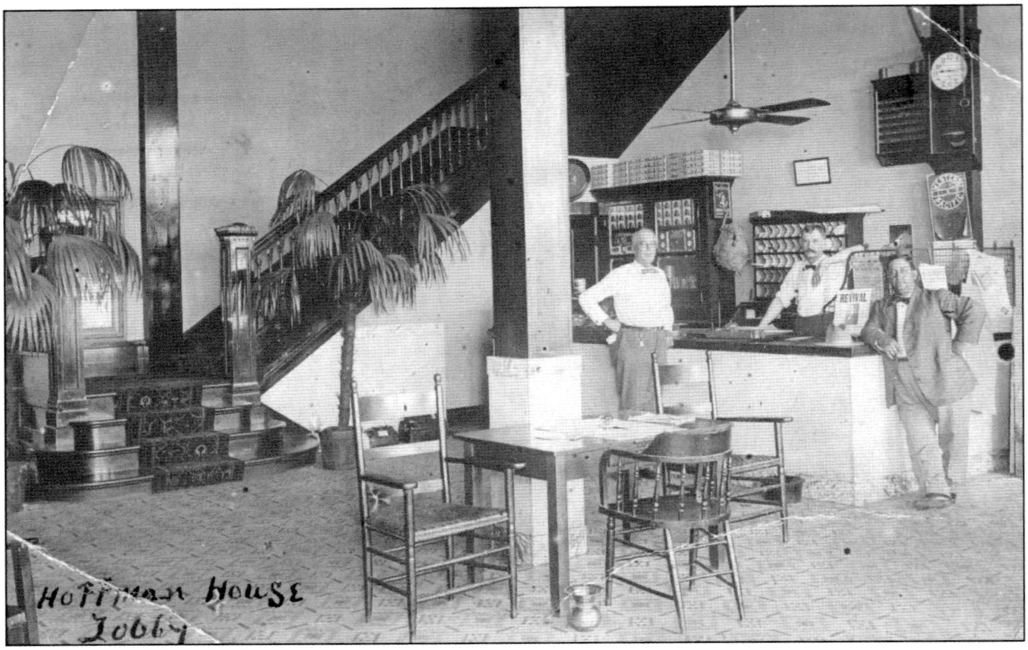

Where Markham Street met Victory Street at the train depot, several hotels were established to cater to those train passengers desiring to stay near the station and who did not demand a lot of luxury. The Hoffman House lobby (above) is seen in 1911 at 9:15 a.m., as indicated by the clock high on the wall. A Revival poster is on the desk. Still in business around 1940, the Hoffman had apparently added a more modern annex and become the Hoffman Hotel. The streetcar (below) bears the destination "Fair Park" on the front. As passenger train traffic faded, the Hoffman started to fade as well. It became rundown and was closed up by 1970. In 1973, it was destroyed in a fire, which may have been started by vagrants.

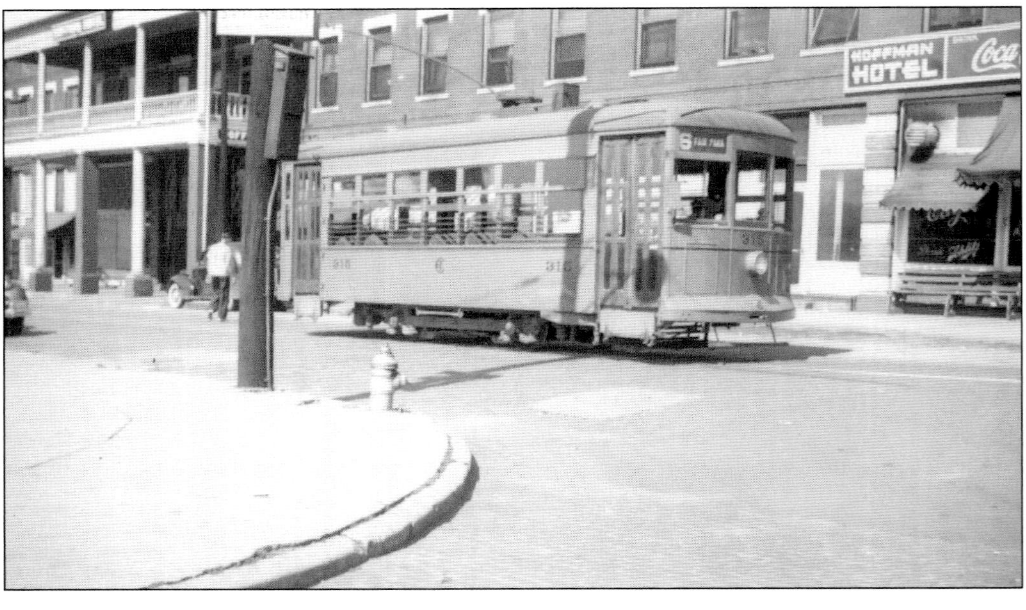

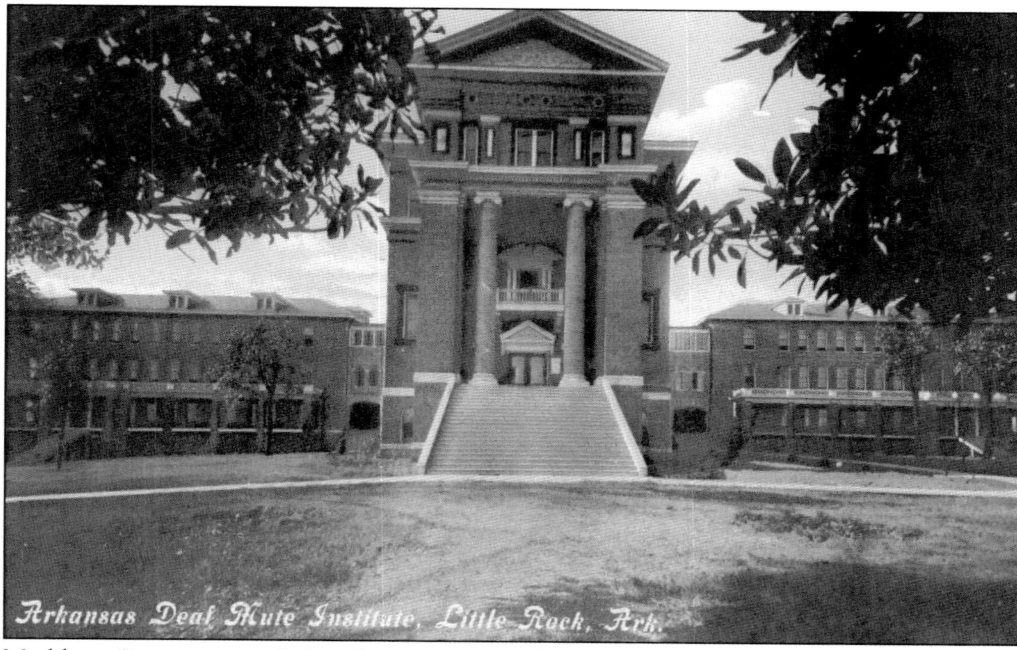

Markham Street once ended at the train station, but it was destined to become a much longer and more significant thoroughfare in the city, with the help of a two-block jump south. West Markham Street begins a few blocks past the state capitol, taking up the path of Third Street near the Arkansas School for the Deaf. Seen here a century ago, the institute still educates hundreds of young people each year.

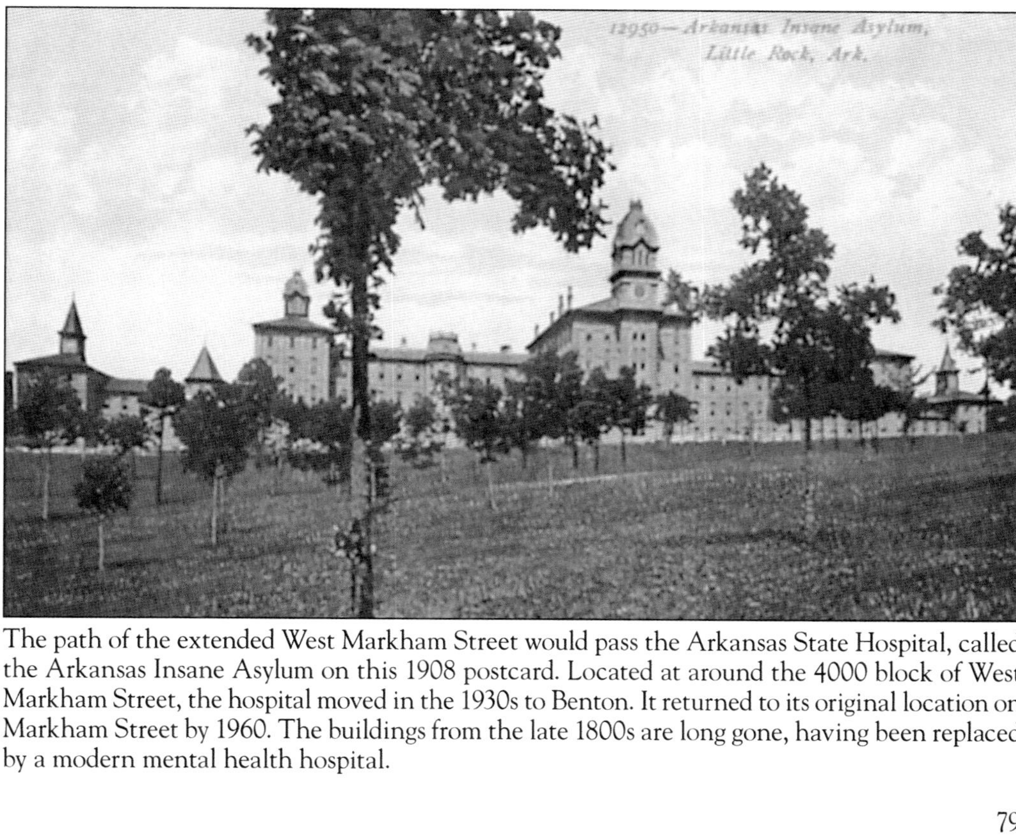

The path of the extended West Markham Street would pass the Arkansas State Hospital, called the Arkansas Insane Asylum on this 1908 postcard. Located at around the 4000 block of West Markham Street, the hospital moved in the 1930s to Benton. It returned to its original location on Markham Street by 1960. The buildings from the late 1800s are long gone, having been replaced by a modern mental health hospital.

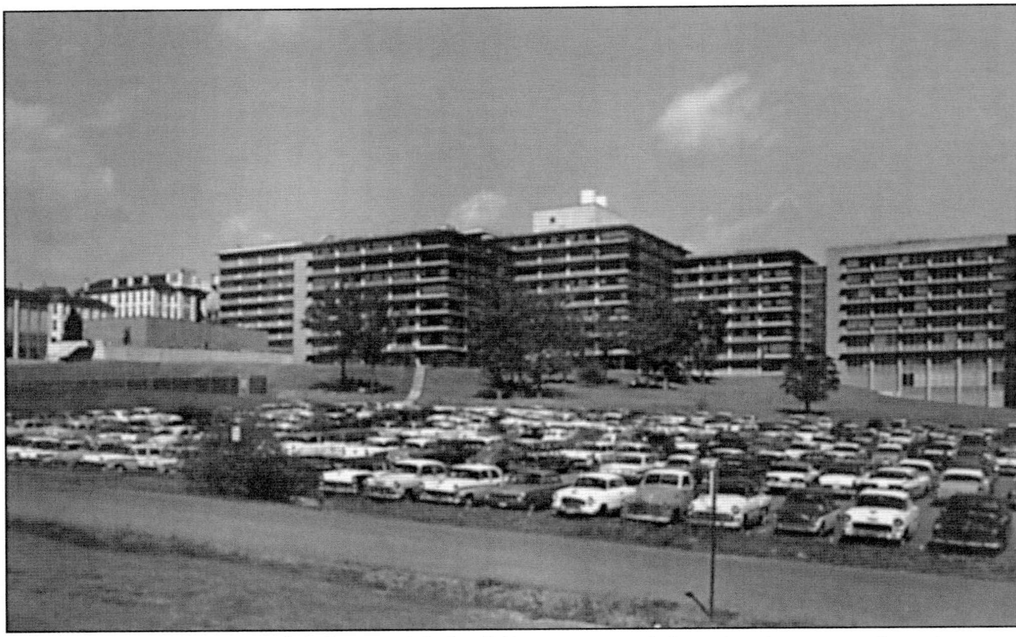

In 1956, the University of Arkansas Medical Center moved from its downtown location near MacArthur Park to a $20 million complex located at 4300 West Markham Street. The UAMS facilities still occupy the site today, much expanded and updated. UAMS serves as the state's only medical school for physicians. The buildings of Arkansas State Hospital, dating from the late 1800s, are visible here in the upper left.

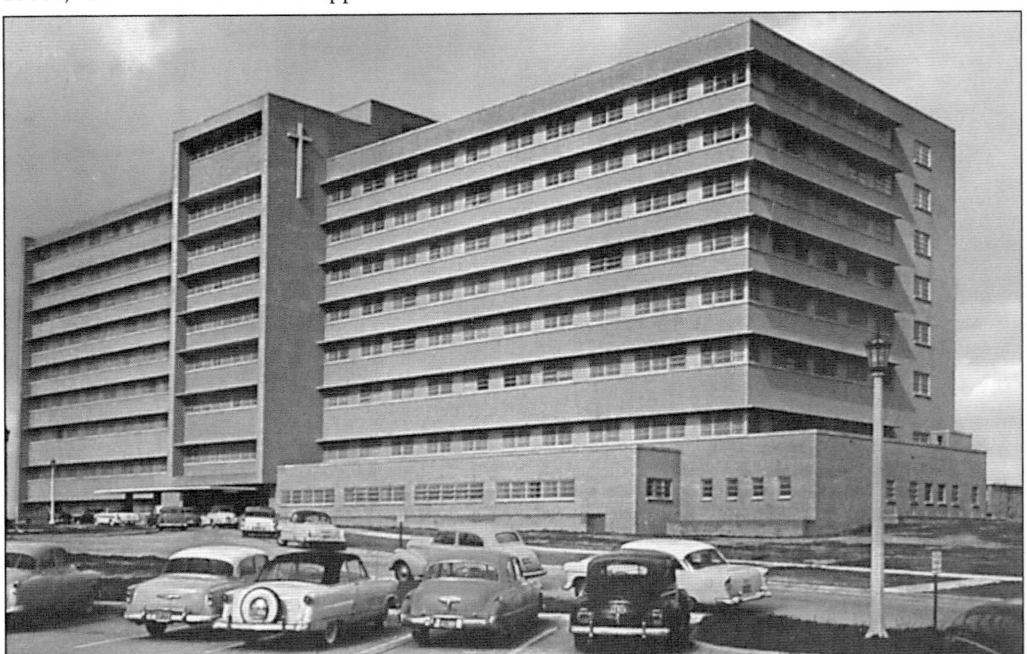

In 1956, St. Vincent's Infirmary left its Cross Street location, where it had been for half a century, and moved to this modern campus at the corner of West Markham Street and Hayes Street (today University Avenue). The hospital still occupies that corner and is a much larger, state-of-the-art health campus.

Four
Capitol Avenue

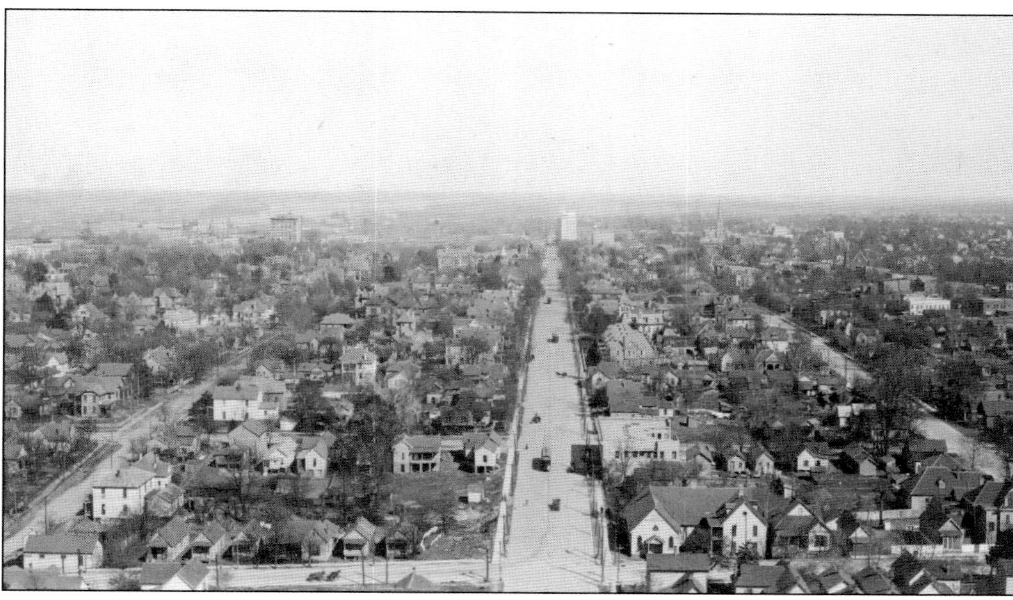

Capitol Avenue began the 20th century as Fifth Street, a major east-west thoroughfare in the growing city. This 1910 photograph was taken from atop the unfinished new state capitol building at the western edge of the city. The view looks down Fifth Street toward Main Street, where the State National Bank building rises. Streetcars go up and down the wide avenue, which at the time was lined with large homes and stately churches.

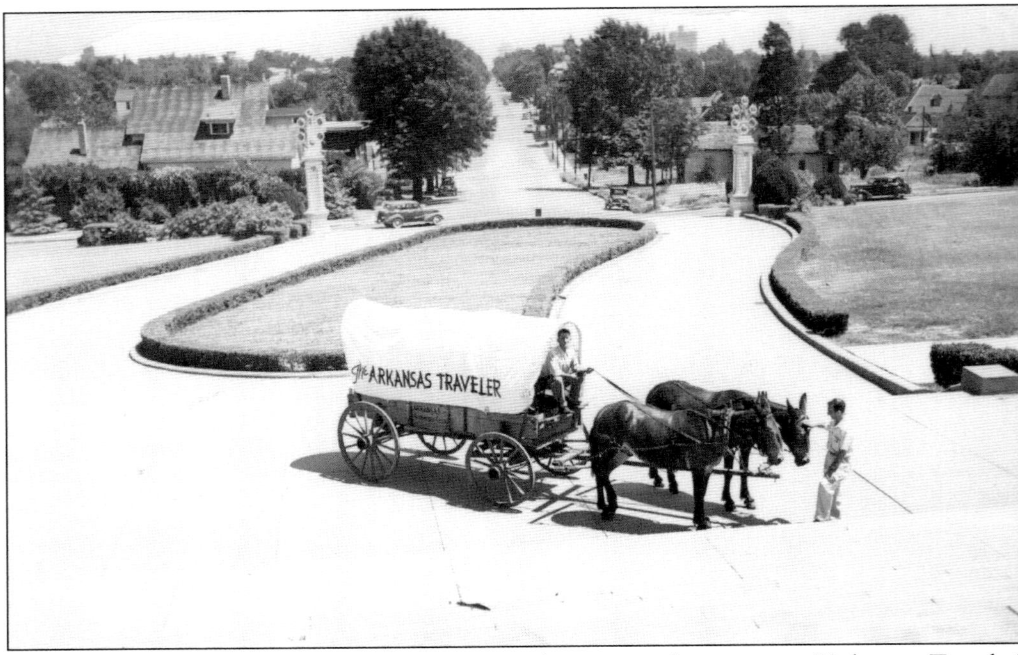

In 1940, the Arkansas Automobile Club promoted its services by posing an "Arkansas Traveler" covered wagon at various sites around Little Rock. The mule-drawn conveyance is seen here in front of the Arkansas State Capitol building. Beyond the wagon is tree-lined Capitol Avenue. The Woodlane Apartments building is on the left; it and most of the trees on Capitol Avenue are gone.

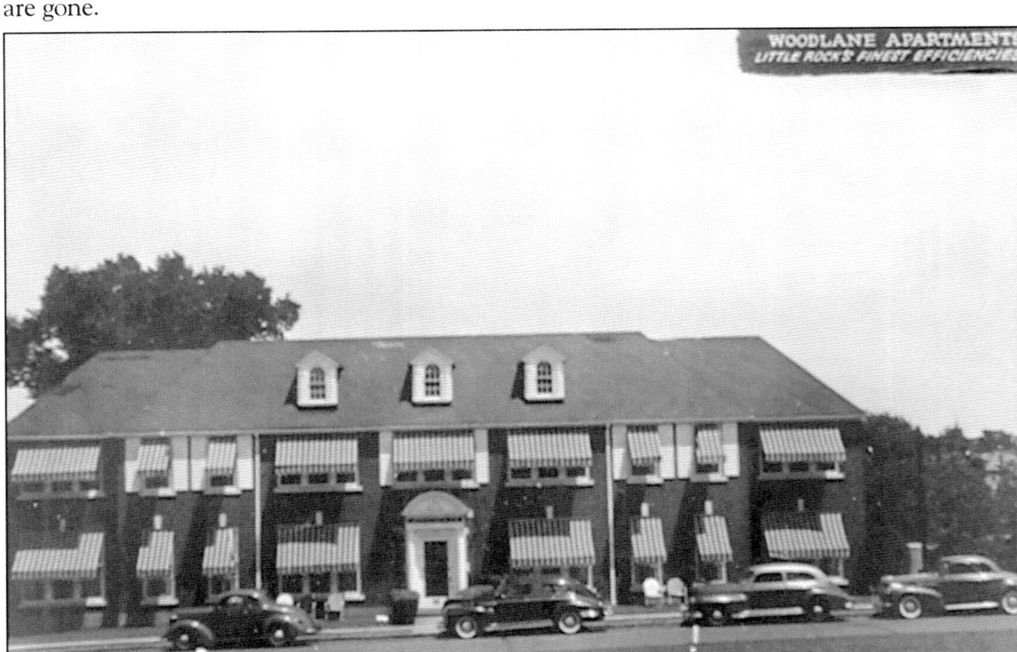

The Woodlane Apartments stood on the corner of Woodlane Street and Capitol Avenue, directly across from the capitol building, for some 30 years. Outfitted with crisp new striped awnings, the establishment advertised itself as "Little Rock's Finest Efficiencies." The building was razed years ago, and the site is now a parking lot for visitors to the state capitol building.

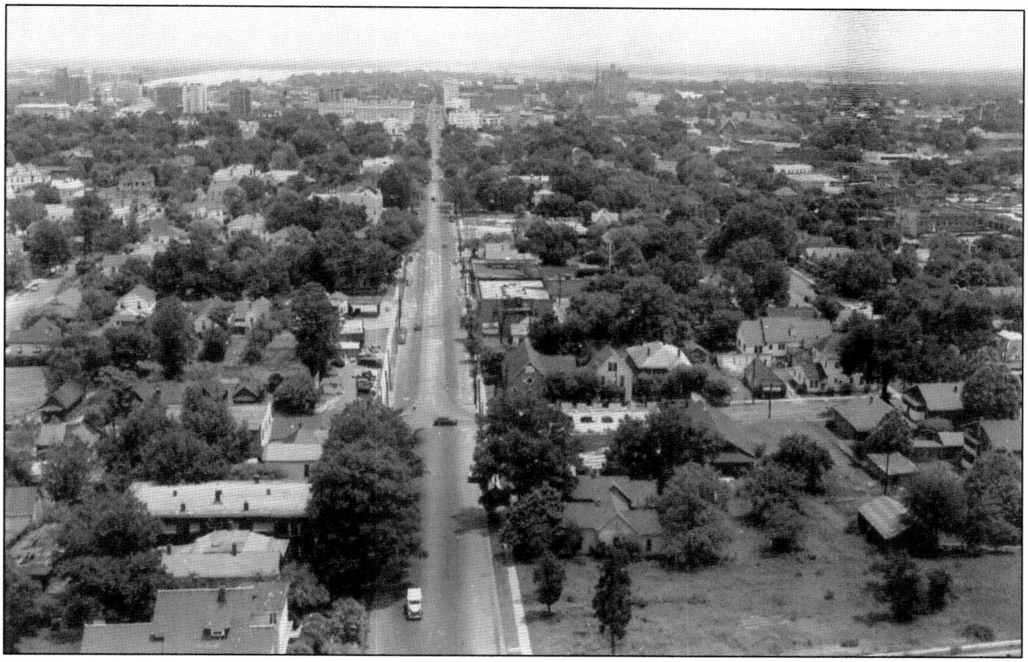

This c. 1940 photograph, taken from atop the capitol dome, looks east down Capitol Avenue. The grassy corner of Woodlane Street and Capitol Avenue in the foreground is today the site of the 501 Building, erected in 1955 as the National Old Line Insurance Building. Just beyond it is where the Victory Building was later erected. (Courtesy of David Ware, capitol historian, office of Secretary of State Mark Martin.)

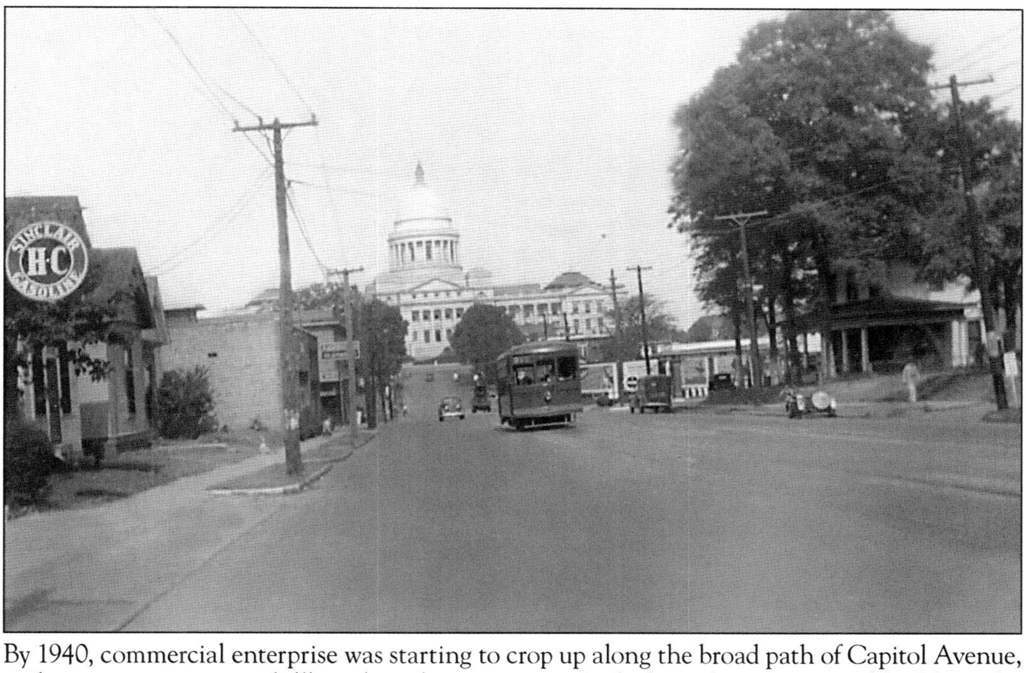

By 1940, commercial enterprise was starting to crop up along the broad path of Capitol Avenue, with trees giving way to billboards and gas stations. Aside from the state capitol building, the only surviving structure visible here is the white house on the right, which for many years has been the home of Frances Flower Shop.

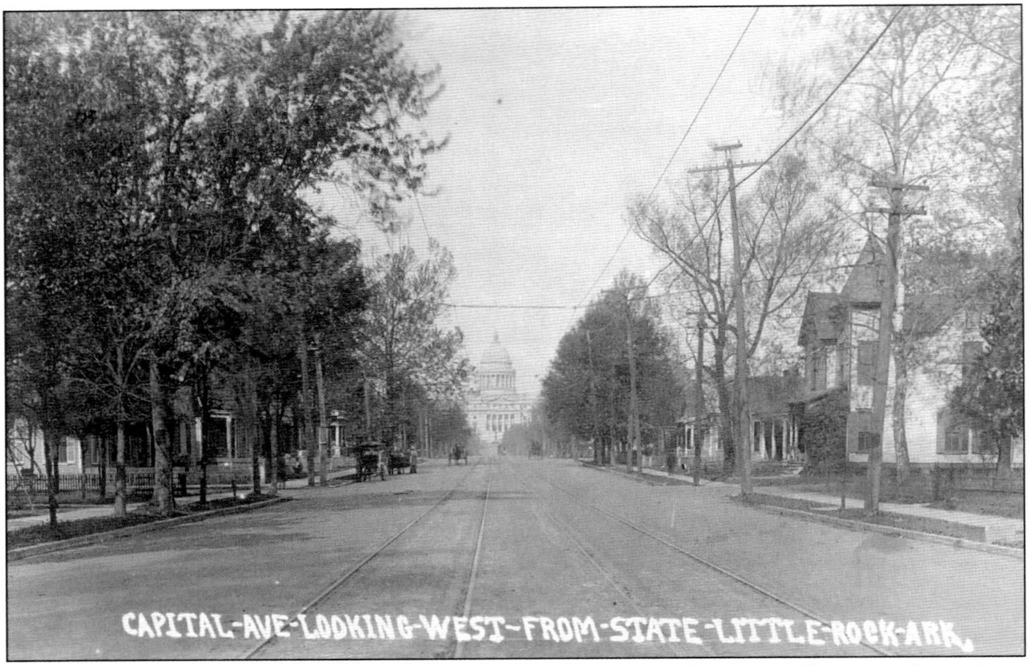

This 1914 photograph, looking west from State Street and Capitol Avenue, illustrates the striking image the new capitol building made as it rose at the end of the street, framed by the trees shading large homes. The homes and trees, like the streetcar tracks and overhead lines, have disappeared.

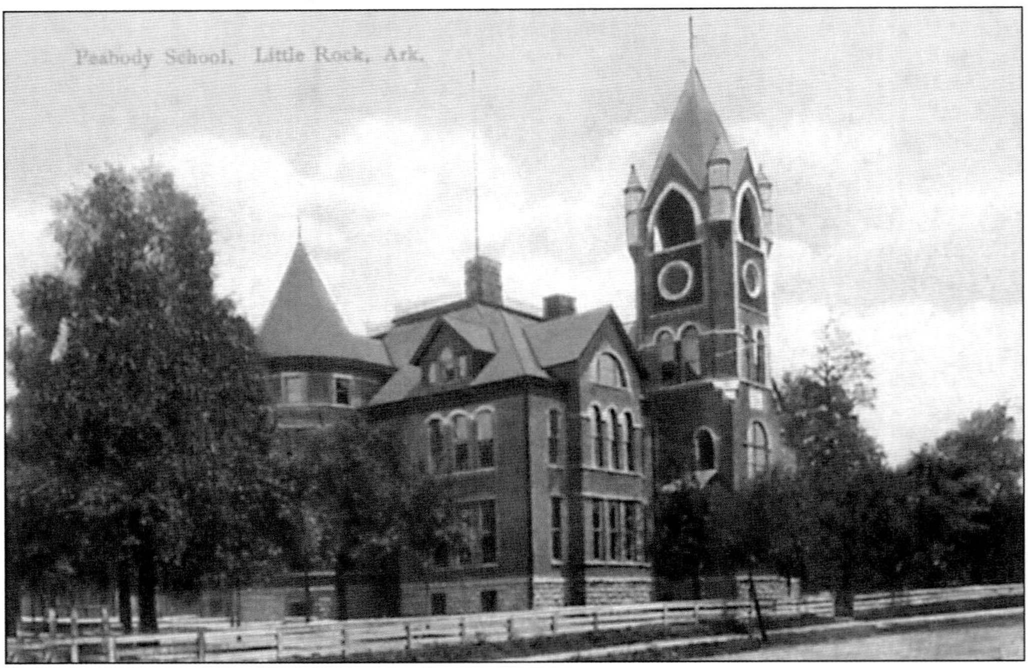

The Peabody School, presumably named for the coal baron Francis Peabody, was built on the dirt path of Fifth Street in 1890 between Gaines and State Streets. In 1911, the Peabody and several other public schools were marshaled into service to help house the influx of 12,000 old soldiers attending the United Confederate Veterans' reunion. One old gentleman reportedly died when he fell out of an upper window of the Peabody School.

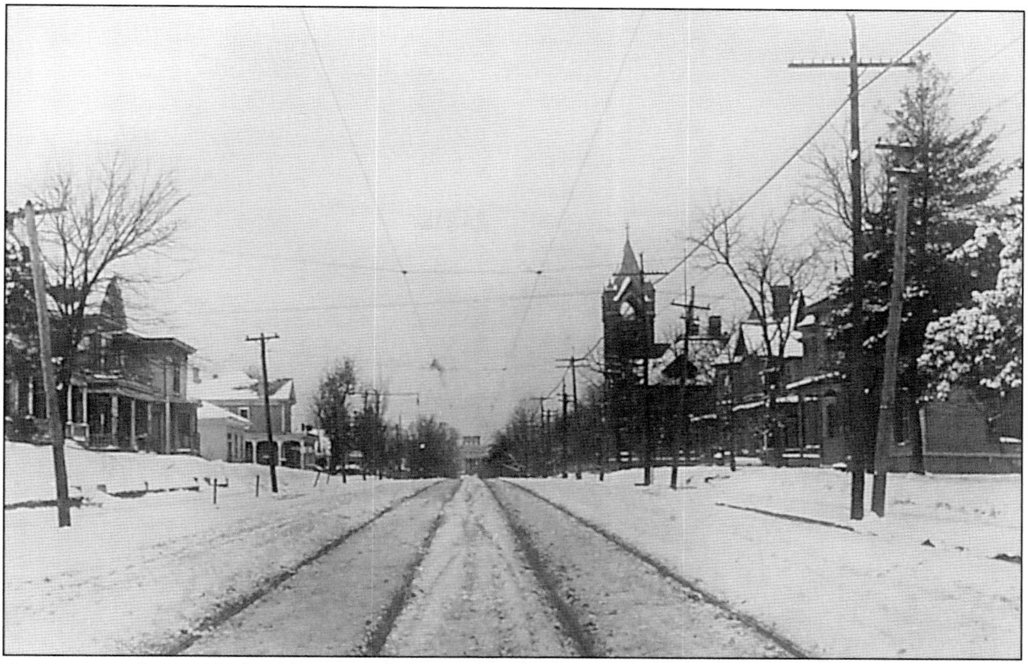

On a snowy day in 1905, a photographer stood looking west on Capitol Avenue from about Gaines Street. The Arkansas State Capitol building rises in the distance. Still under construction, the building's dome has not yet been erected. The Peabody School (right) stands out among the large homes lining the empty street.

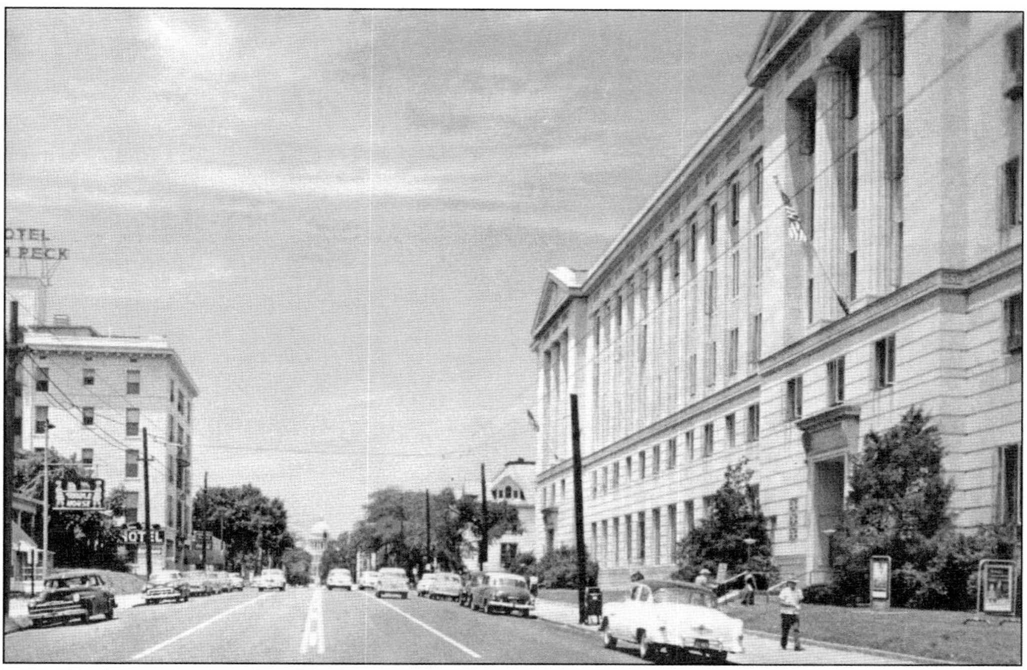

By 1955, the Peabody School had lost its tower and been painted white. It is visible in this postcard image just beyond the combined US Courthouse and Post Office that had been erected in the 1930s. Most of the large homes from earlier years are gone; the Toddle House eatery is near the Sam Peck Hotel across the street. The Peabody School was razed to make way for the US Federal Building.

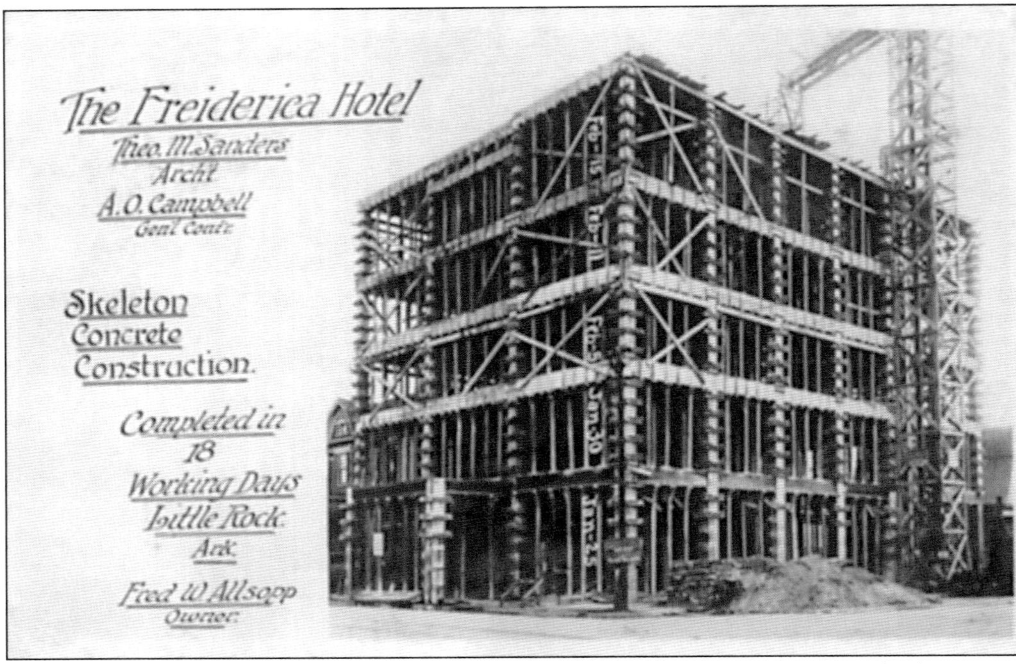

In 1910, businessman Fred Allsopp desired to build the finest hotel in town outside the central business district. He began construction of the Freiderica Hotel at the northwest corner of Fifth and Gaines Streets. The 1913 card (above) brags about completing the concrete framework in only 18 days. The finished hotel stood out on an avenue that was for the most part still lined with large homes, but the new state capitol building a few blocks to the west was beginning to bring increased traffic. Side entrances to the hotel had smaller businesses, such as a barbershop and laundry. Over the next century, the hotel would change ownership eight times; it was known as the Sam Peck for some 40 years. The building, proudly restored, is the Legacy Hotel by Ramada.

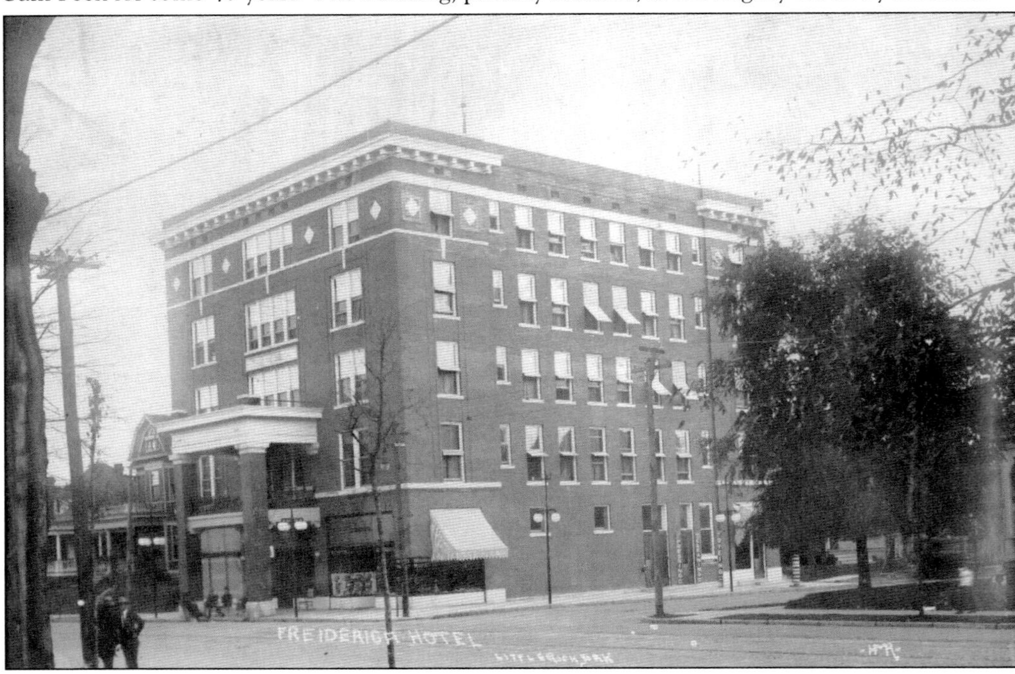

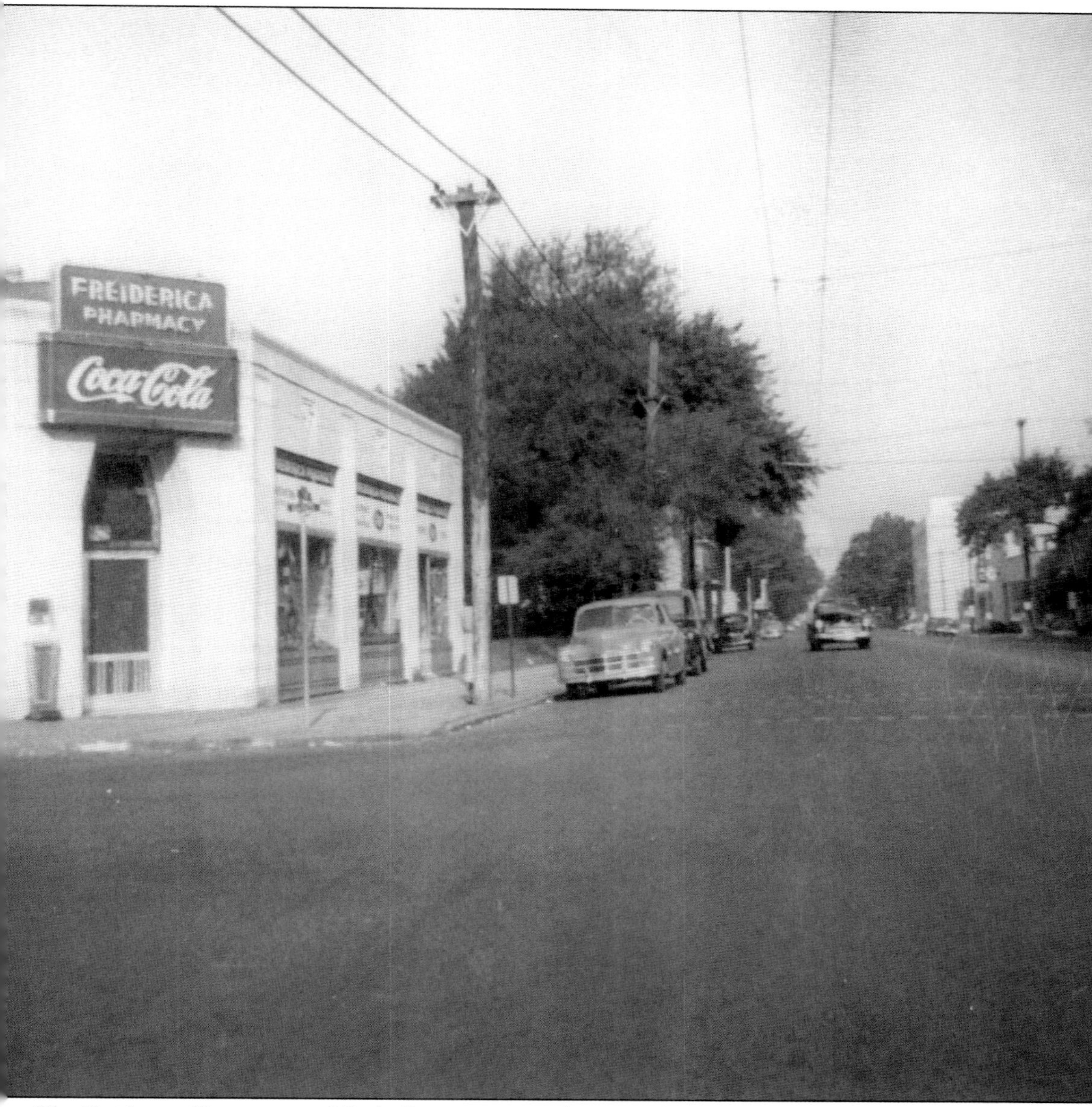

The Freiderica Pharmacy and Soda Fountain started out inside the hotel of the same name; by 1950, it had its own building at the corner of Capitol Avenue and Gaines Street. Beneath the Coca-Cola sign on the entrance is a "Your Weight and Fortune" scale. Freiderica Pharmacy still does business today, now located inside the Regions Bank building. The little white building at Capitol Avenue and Gaines Street still survives, now standing vacant.

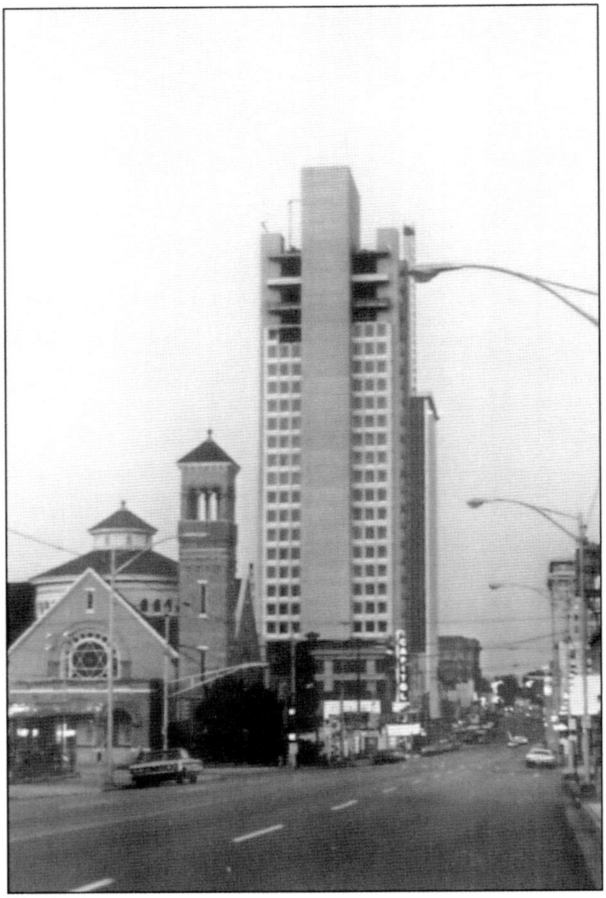

This 1968 photograph looks east on Capitol Avenue, across the intersection with Broadway, revealing a markedly changing street scene. The 23-story Worthen Bank building rose just beyond the Capitol Theater and the Jewish synagogue. The distinctive building was the tallest in the state until the First National Bank tower was erected five years later. The synagogue and the theater were both razed. (Courtesy of Butler Center for Arkansas Studies.)

This west-facing photograph shows a flatbed truck set up as a stage in the middle of Capitol Avenue in 1973. Dressed in coordinating outfits of the day, the live act may have been part of a music festival or other celebration. The Capitol Theater and Jewish synagogue, on the right just past Worthen Bank, would be razed within two years to make way for the First National Bank tower. (Courtesy of Butler Center for Arkansas Studies.)

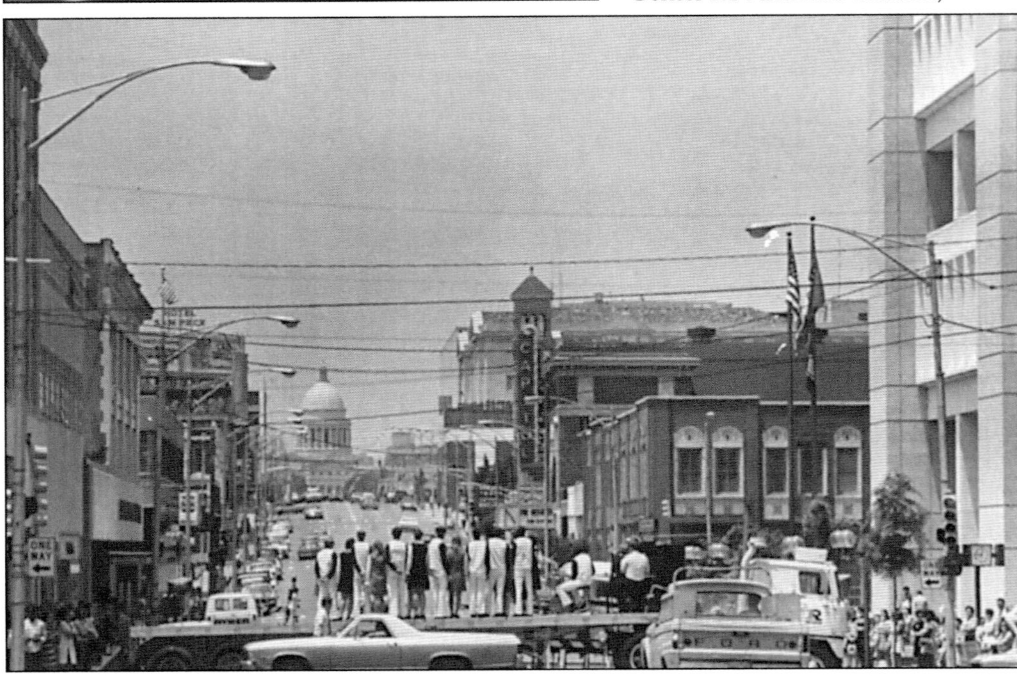

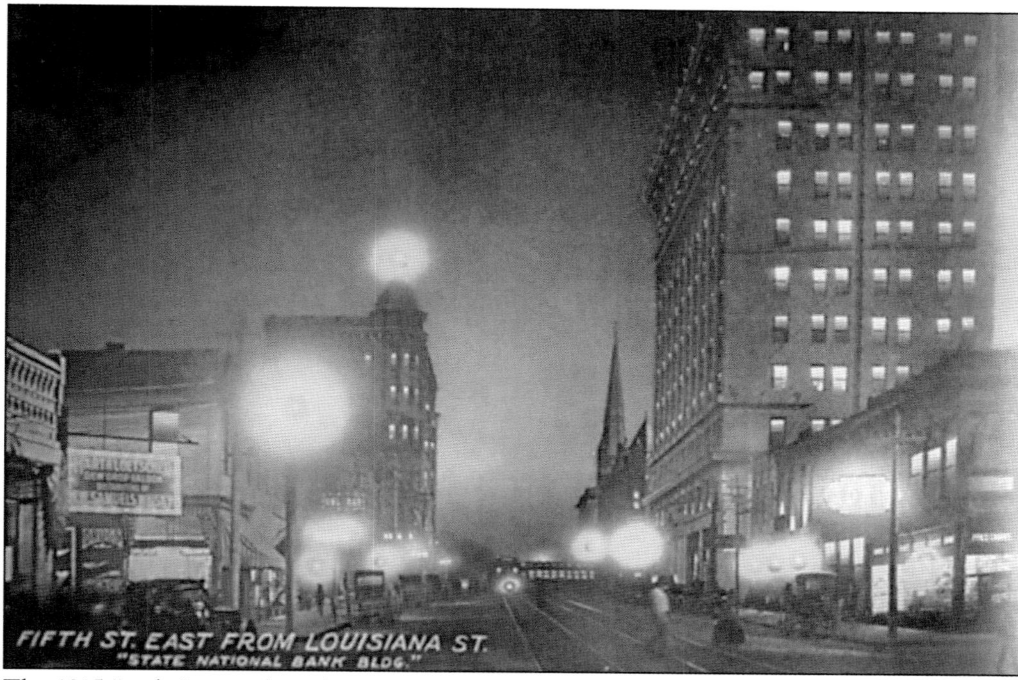

The 1915 "night" view above looks east on Fifth Street (today Capitol Avenue) from Louisiana Street. The 1911 photograph below also looks east from the crossing at Center Street. Both images reveal a host of small merchants and shops, with the Owl Bar and Hart & Loetscher's Dew Drop Saloon on display above. The daytime view includes two grocers (Paul Snodgrass and George Koonce), two meat markets, a French bakery, and the White House Café. Visible at the intersection with Main Street are the Masonic temple (left) and the National Bank Building (right), today's Boyle Building. Also visible is the steeple of the original Christ Episcopal Church. All of the structures in these images have vanished except for the Boyle Building, which was being converted into a luxury hotel in 2014.

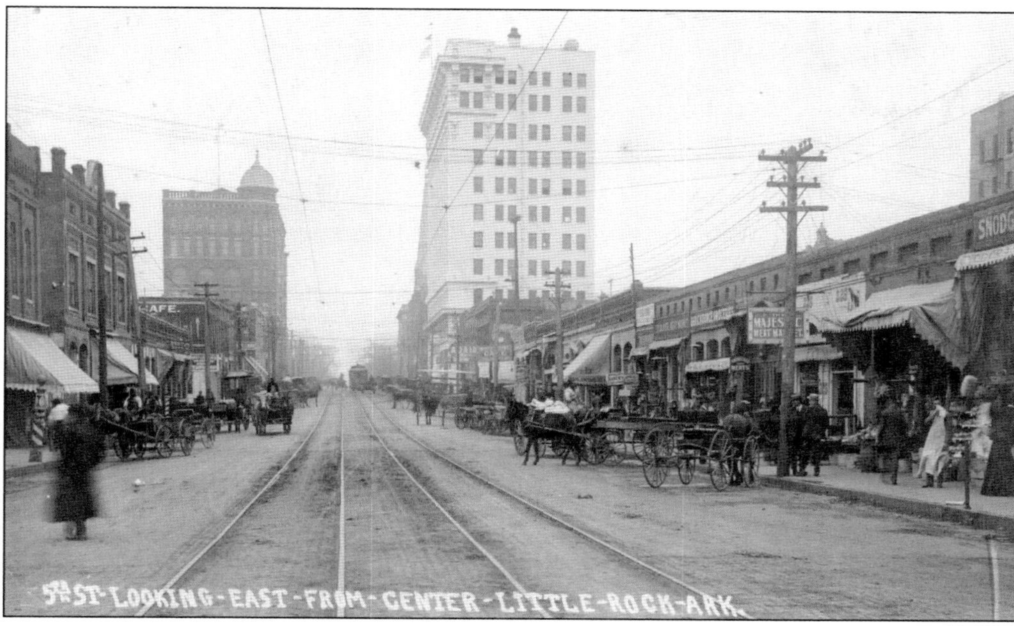

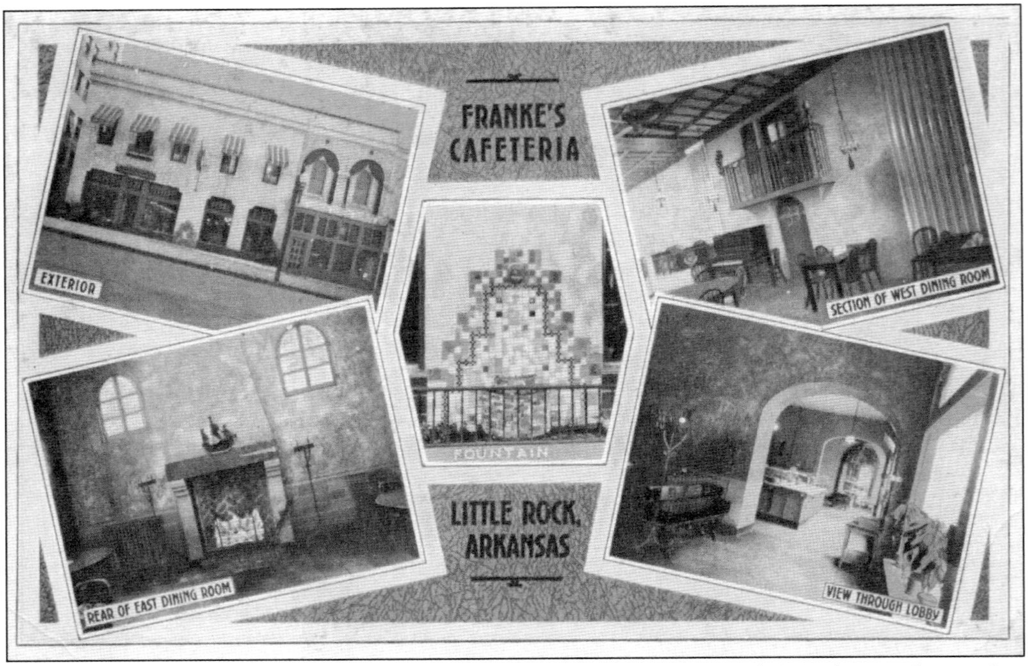

C.A. Franke opened a bakery in 1919 that would soon evolve into Franke's Cafeteria, featured in the 1930 postcard above. Its original location was on Capitol Avenue, a half block west of Main Street. The structure presented unique design details, including arched windows, tile fountain, brick fireplace, balcony, and twin dining rooms. Also notable are the welcoming lobby and a piano for dinner music. The back of the postcard claims that the location fed over 2,000 hungry people a day. The same building is seen below in 1970, with the same features and a sign noting a Duncan Hines recommendation. The structure is gone today, but Franke's continues to serve after almost a century, with locations inside the downtown Regions Bank building and in west Little Rock. (Below, courtesy of Butler Center for Arkansas Studies.)

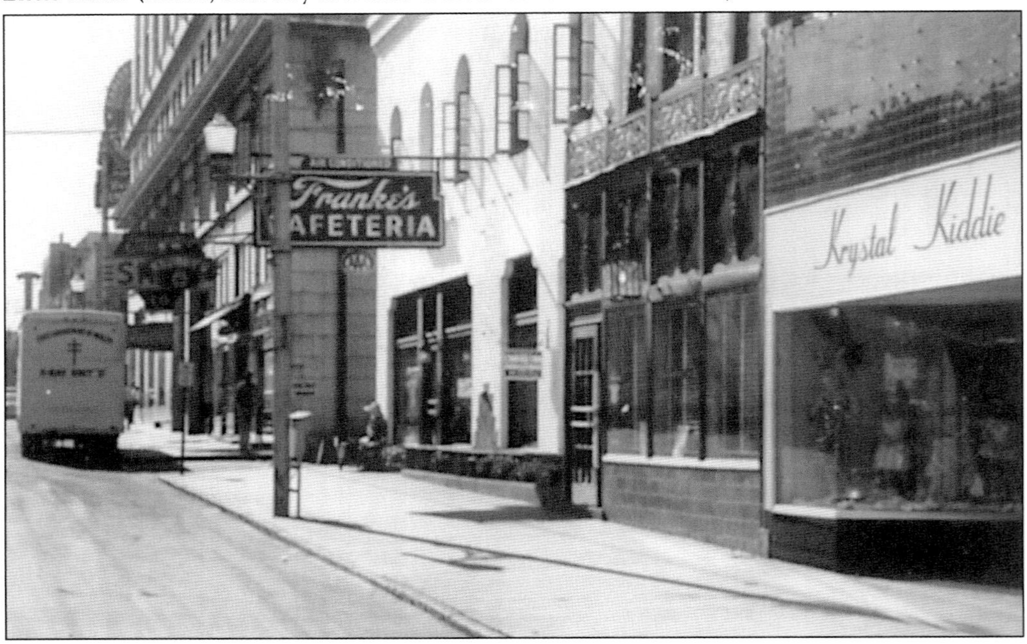

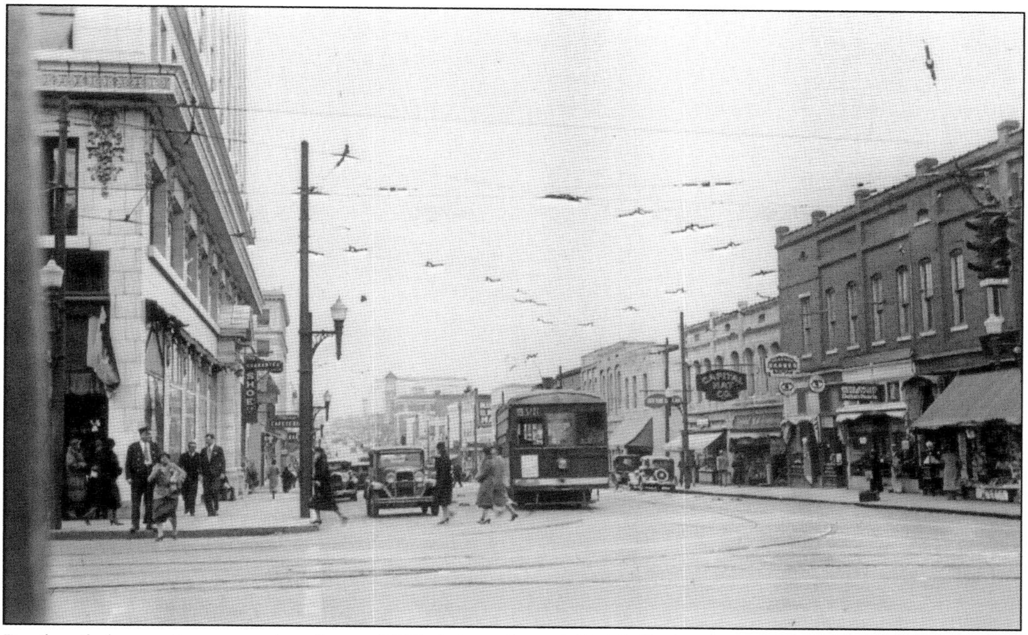

Both of these photographs, from 1933 (above) and 1960 (below), were taken looking across Main Street facing west toward the Arkansas State Capitol building. The photographs, captured almost three decades apart, both show the Boyle Building on the left, as well as a line of early-20th-century storefronts stretching up both sides of Capitol Avenue. The above image shows the Guarantee Shoe shop, Franke's Cafeteria, and the Capital Hat Company. The Jewish synagogue rises above the Capitol Theater marquee in the distance, with the US Courthouse beyond. These same locations persisted into the 1960s, though the styles of clothing and transportation on the street had changed. Today, the only identifiable landmarks left are the Boyle Building, the US Courthouse, and the state capitol building. All of the other structures gave way to modern buildings and their ubiquitous parking lots. (Above, courtesy of UALR Center for Arkansas History and Culture.)

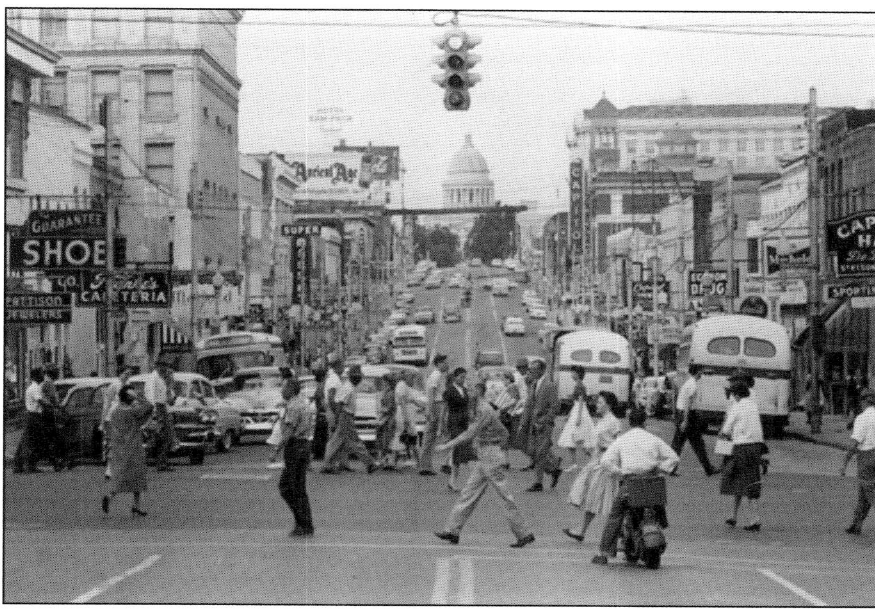

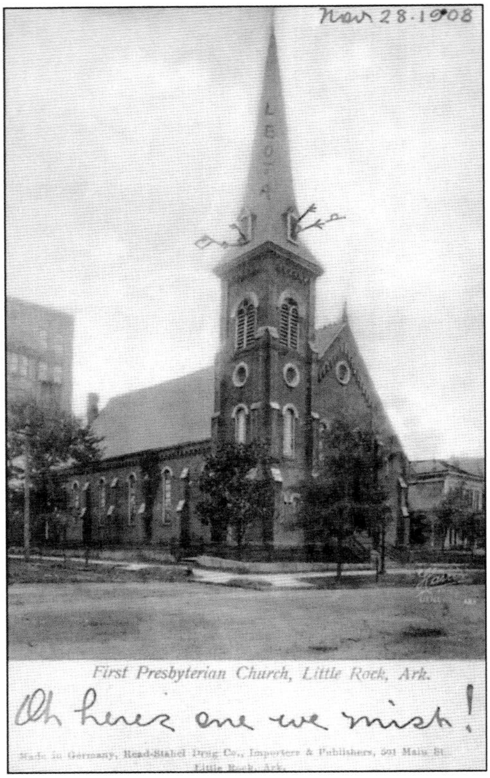

First Presbyterian Church was organized in 1828. Its congregation met in a rented log cabin near the river. This building was erected in 1869, the first church to be constructed in Little Rock after the Civil War. Seen here in 1908, it was located at the northwest corner of Fifth and Scott Streets. The congregation outgrew this building and moved to a larger home three blocks south in 1921. The old church was razed decades ago; a parking lot marks the space today.

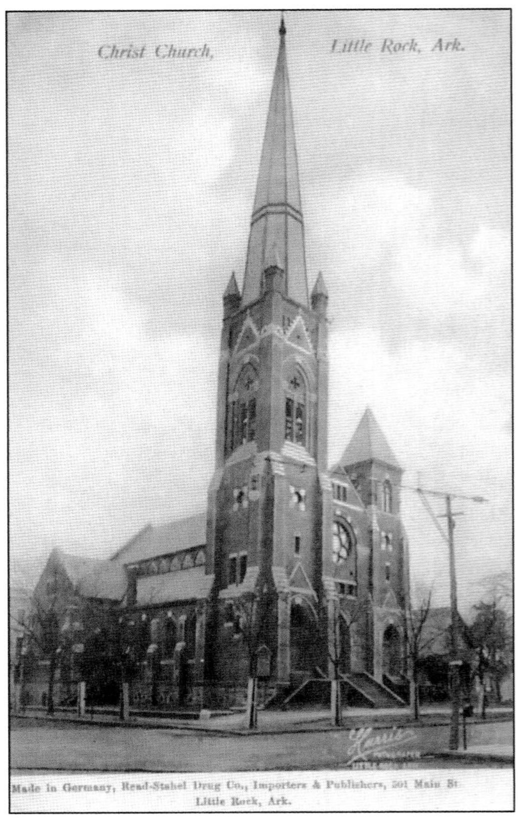

Christ Episcopal Church was built in 1887 at the southeast corner of Fifth and Scott Streets, diagonal from the First Presbyterian Church. It replaced a smaller church that had been destroyed in a lightning fire. After 50 years of service, fire struck again; this building was burned to the ground in 1938. A replacement built of stone in the Neo-Gothic style was erected on the same corner and still holds worship services today.

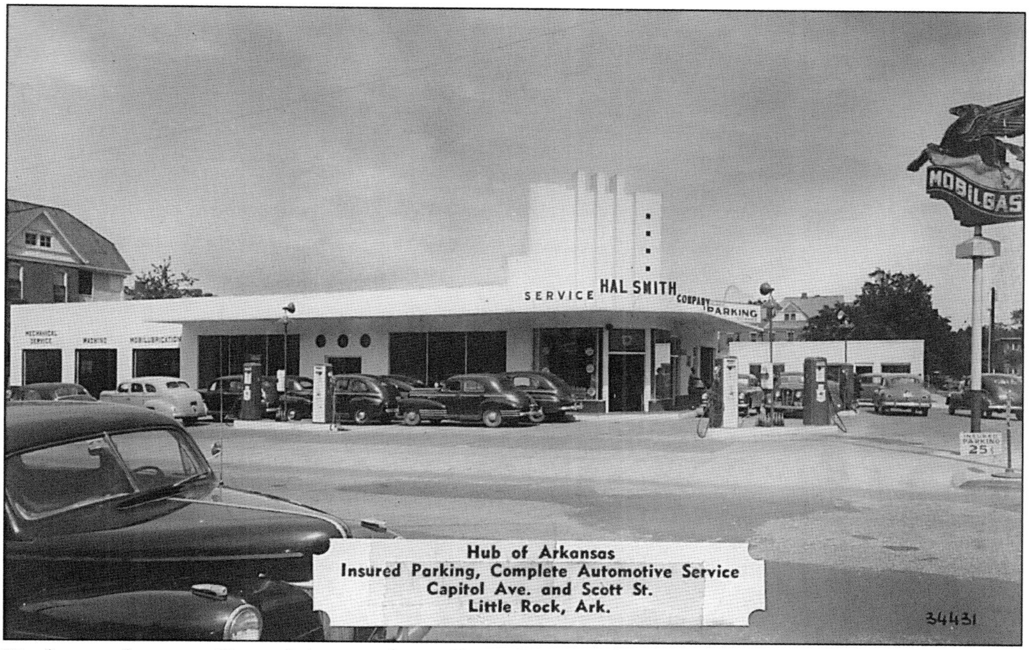

To the north across Capitol Avenue from Christ Episcopal Church stood the "Hub of Arkansas," Hal Smith's clean and modern Mobil service station. The corner was marked with a prominent neon-lit Mobilgas sign with the well-known red Pegasus logo, seen here around 1950. Smith advertised "insured parking" for 25¢, hoping to capture shoppers headed to Main Street two blocks away. Today, the site is a large parking lot.

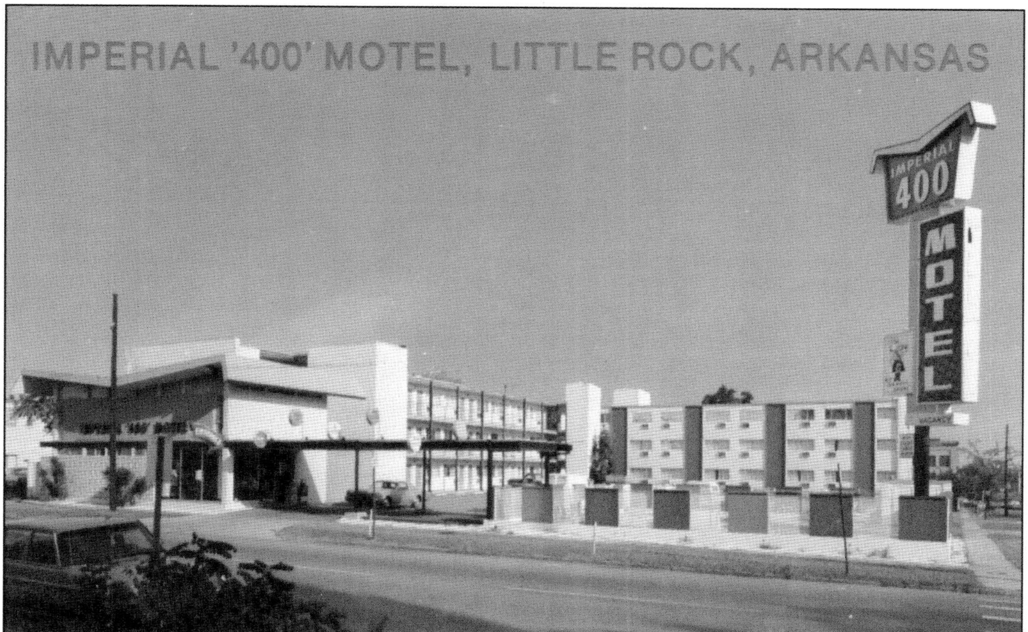

The Imperial 400 Motel at 322 East Capitol Avenue was an example of the lodging that developed between Interstate 30 to the east and downtown Little Rock to the west. The motel, seen here in 1982, was known for its loud colors; the sign sports a Scotch plaid background and kilted mascot. The motel began to deteriorate in the 1980s and was eventually razed.

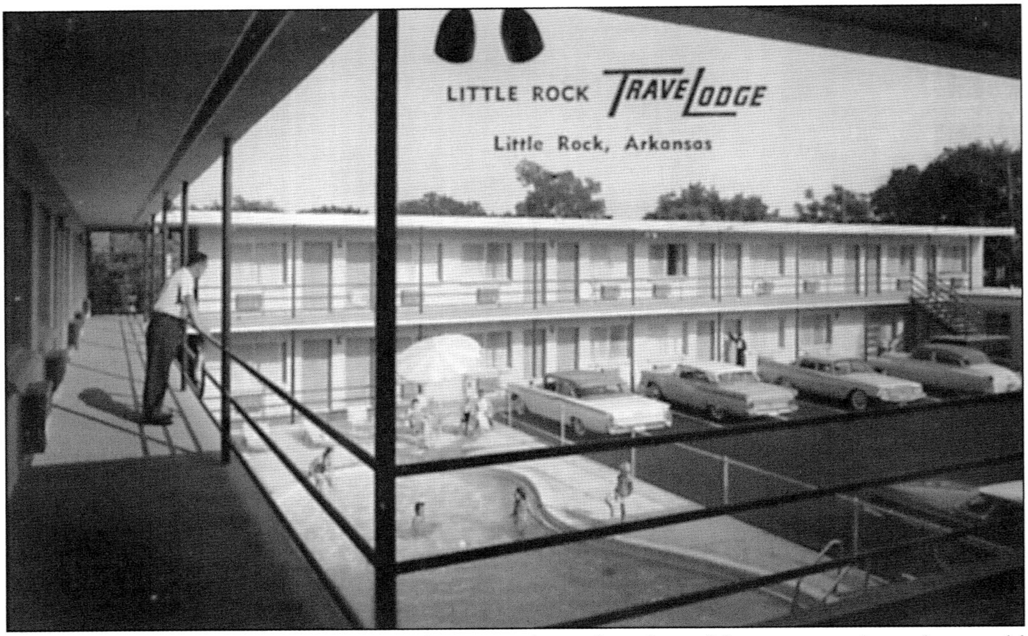

The motoring public was beginning to favor motels on the edges of downtown, where they could park at the door. Such demand gave rise to the TraveLodge at 308 East Capitol Avenue, which took business from the downtown hotels. In this 1957 view, patrons enjoy the motel's kidney-shaped pool and room service from the adjoining Toddle House café. The lodge is gone today, replaced by the bus transfer facilities of Central Arkansas Transit.

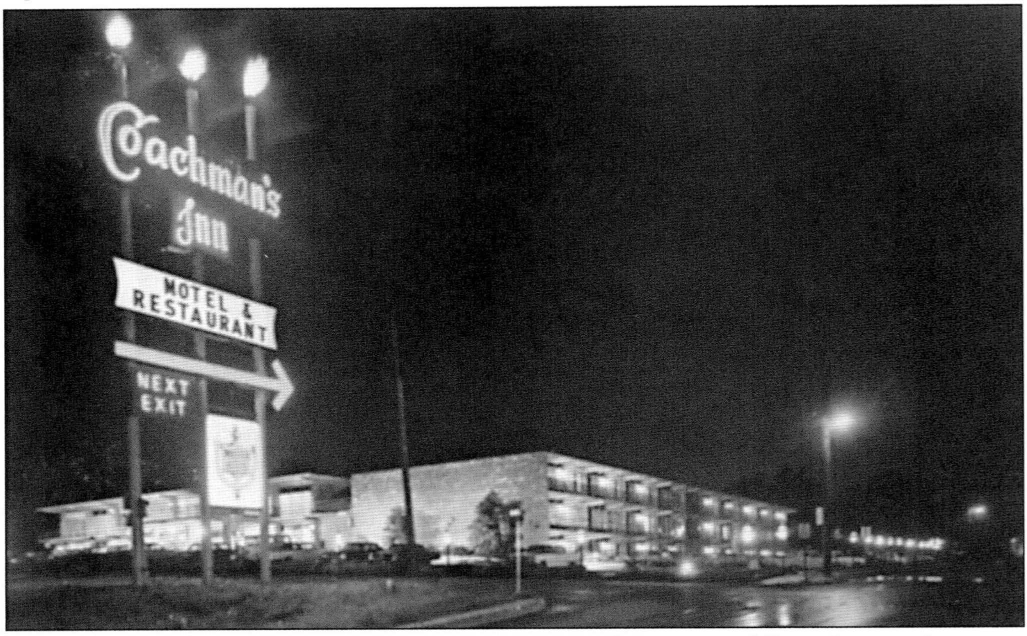

In the 1950s, the Coachman's Inn was erected at Capitol Avenue and Ferry Street, adjacent to the new Interstate 30. It represented an investment for Jack and Witt Stephens, who had founded the largest brokerage firm off Wall Street. The facility was the location of the first meeting of the Political Animals Club in 1983. The inn was razed in the 1990s to make way for Little Rock's main post office.

Five

Broadway

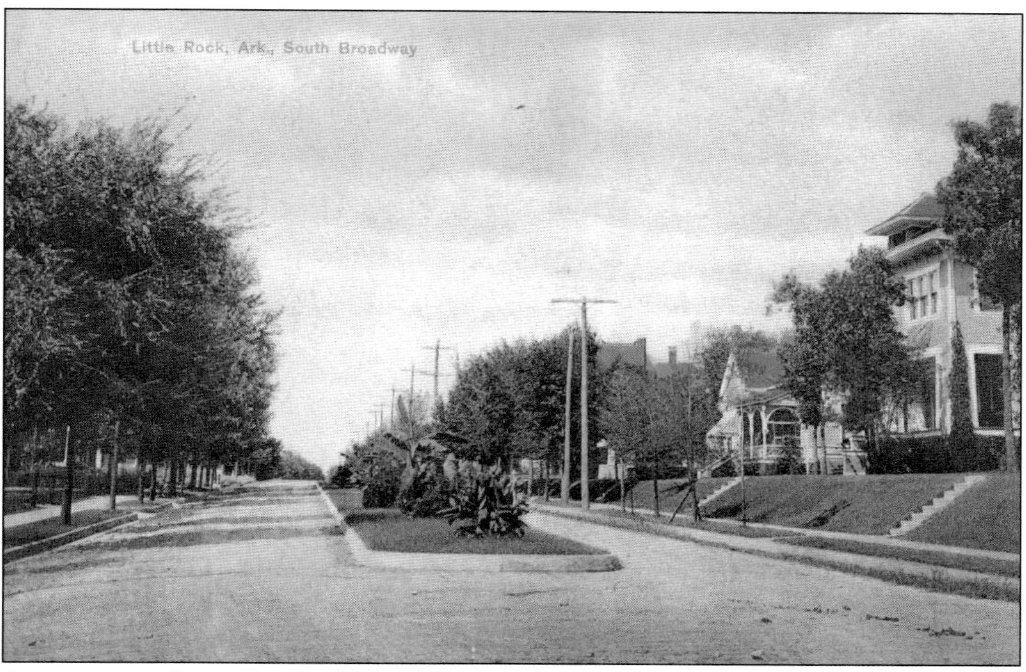

A century ago, the southern end of Little Rock's Broadway boasted many fine homes, a testament to the success of local merchants and professional men, who generally worked by day a few blocks north and east. Seen at right around 1910 is the Egyptian Revival home of John R. Fordyce II, a former US Army engineer who oversaw construction of Camp Pike near Argenta (today North Little Rock) during World War I.

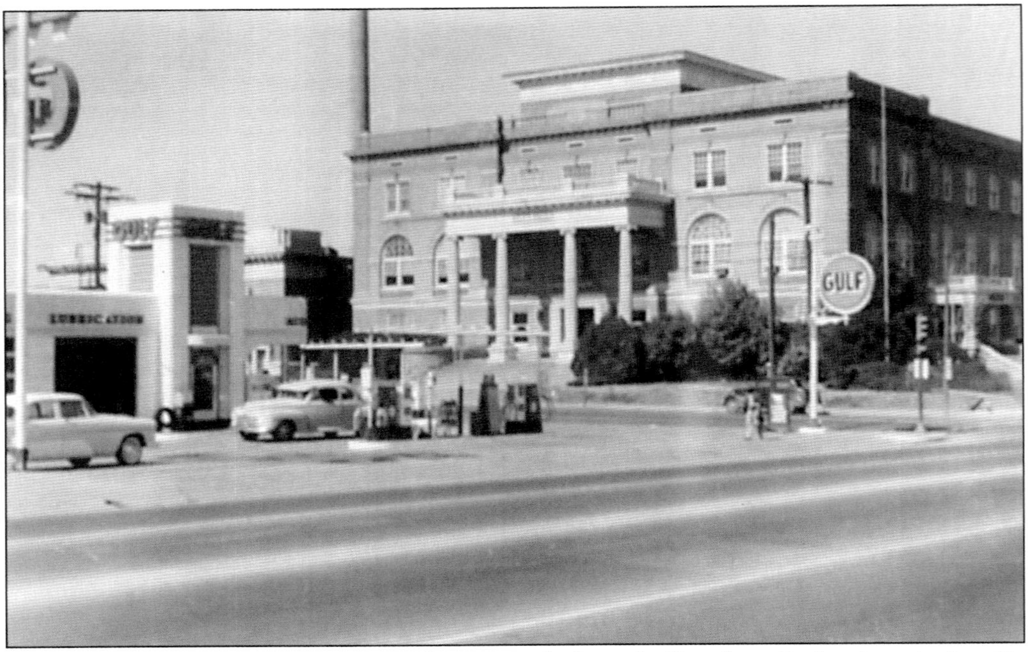

The northern end of Little Rock's Broadway started where the Broadway Bridge deposited traffic next to city hall, which had seen its deteriorating dome removed in 1956. US Highway 67/70 followed Broadway through the city, leading to a number of gas stations being built along the way. This Gulf station, seen around the time of Little Rock's integration crisis in 1957, offered gas and auto service to locals and those just driving through.

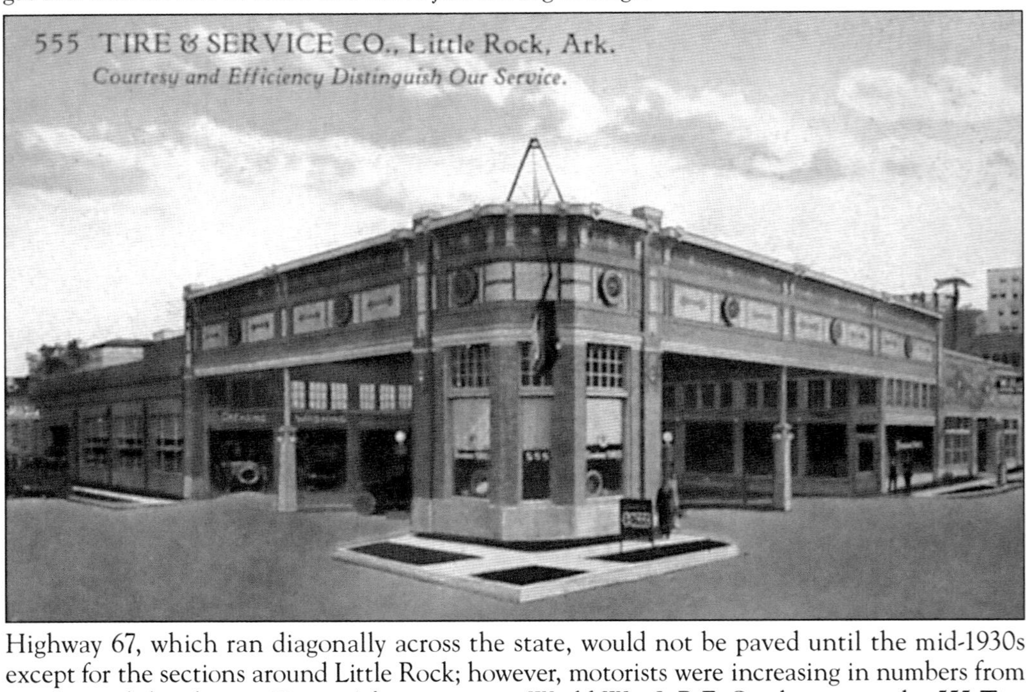

Highway 67, which ran diagonally across the state, would not be paved until the mid-1930s except for the sections around Little Rock; however, motorists were increasing in numbers from points north heading to Texas. After serving in World War I, R.E. Stueber set up the 555 Tire & Service Company on the east side of Broadway at Third Street. In 1925, it was billed as "The Home of *Good* Service."

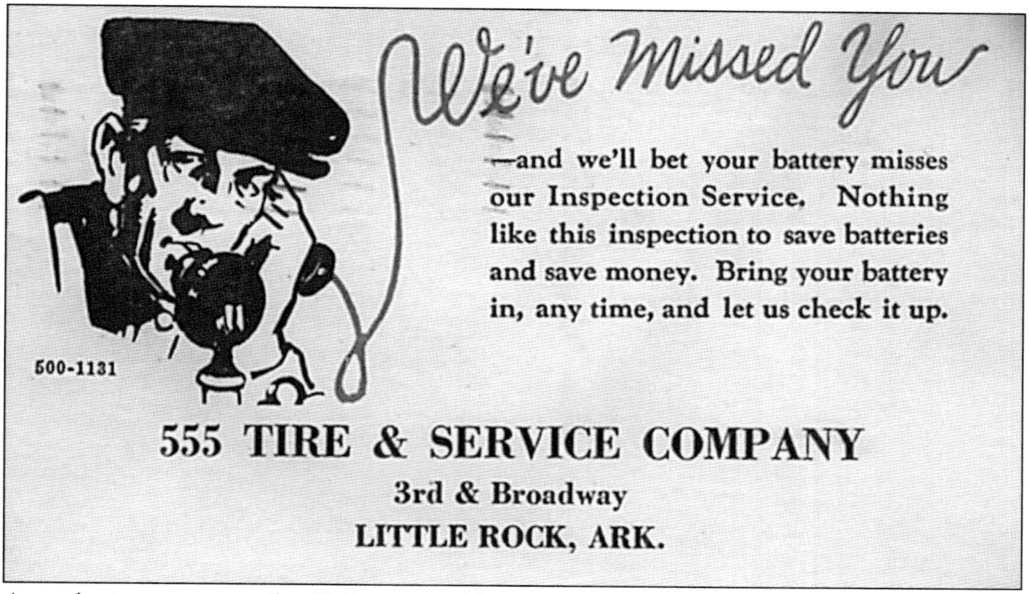

As its business grew in the 1920s, the 555 Tire & Service Company started reaching out to its past customers with postcards, reminding them to bring their cars in for service. The firm, named for its phone number, offered roadside assistance to all who called. Until the coming of Interstate 30 in the 1960s, Highway 67/70 would bring thousands of cars down Broadway from points northeast and southwest.

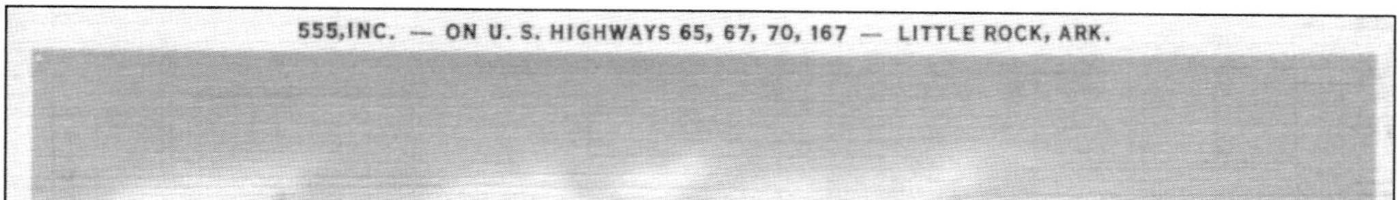

The 555 expanded up Broadway to Second Street, advertising "The World's Largest Service Station." Stueber's enterprise had a variety of features, such as a rooftop tank to catch rainwater for use in washing cars and filling radiators. A pit beneath the car wash bays caught mud from the unpaved roads to prevent clogging the sewer lines. Comfortable customer lounges for men and women provided a phone-message board, especially helpful to physicians and other busy professionals.

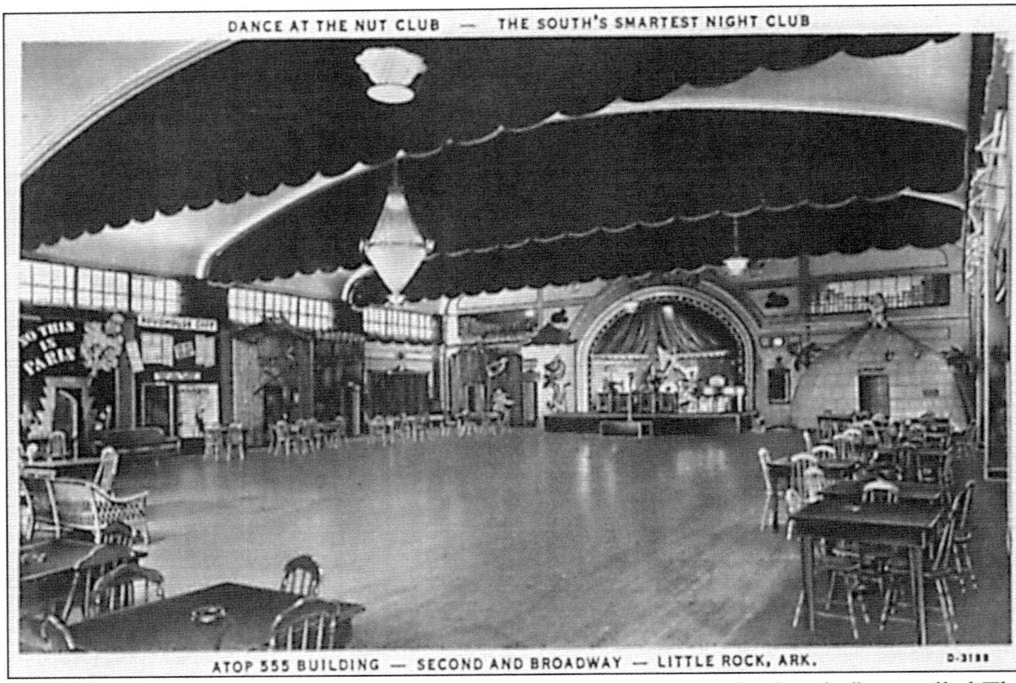

Around 1940, the enormous 555 Building opened a dance hall on the fourth floor, called The Nut Club, and proclaimed it "The South's Smartest Night Club," offering "The Largest Dance Floor and the Best Music in the City—Beer and Good Things to Eat." Admission was 40¢ per person. A dance contest, with prizes, was held every Friday, and Saturday was "Whoopee Nite." Music was provided by Frankie Littlefield and his 10-piece band.

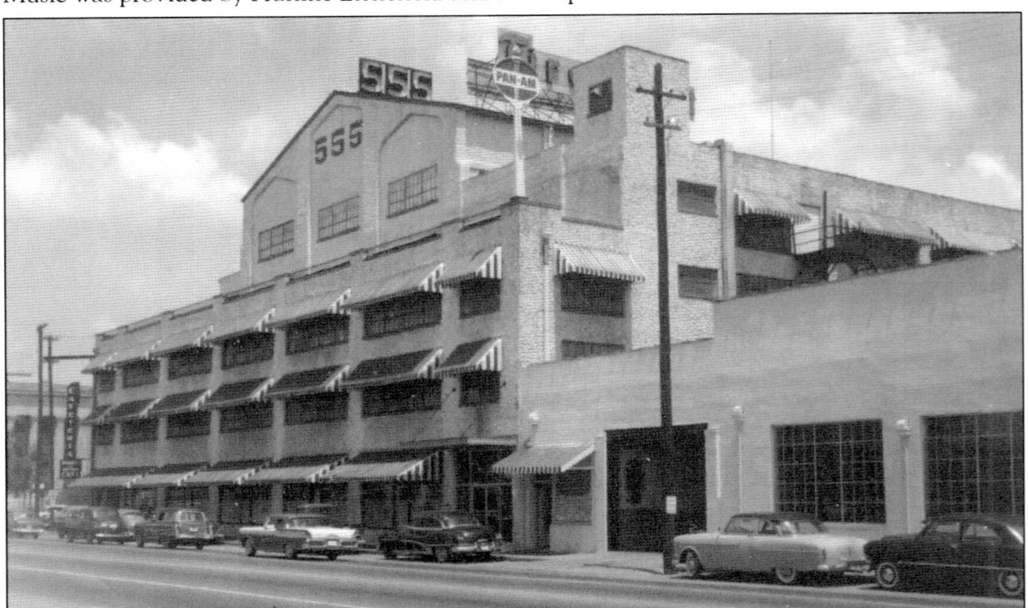

The coming of Interstates 30 and 40 in the 1960s siphoned off much of the traffic that had helped the 555 to expand over the years. During the 1950s, however, it was still a huge presence on Broadway. In this 1957 photograph, Robinson Auditorium is seen on the far left, facing Markham Street and across from the 555's cafeteria. (Courtesy of Butler Center for Arkansas Studies.)

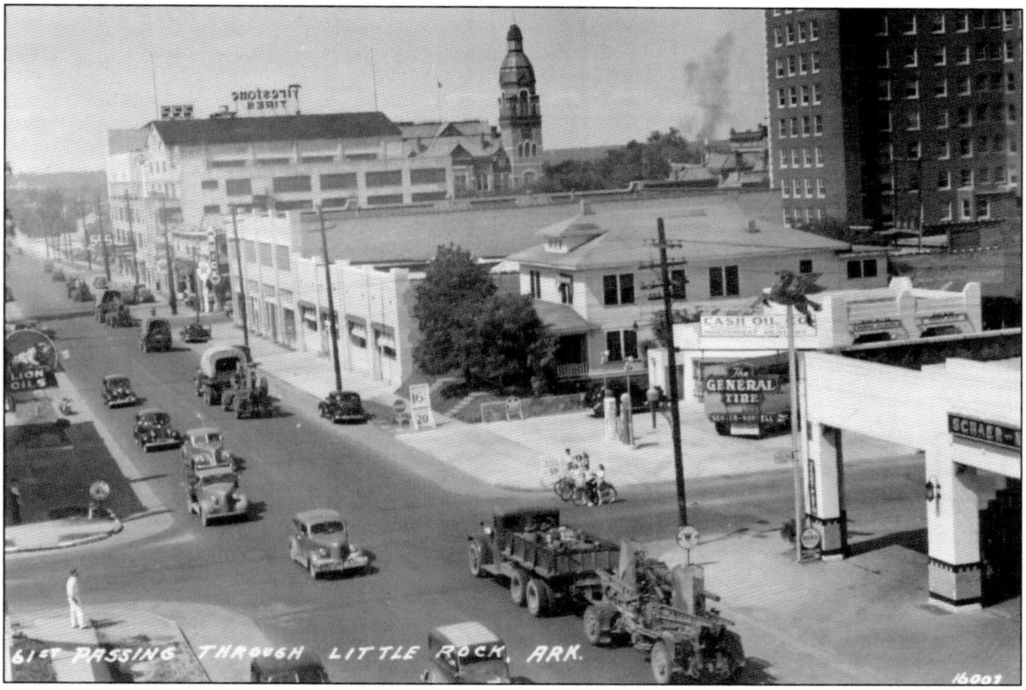

In 1940, Camp Robinson, across the river, housed up to 50,000 soldiers at a time. This often generated a flood of traffic onto Broadway, as troops moved up and down Highways 67, 167, and 70 on maneuvers. The 555, with a Model T automobile on the roof, is seen in the distance. The tower of the Pulaski County Courthouse rises to the right. Gas sold for 16¢ per gallon.

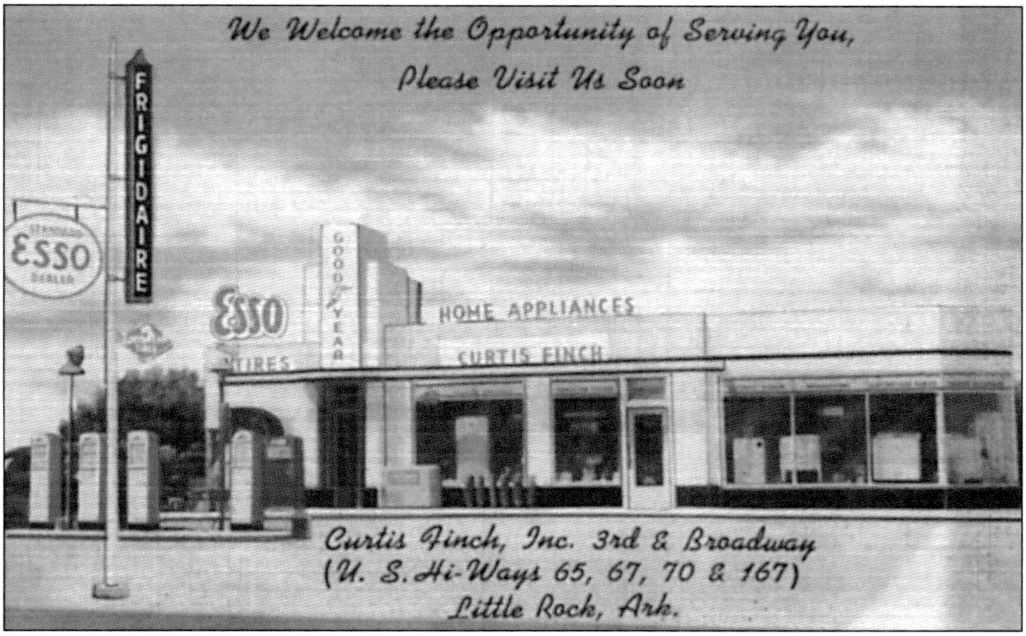

For decades, Curtis Finch was a successful retailer in Little Rock, initially with a combined automobile service and appliance store at Third Street and Broadway. On the back of this 1949 postcard, the dealership offered four-ply tires for $8.88, "absolutely guaranteed for ONE year. We have 156 tires to sell at this price." Today, the site is a parking lot.

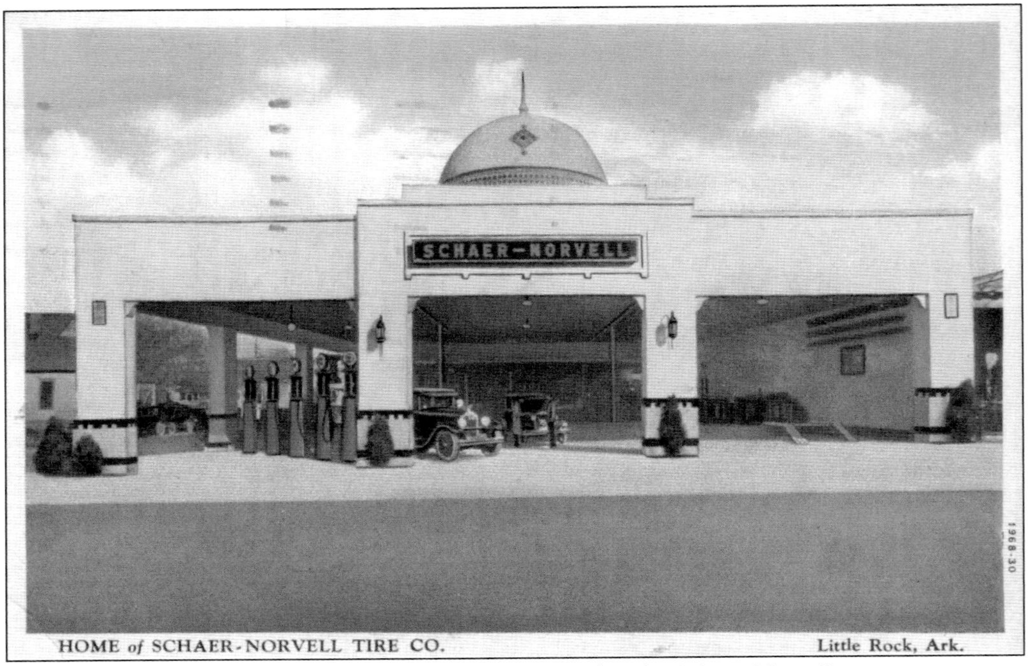

Motorists on the way home to New York in 1939 stopped at the Schaer-Norvell service station, at Fourth Street and Broadway, mailing a postcard telling friends they were in Little Rock. Printed on the card with the tire company's phone number was the request, "Invite Us to Your Next Blowout." The wonderful yellow-domed structure was gone by the 1950s.

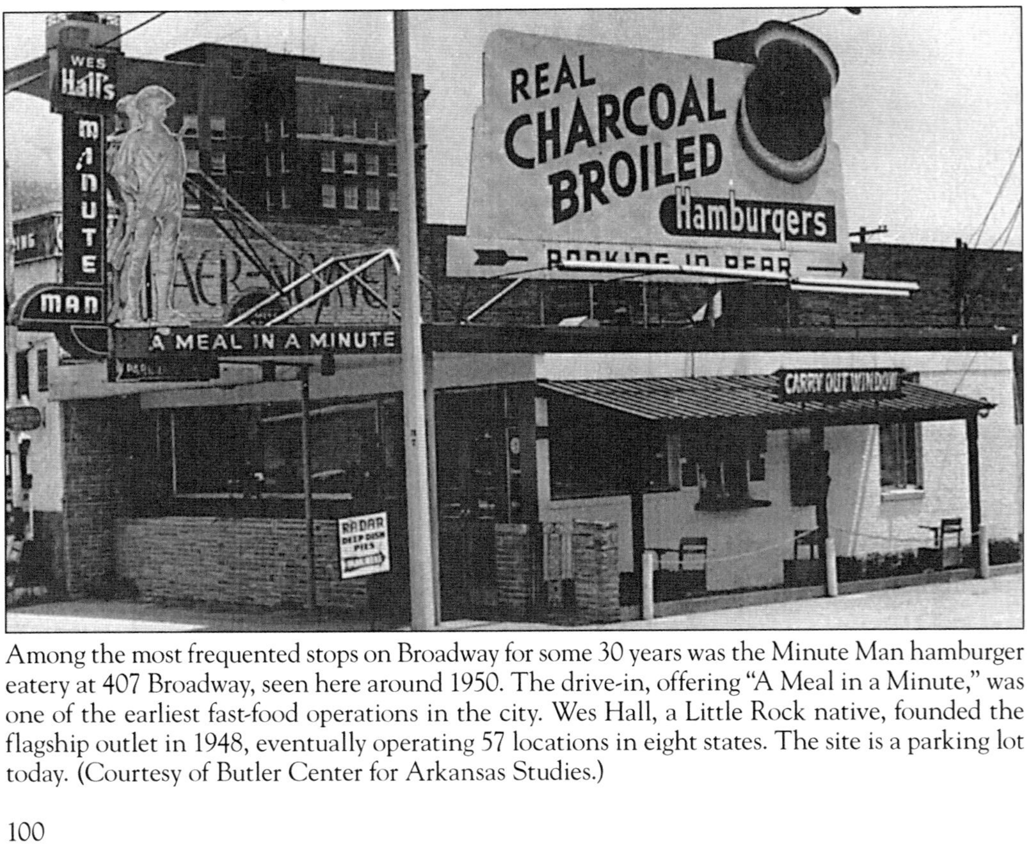

Among the most frequented stops on Broadway for some 30 years was the Minute Man hamburger eatery at 407 Broadway, seen here around 1950. The drive-in, offering "A Meal in a Minute," was one of the earliest fast-food operations in the city. Wes Hall, a Little Rock native, founded the flagship outlet in 1948, eventually operating 57 locations in eight states. The site is a parking lot today. (Courtesy of Butler Center for Arkansas Studies.)

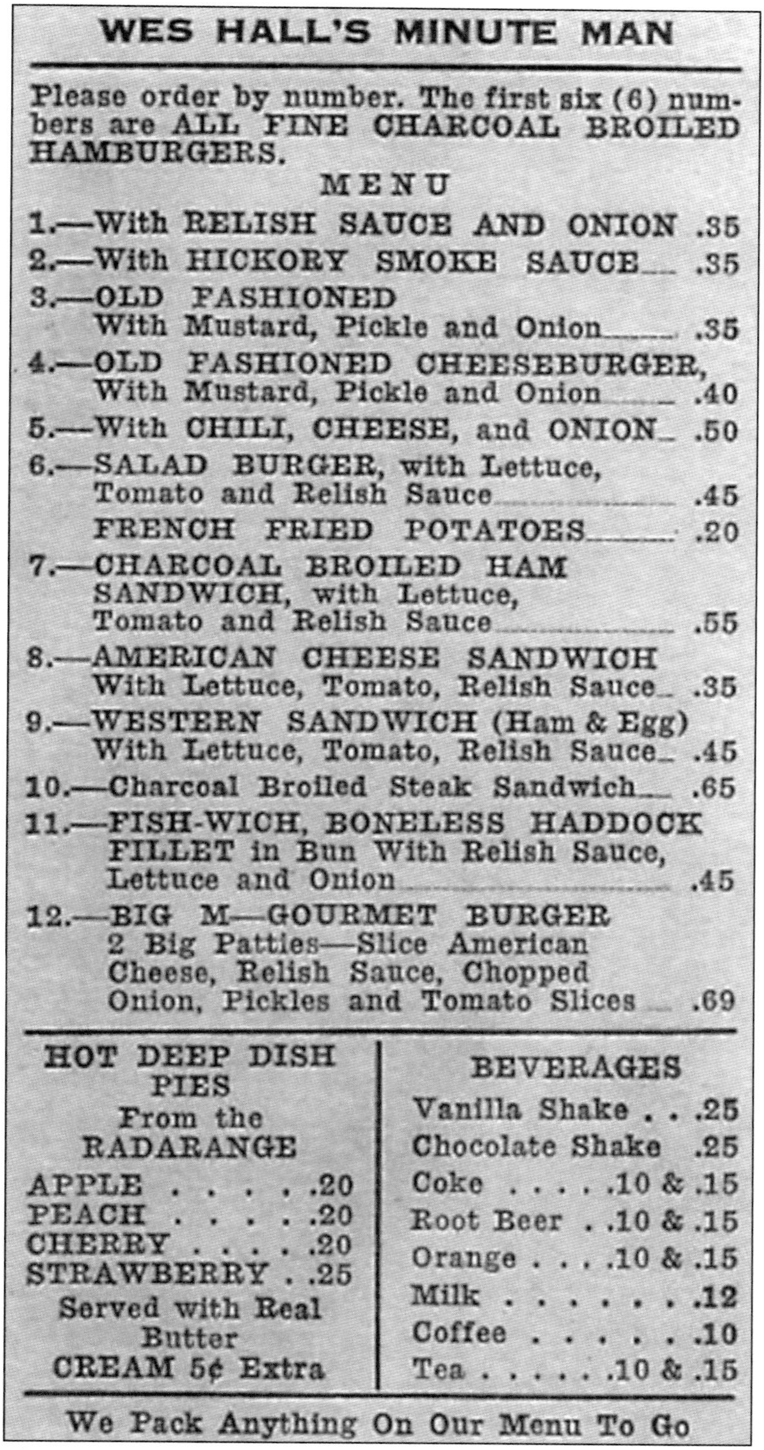

WES HALL'S MINUTE MAN

Please order by number. The first six (6) numbers are ALL FINE CHARCOAL BROILED HAMBURGERS.

MENU

1.—With RELISH SAUCE AND ONION .35
2.—With HICKORY SMOKE SAUCE .35
3.—OLD FASHIONED With Mustard, Pickle and Onion .35
4.—OLD FASHIONED CHEESEBURGER, With Mustard, Pickle and Onion .40
5.—With CHILI, CHEESE, and ONION .50
6.—SALAD BURGER, with Lettuce, Tomato and Relish Sauce .45
FRENCH FRIED POTATOES .20
7.—CHARCOAL BROILED HAM SANDWICH, with Lettuce, Tomato and Relish Sauce .55
8.—AMERICAN CHEESE SANDWICH With Lettuce, Tomato, Relish Sauce .35
9.—WESTERN SANDWICH (Ham & Egg) With Lettuce, Tomato, Relish Sauce .45
10.—Charcoal Broiled Steak Sandwich .65
11.—FISH-WICH, BONELESS HADDOCK FILLET in Bun With Relish Sauce, Lettuce and Onion .45
12.—BIG M—GOURMET BURGER 2 Big Patties—Slice American Cheese, Relish Sauce, Chopped Onion, Pickles and Tomato Slices .69

HOT DEEP DISH PIES From the RADARANGE

APPLE 20
PEACH 20
CHERRY 20
STRAWBERRY . .25

Served with Real Butter
CREAM 5¢ Extra

BEVERAGES

Vanilla Shake . . .25
Chocolate Shake .25
Coke . . . . .10 & .15
Root Beer . .10 & .15
Orange . . . .10 & .15
Milk 12
Coffee 10
Tea . . . . . .10 & .15

We Pack Anything On Our Menu To Go

The menu at the Minute Man in 1955 offered hamburgers starting at 35¢, soft drinks for a dime, shakes for a quarter, and the trademark Radarange hot deep-dish pies "with real butter" for 20¢. The use of radar (microwave) ovens was a novel concept at the time. The most expensive item on the menu was a loaded double-patty Big M burger, at 69¢.

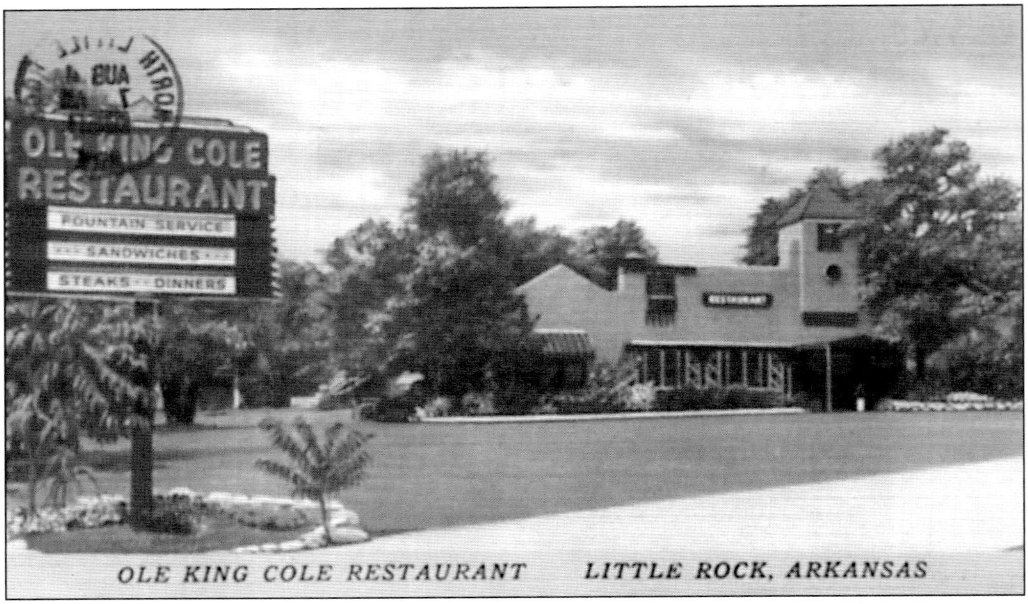

Ole King Cole Restaurant was located at Fifth and Main Streets, where at mid-century it was advertised on the back of this card as "Arkansas' oldest drive-in restaurant." While retaining the drive-in feature, the establishment became well regarded as a "sit-down" family eatery, known for such dishes as eggplant casserole. Today, the corner is occupied by the expanded US Courthouse.

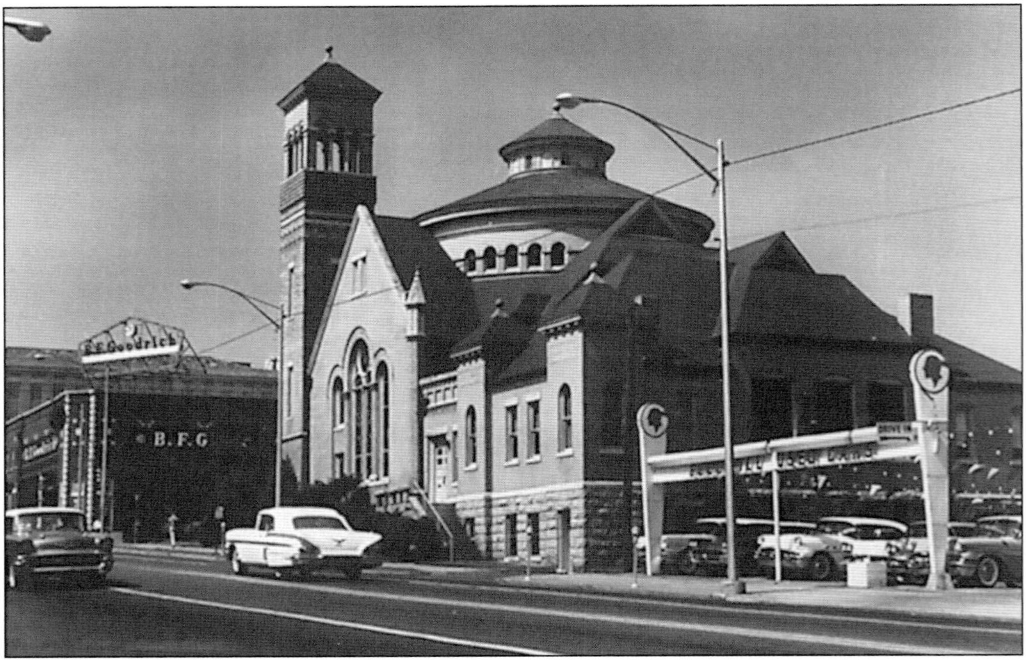

Temple B'nai Israel, designed by architect Charles Thompson and seen here around 1957, was erected at the northeast corner of Broadway and Capitol Avenue in 1897. At the time, Broadway was still unpaved, dusty on some days and muddy on others, as the Jewish worshipers of Little Rock made their way to the handsome building. The temple was razed in 1972 to make way for the 30-story First National Bank building, today the home of Regions Bank. (Courtesy of Butler Center for Arkansas Studies.)

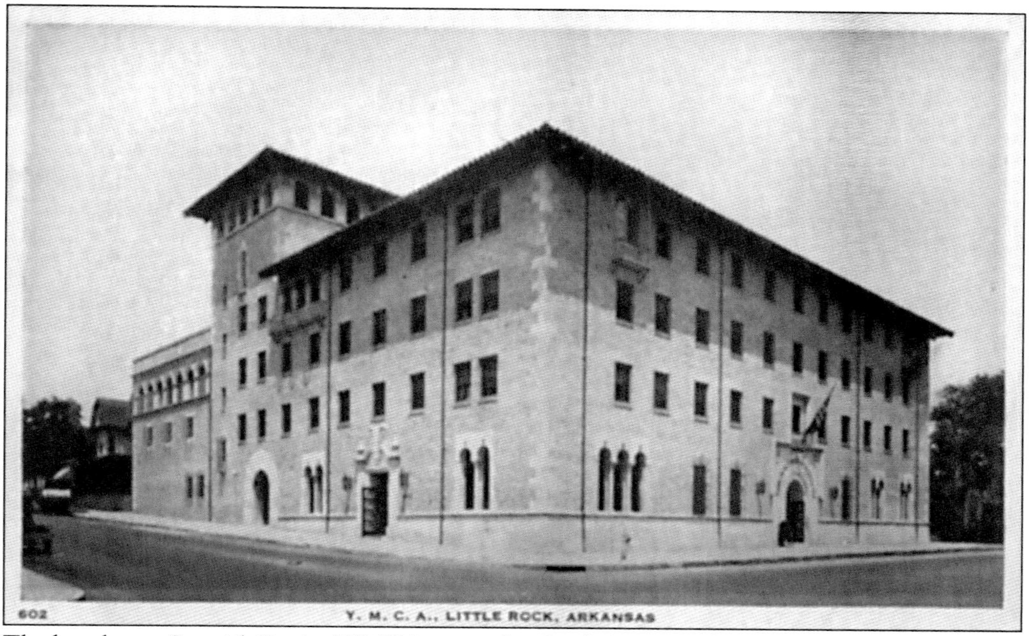

The handsome Spanish Revival YMCA opened at Sixth Street and Broadway in 1928, providing recreation and lodging for decades. It boasted two gyms, a pool and sauna, and a lovely interior courtyard. Beset with declining membership and financial pressures due to demographic shifts, the YMCA closed its facility at the historic building in 1996. Its ground floor hosts a smoothie café, but much of the rest of the massive structure remains empty.

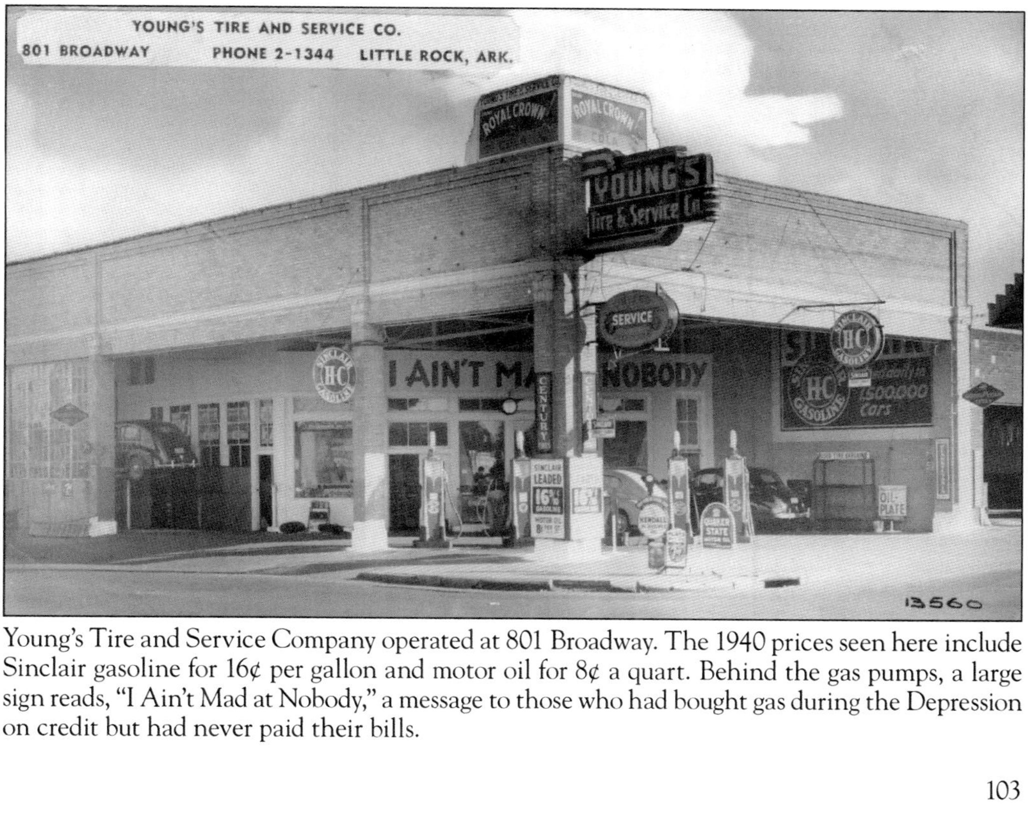

Young's Tire and Service Company operated at 801 Broadway. The 1940 prices seen here include Sinclair gasoline for 16¢ per gallon and motor oil for 8¢ a quart. Behind the gas pumps, a large sign reads, "I Ain't Mad at Nobody," a message to those who had bought gas during the Depression on credit but had never paid their bills.

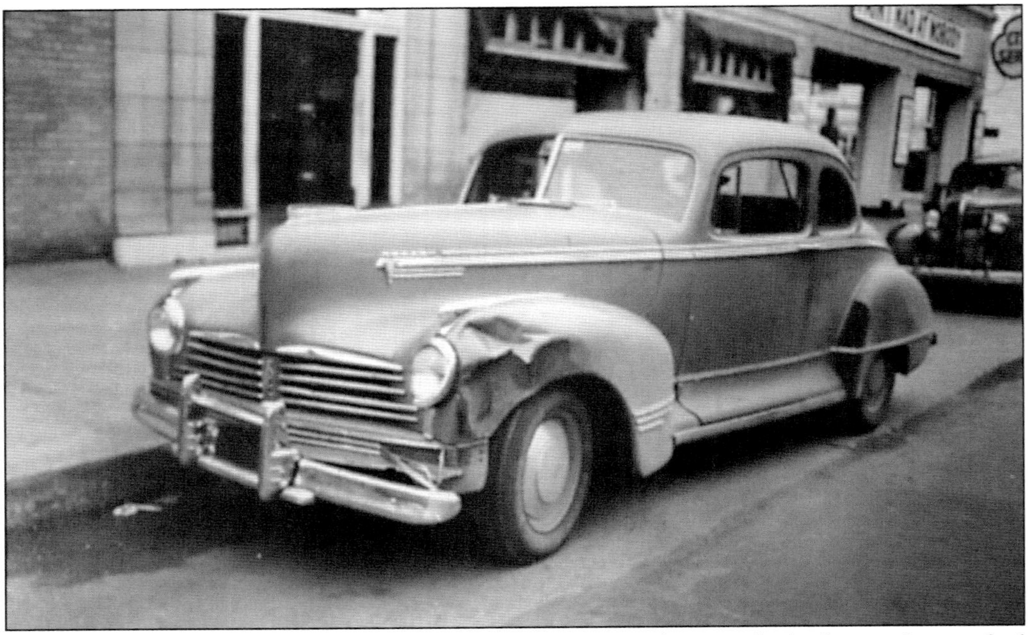

Following a fender bender, the Little Rock Police Department photographed a damaged car parked in front of Young's Tire and Service Company. The station had moved its "I Ain't Mad at Nobody" sign to the outside wall of the business. The building was razed years ago.

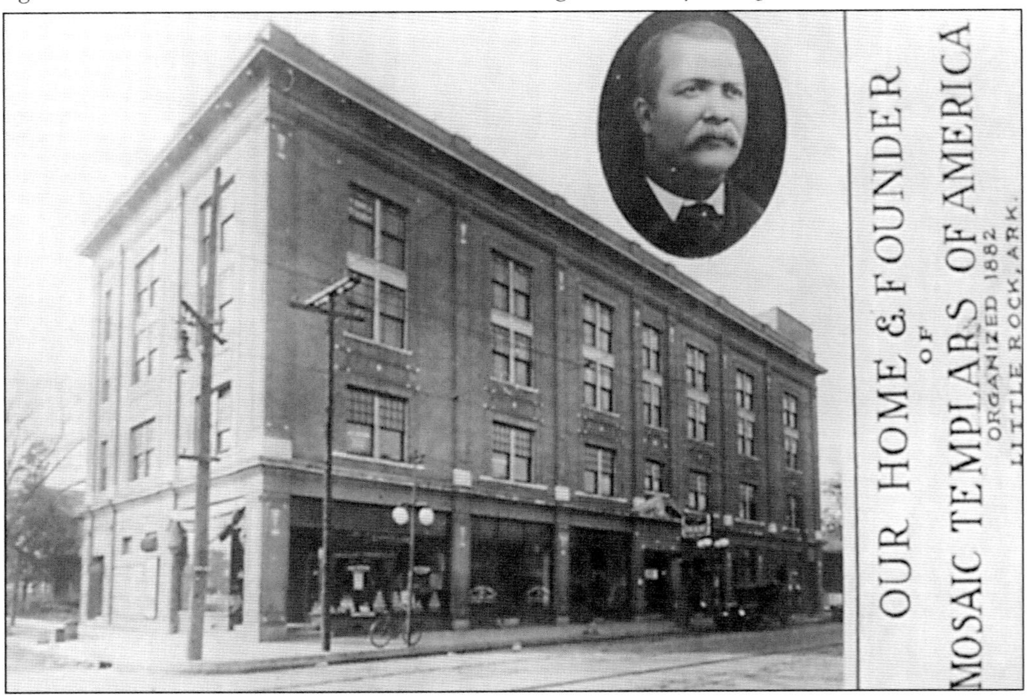

Mosaic Templars of America was founded in 1882 by two former slaves to sell insurance to African American families. In 1913, the lodge opened this impressive building at the southwest corner of Ninth Street and Broadway. It also operated a business college, a nursing school, and a building and loan for black citizens. The historic structure burned down in 2005, but it was rebuilt. Today, it operates as a museum incorporating the Arkansas Black Hall of Fame.

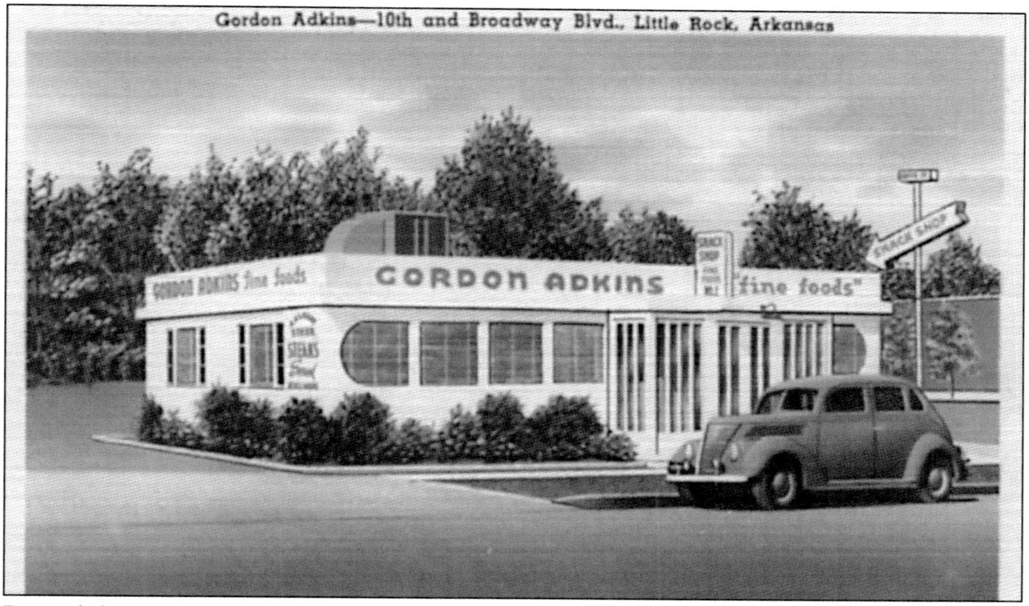

Beyond the competing gas stations on the first few blocks of Broadway, motorists on the path of the busy highway in 1950 found a variety of dining options. The Gordon Adkins No. 2 operated at Tenth Street and Broadway, advertising "Steer Steaks Served at All Hours." The business had previously been the Ritz Grill. It was razed decades ago, as family-owned eateries yielded to uniform franchise outlets.

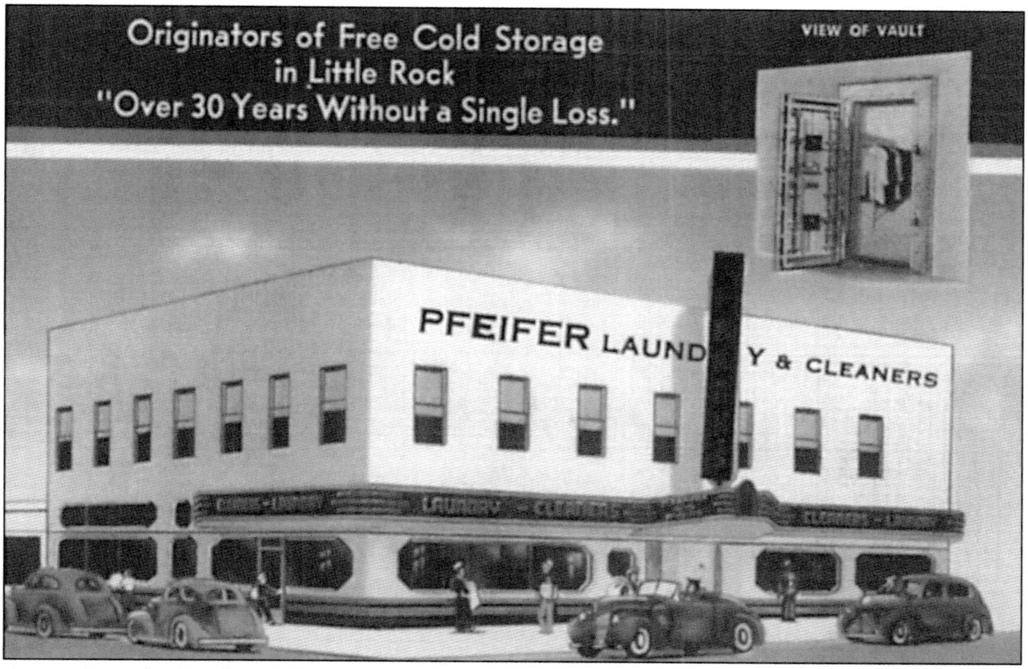

Across from the Gordon Adkins restaurant was the two-story Pfeifer Laundry & Cleaners, which advertised as the "Originators of Free Cold Storage in Little Rock—Over 30 Years Without a Single Loss." In this 1945 advertising card, a view of the cold-storage vault is included. The business offered the "latest methods in cleansing" as well as a dyeing service. The building has been gone for decades.

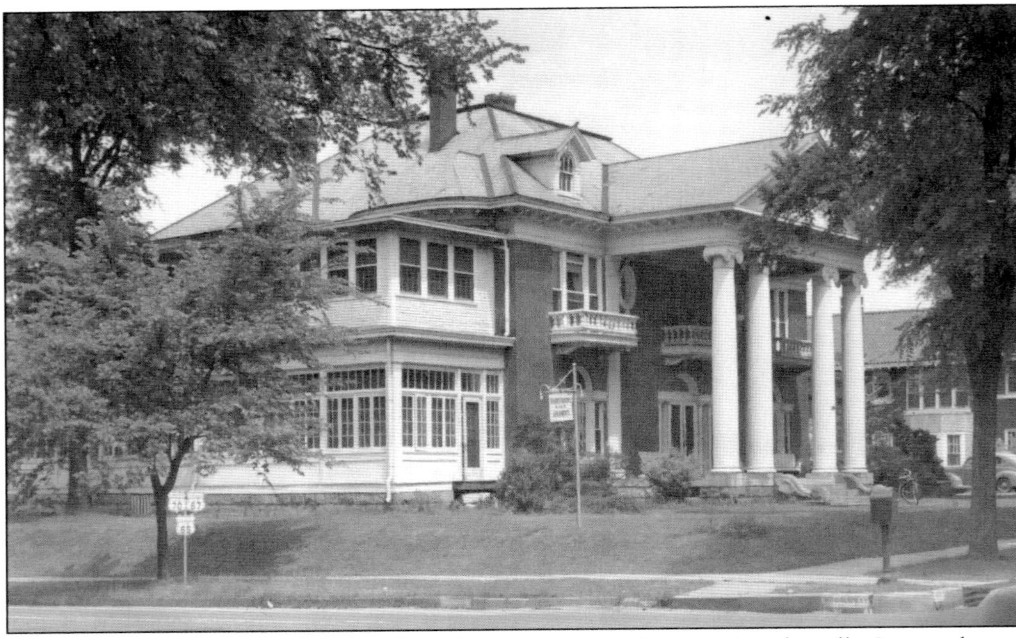

Beyond Tenth Street, Broadway's wide path saw commercial enterprises dwindle. Large, elegant homes graced the route all the way to its terminus at Roosevelt Road. At the northeast corner of Broadway and Eighteenth Street, a former mansion had by 1940 become Garm's Tourist Home, renting rooms for $2 a day. A triple highway marker is visible at the street. Today, a small office occupies the site, as the grand home was razed long ago.

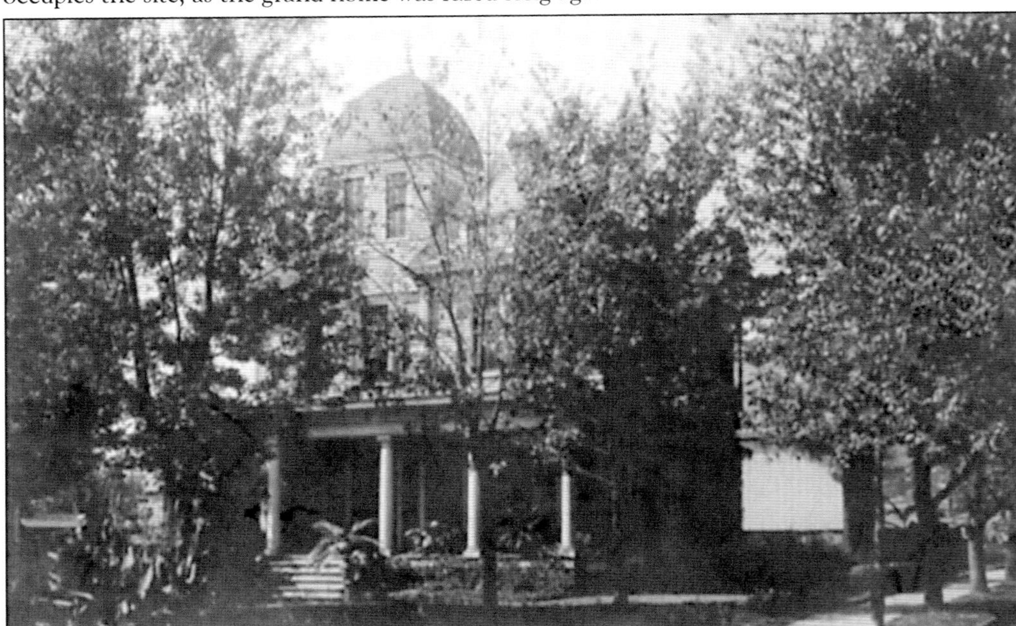

The medical and surgical practice of Dr. R.W. Lindsey afforded him the means to build a striking home at 2100 Broadway. In this 1910 photograph, a weather vane and lightning rod are seen on the home's topmost turret; the porch and yard are adorned with roses, ferns, and tropical plants. One of Dr. Lindsey's neighbors on Broadway was Joseph T. Robinson, a prominent figure in Arkansas history and national politics. Dr. Lindsey's home is no longer standing.

Six

Roosevelt Road and a Highway before the Interstate

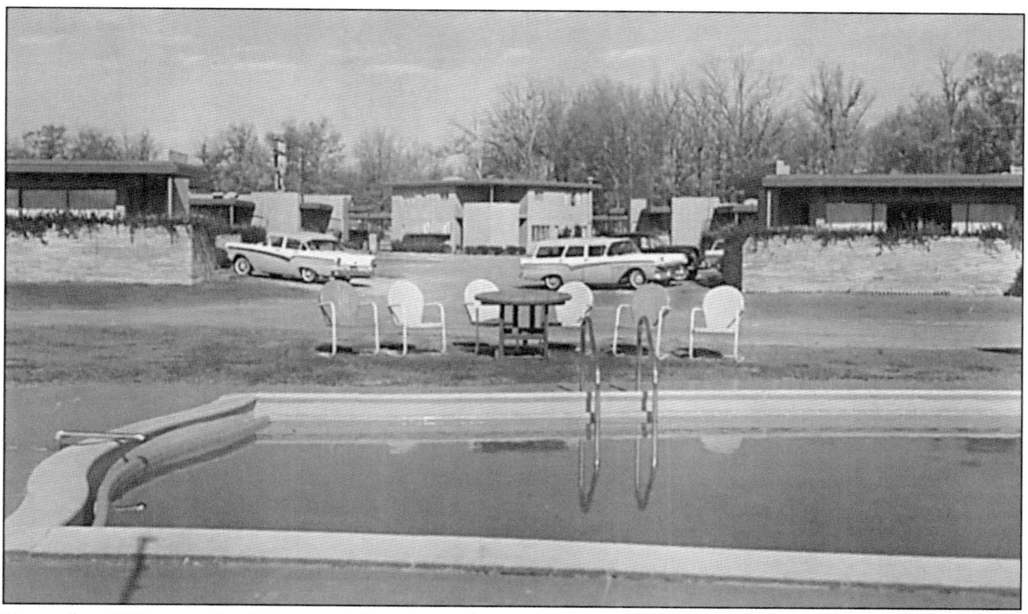

From the 1920s, much of the north/south traffic in the nation moved along US Highways 67/70 and 65 through Little Rock, exiting downtown onto Roosevelt Road and Asher Avenue. Commerce sprang up to service these motorists, such as the Rose Courts at Highway 65 and Roosevelt Road. The rooms were located in pods placed around landscaped grounds and a pool. No trace remains today of the business, seen here in 1957.

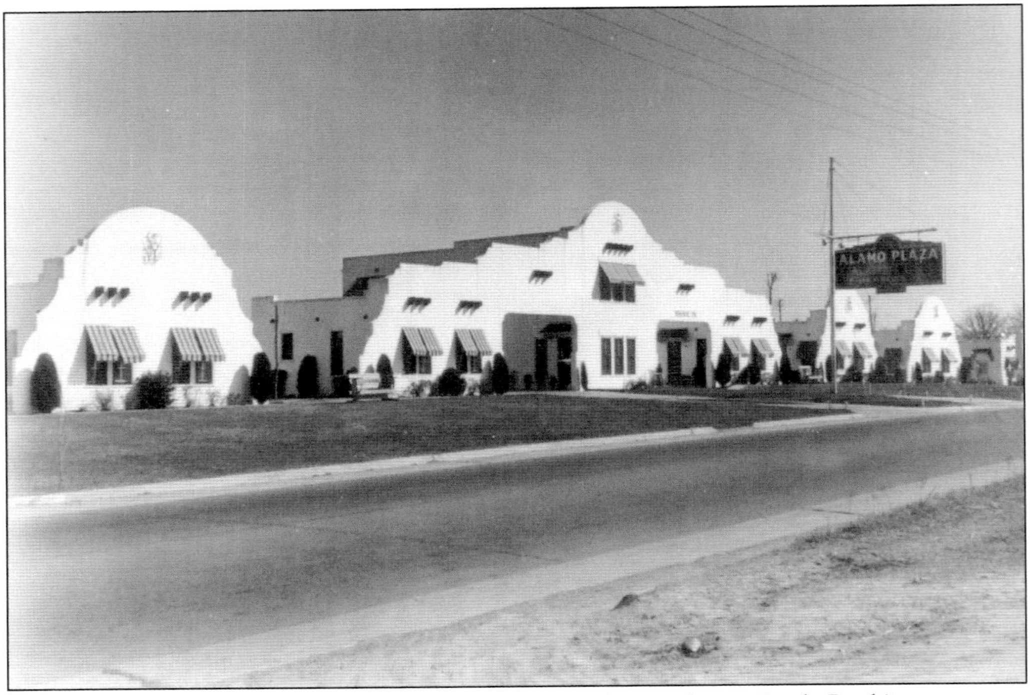

The Alamo Plaza was part of a chain that spread over the Southwest. Little Rock's version was erected at 3200 Roosevelt Road in the 1930s. The tourist court, in its trademark "Alamo" design, hosted guests for around $2 a night in the 1940s. (Courtesy of Arkansas History Commission.)

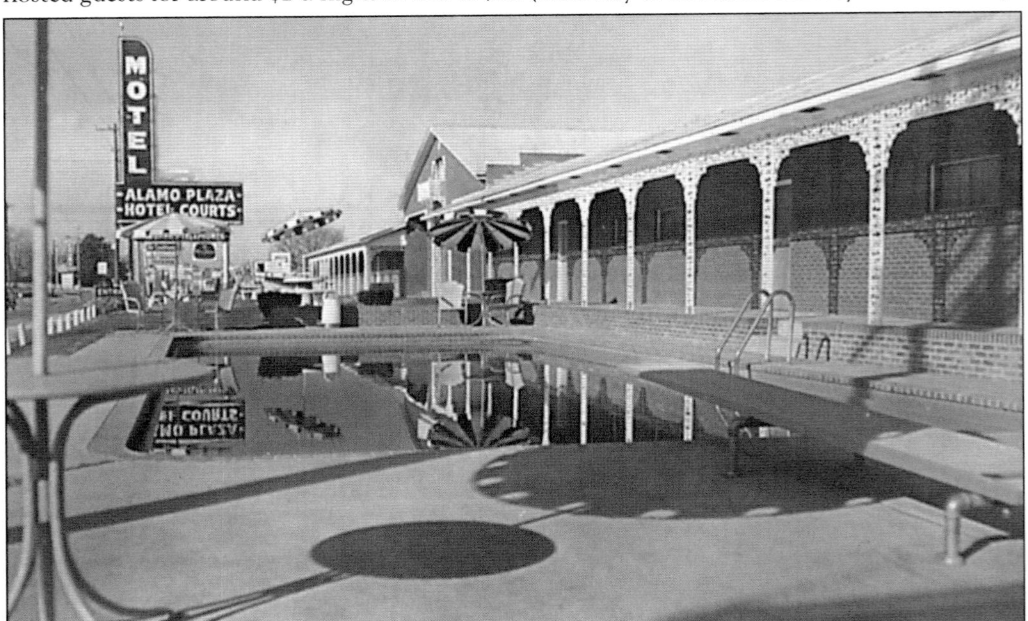

By 1960, the Alamo Plaza Hotel Courts had been rebuilt, abandoning the Southwestern style but retaining the name. This deluxe facility offered 24-hour food and valet service, airport transportation, and babysitting. The coming of Interstate 30 in the mid-1960s caused the cross-country auto traffic to bypass Roosevelt Road. The business was razed in the 1980s. A McDonald's briefly occupied the site, which is vacant today.

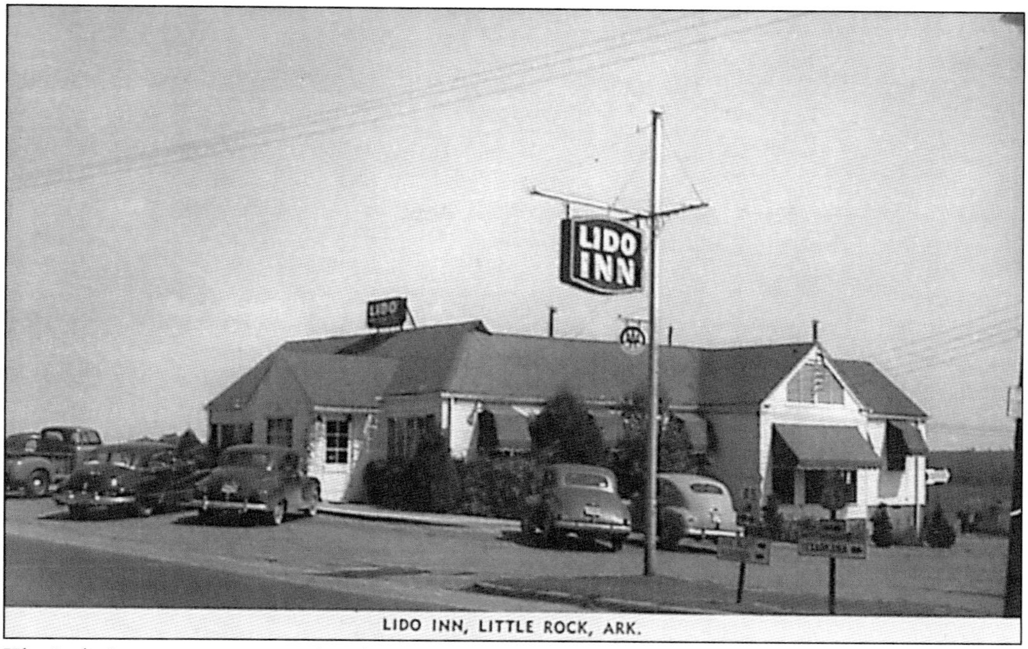

The Lido Inn restaurant stood at the corner of Main Street and Roosevelt Road, poised to attract hungry motorists entering and exiting Little Rock. The postcard advertised, "This is one of Little Rock's smartest eating places—completely air conditioned." No trace remains of the business; a shopping complex now occupies the corner location.

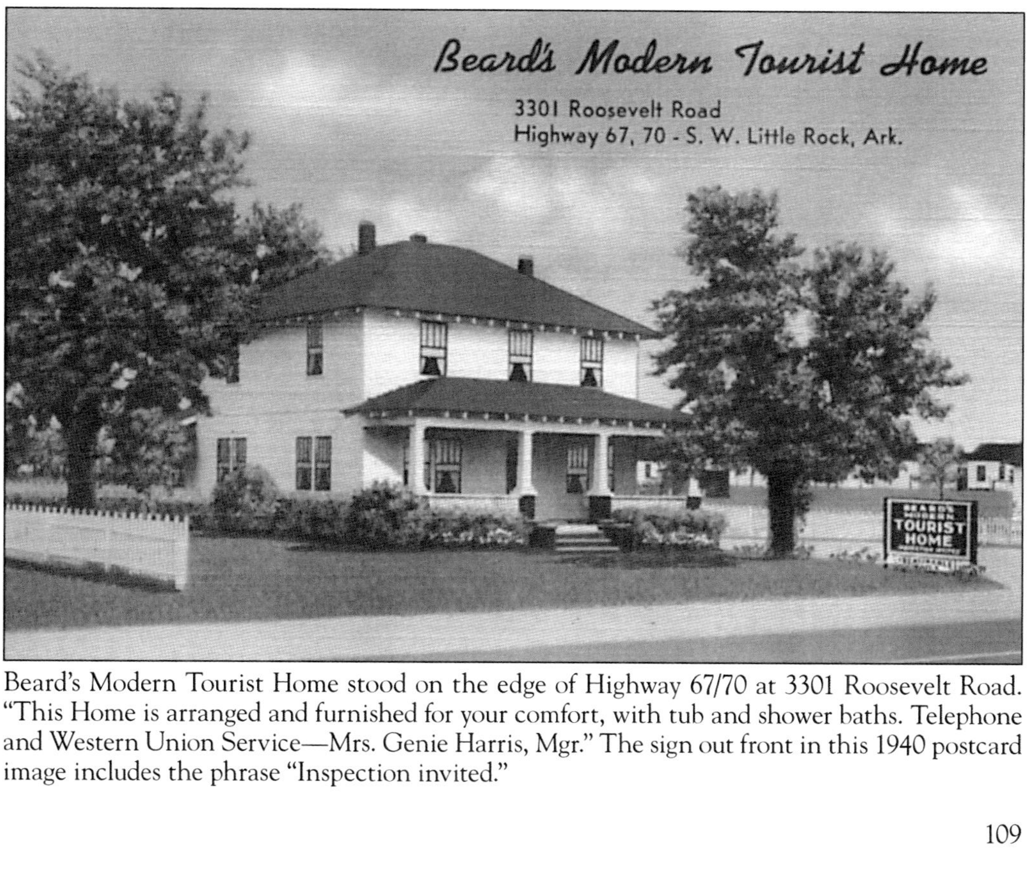

Beard's Modern Tourist Home stood on the edge of Highway 67/70 at 3301 Roosevelt Road. "This Home is arranged and furnished for your comfort, with tub and shower baths. Telephone and Western Union Service—Mrs. Genie Harris, Mgr." The sign out front in this 1940 postcard image includes the phrase "Inspection invited."

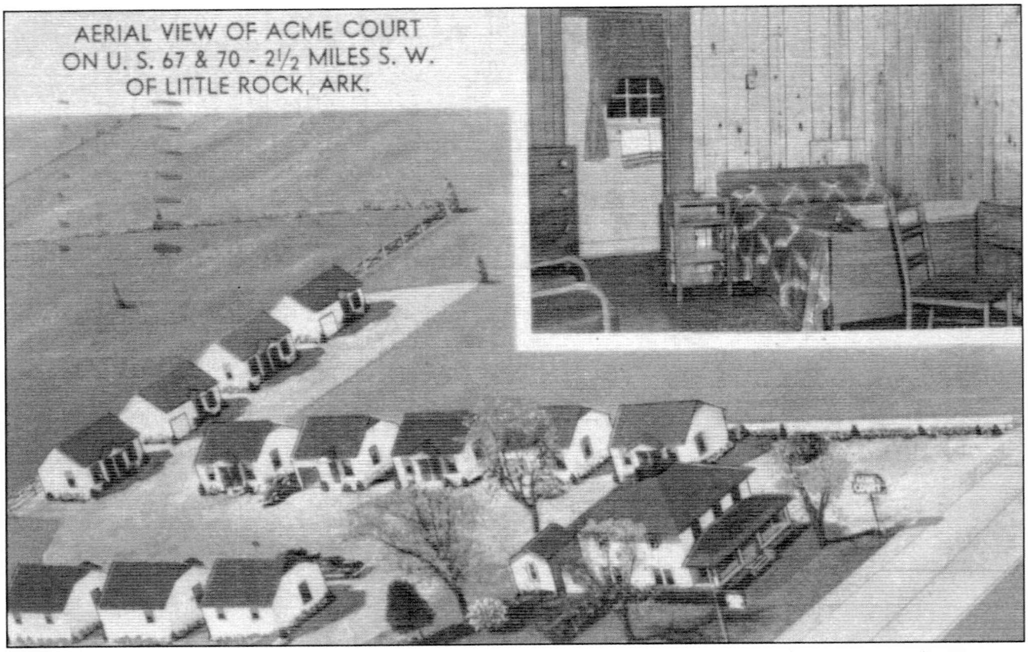

A few years after the postcard on the previous page was produced, the former Beard's Tourist Home had been transformed into the Acme Court. The original building, which had been the tourist home, still fronted the business at the road, while its set of individual cottages had been expanded into the farm fields behind the house. This 1949 postcard still listed the owner as B.G. Beard, with Genie Harris still the manager.

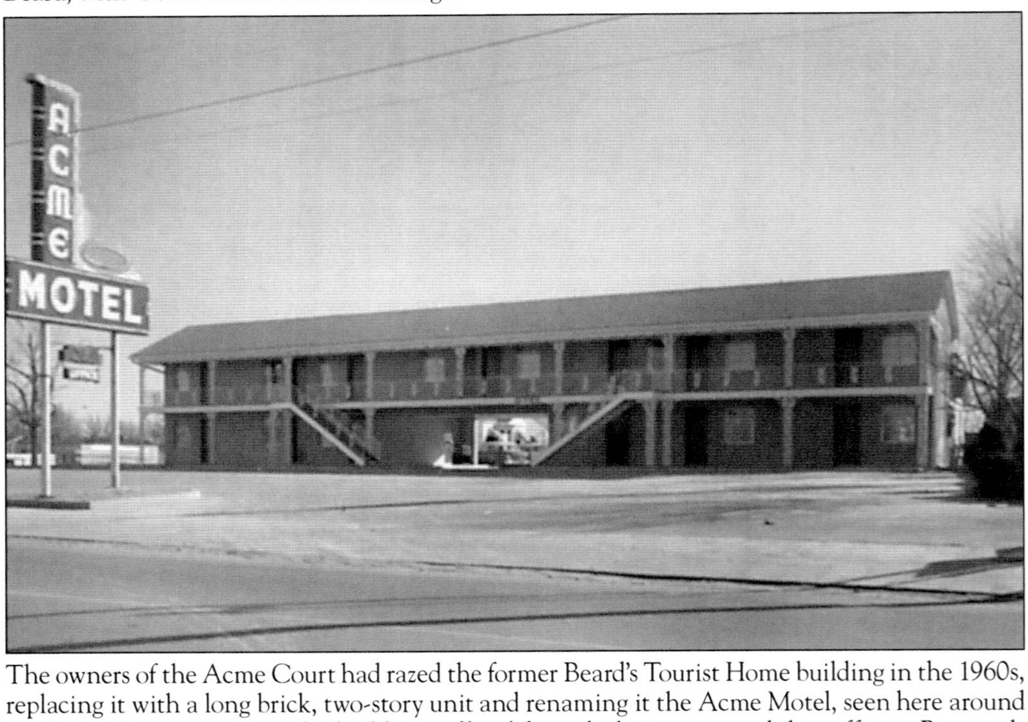

The owners of the Acme Court had razed the former Beard's Tourist Home building in the 1960s, replacing it with a long brick, two-story unit and renaming it the Acme Motel, seen here around 1980. In subsequent years, the building suffered from declining automobile traffic on Roosevelt Road and, as a consequence, fewer guests. It no longer functions as a motel.

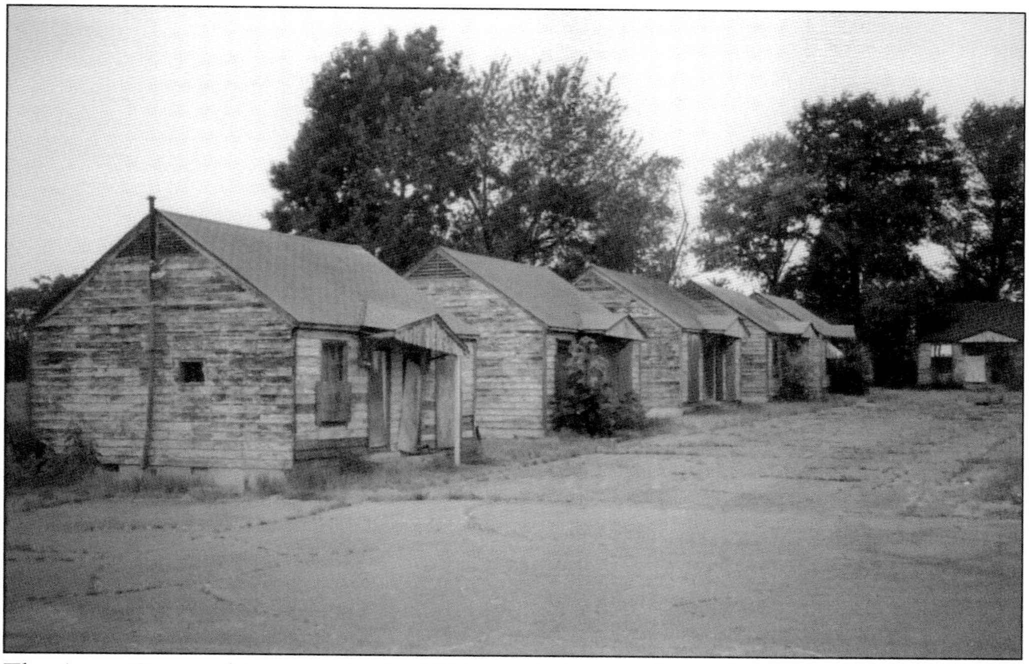

The Acme Court cabins, seen in the 1949 aerial photograph on the previous page, stood for another 50 years, but they were shuttered and decaying by 1998. These cabins were in their original location behind the "modern" Acme Motel. They were razed soon after this photograph was taken. (Photograph by the author.)

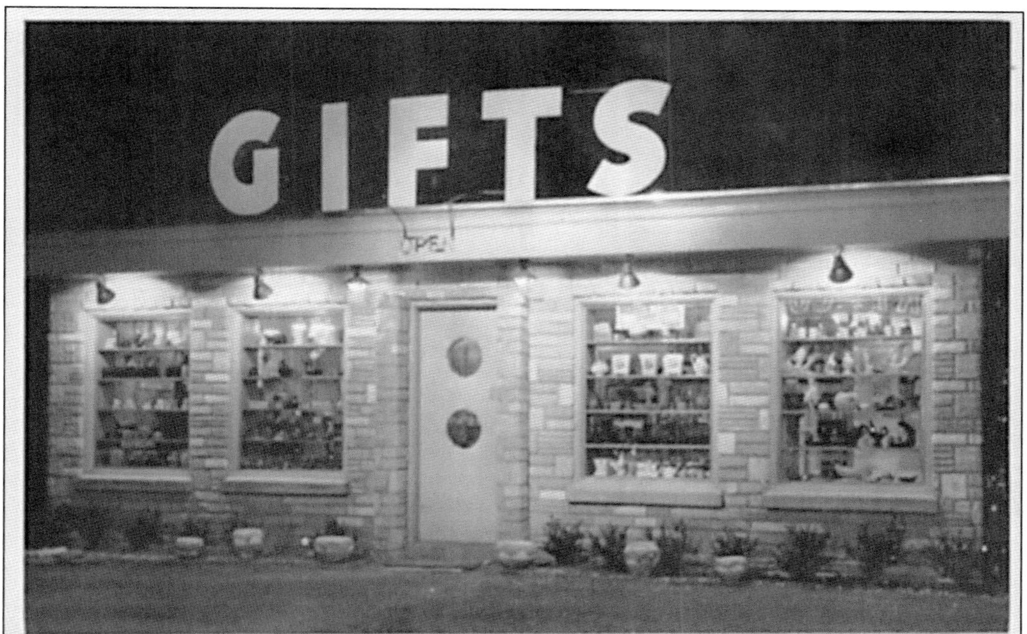

Tourist traffic funneling down busy highway 67/70 found gift shops and other classic "tourist traps" at which to pull off the road to shop. Such was Adkins Gifts at 3604 Roosevelt Road. The shop was shuttered long ago as the interstates took the traffic away, but the building still stands.

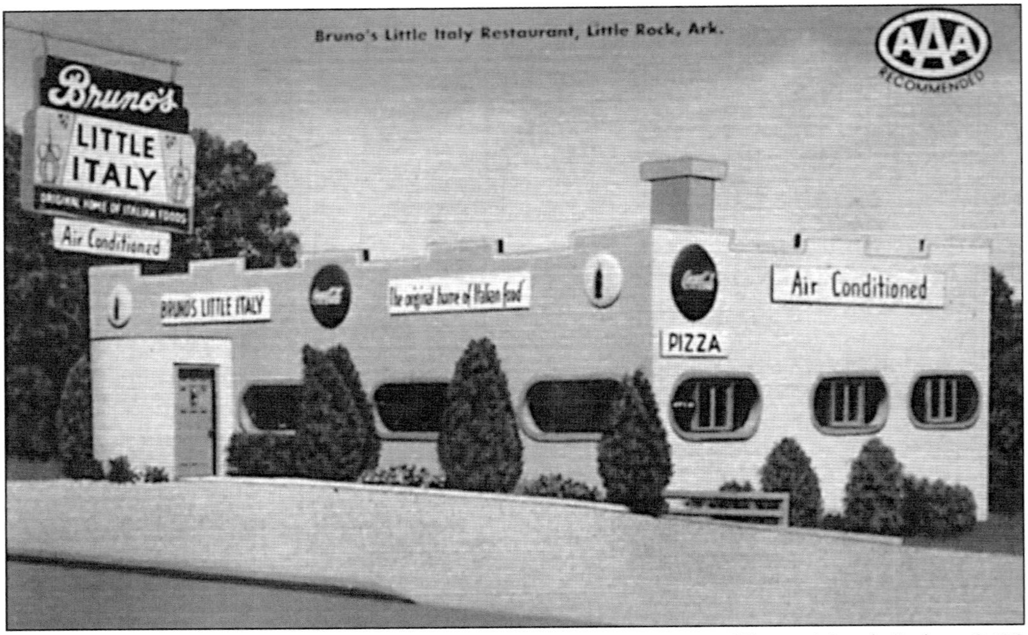

In 1949, Vincent "Jimmy" Bruno, son of an Italian immigrant, opened Bruno's Little Italy at 3400 West Roosevelt Road. The business operated at the site for the next 29 years under the slogan "The Original Home of Italian Food." At one point, the business was ranked 99th among America's 12,000 most-popular restaurants in Darnell's *Guide to Good Eating in the South*.

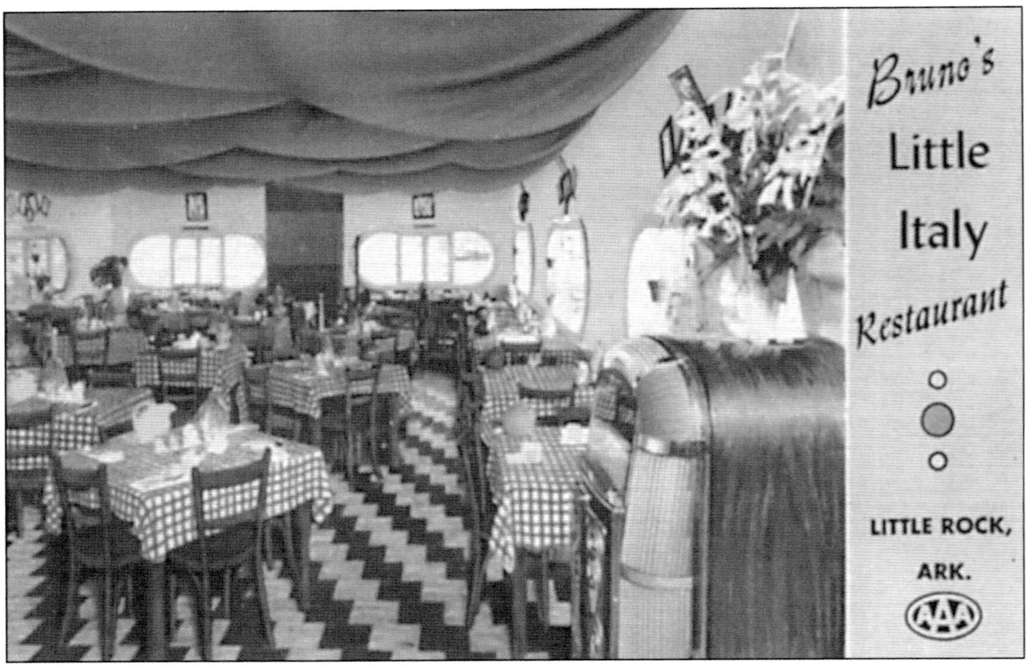

Bruno's Little Italy sported quaint Italian decor, with a jukebox, seen at right in this 1950 view. A menu from that time showed the most expensive item was lobster tails for $2.75. "Round the World Pizza" cost $1.50, and Budweiser beer went for 35¢ a glass. The restaurant moved to West Little Rock in the late 1970s. The empty building still stands, having served as a church at one point.

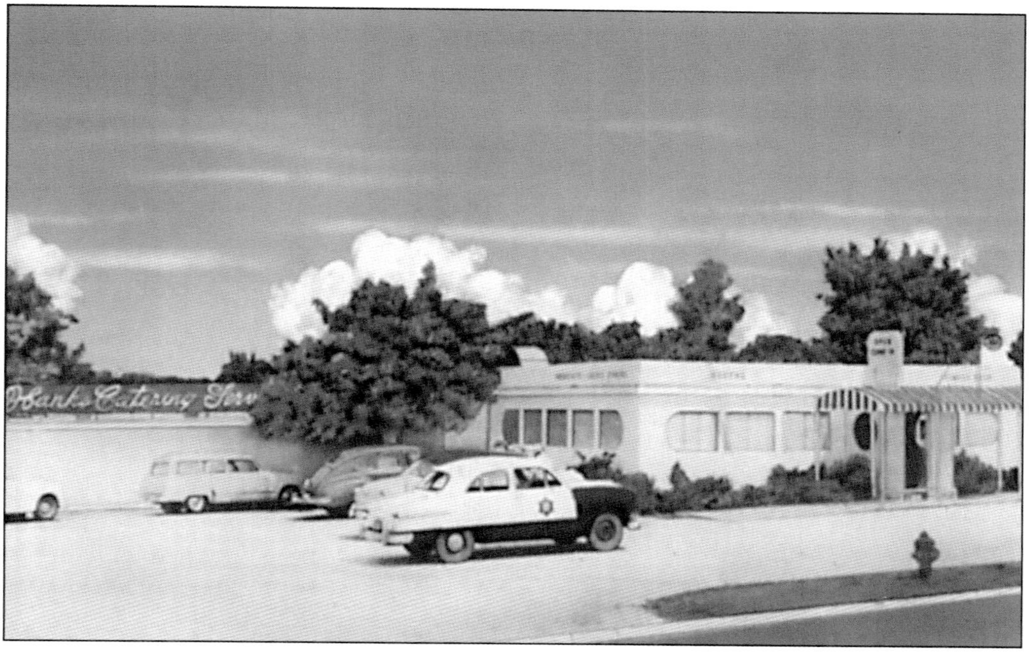

Hank's Dog House opened around 1950 at 3614 Roosevelt Road along the busy route of Highway 76/70. It soon became among the most popular eateries in town. Its first home (above) was the former Gordon Adkin's, which relocated to Broadway downtown. Within a decade, Hank's had been remodeled and expanded (below). Despite the "dog house" name, it was very much an upscale place, with white-jacketed waiters serving steaks and lobster. The postcard advertised Little Rock's only "Oyster Bar." Seating was advertised for up to 350 diners. Today, Hank's is long gone, and the site is a bare concrete slab.

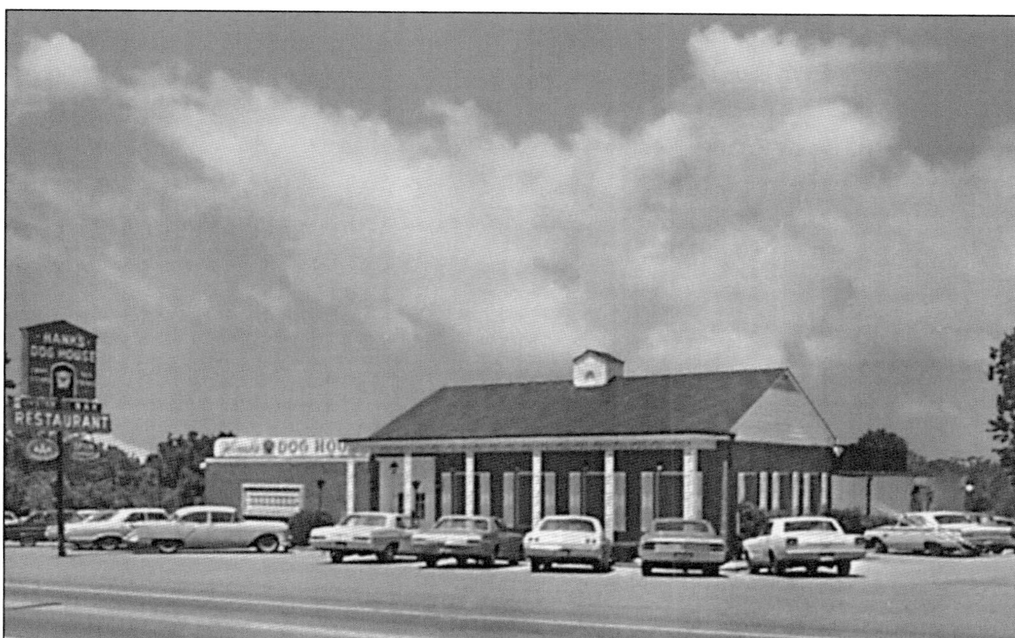

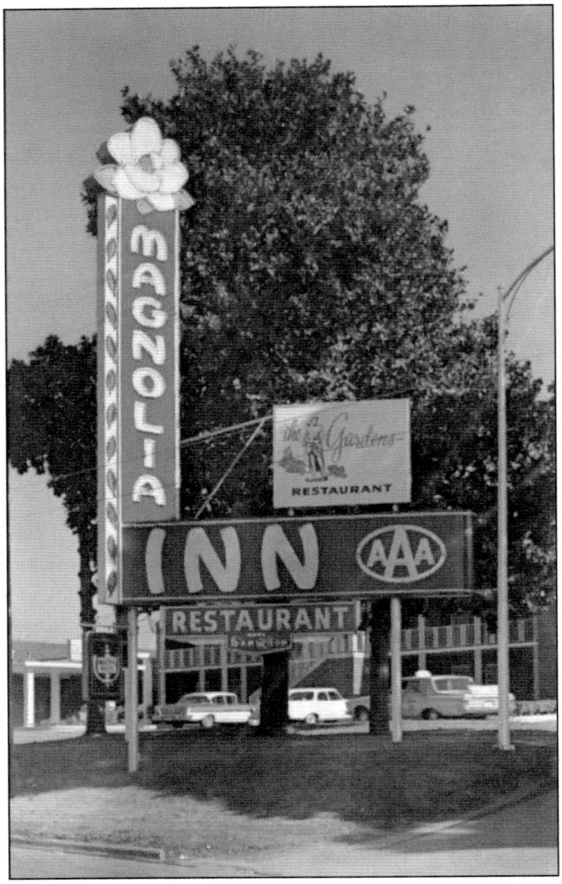

The Magnolia Inn, at 3601 Roosevelt Road, opened around 1950 and featured the Gardens Restaurant. This 1957 postcard proclaimed that it had 112 rooms and suites, a pool, and the "Cadillac Club." The passage of years and the loss of traffic to the interstate was not kind to the Magnolia. Its wonderful sign has vanished, and the building is surrounded by a chain-link fence.

This classic gas station dates to the 1930s, when its gas pumps were operated by uniformed attendants. The building was still in use in 1998, hosting a used-tire outlet and hamburger stand. The price on the "Byrd" pumps read 57¢ a gallon, suggesting that the last gas pumped had been at least two decades previous. Today, the pumps are gone, and the building is falling into disrepair. (Photograph by the author.)

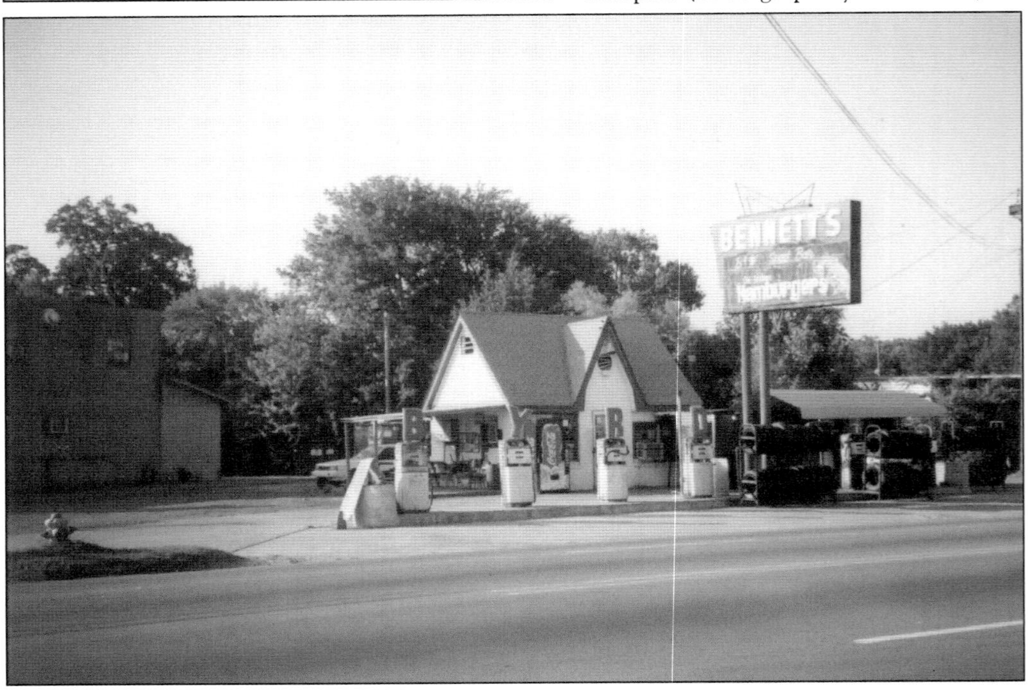

Seven

Parades, Theaters, and Little Rock's First Shopping Mall

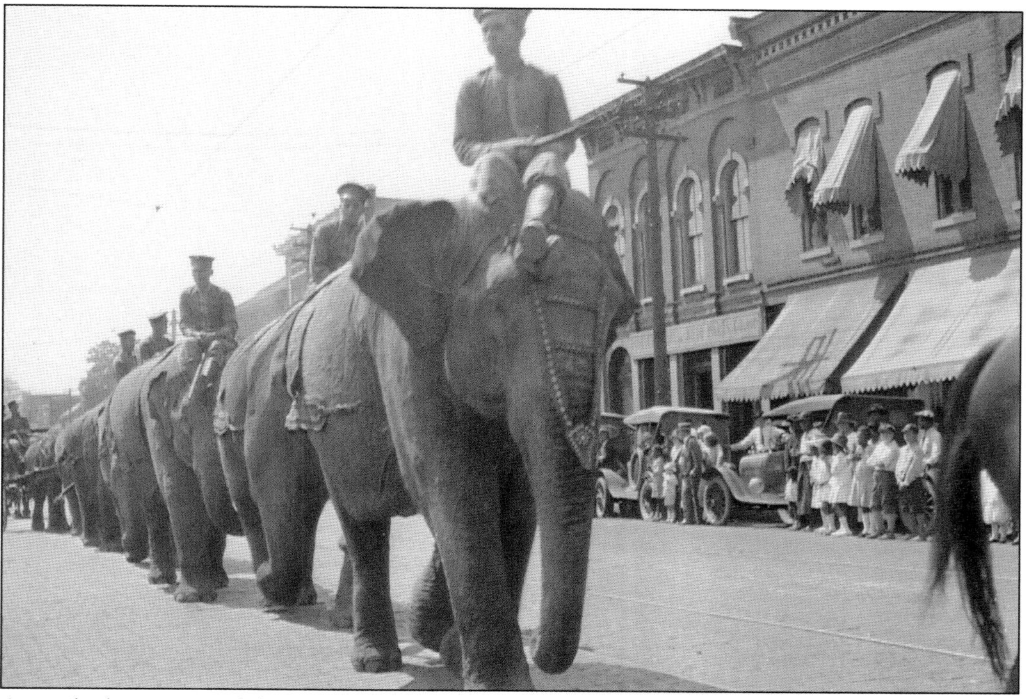

As with shopping and dining, modes of entertainment have changed over the years. Parades were once common along Little Rock's Main Street and Capitol Avenue, and single-screen movie houses dotted the city. Seen here around 1920, the 900 block of Main Street is lined with spectators as the arrival of the circus in town was promoted by a parade of elephants, zebras, and other attractions.

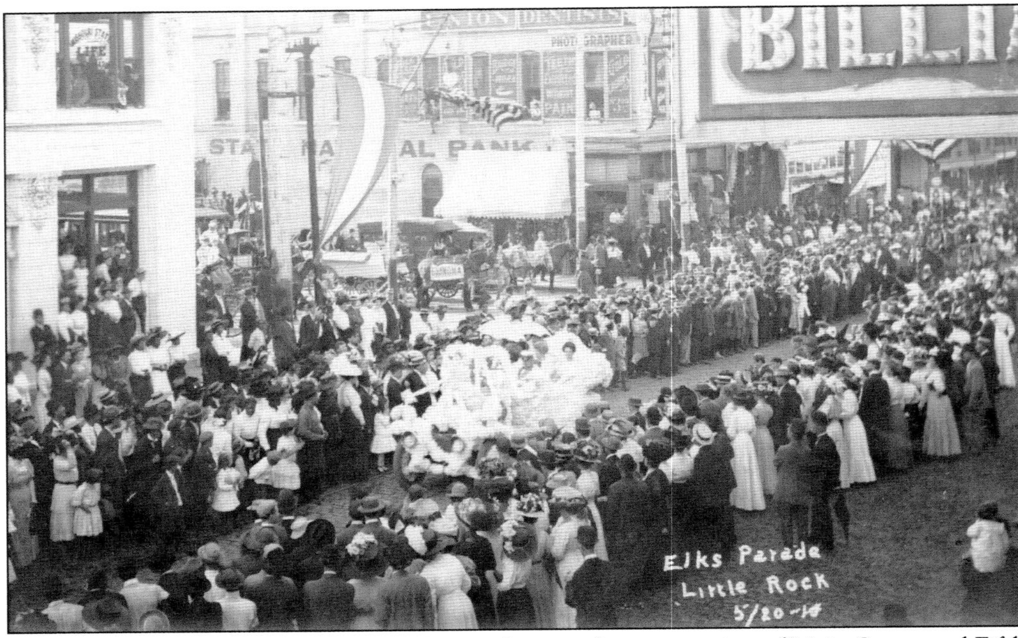

The best place from which to view many parades was the intersection of Main Street and Fifth Street (later Capitol Avenue), as seen here when the Elks Parade filed by onlookers in 1910. Spectators were even hanging out of windows at the insurance office (left) and the Union Dentist office (center). The site of the dentist's practice is a parking lot today, while the office building is being transformed into a hotel.

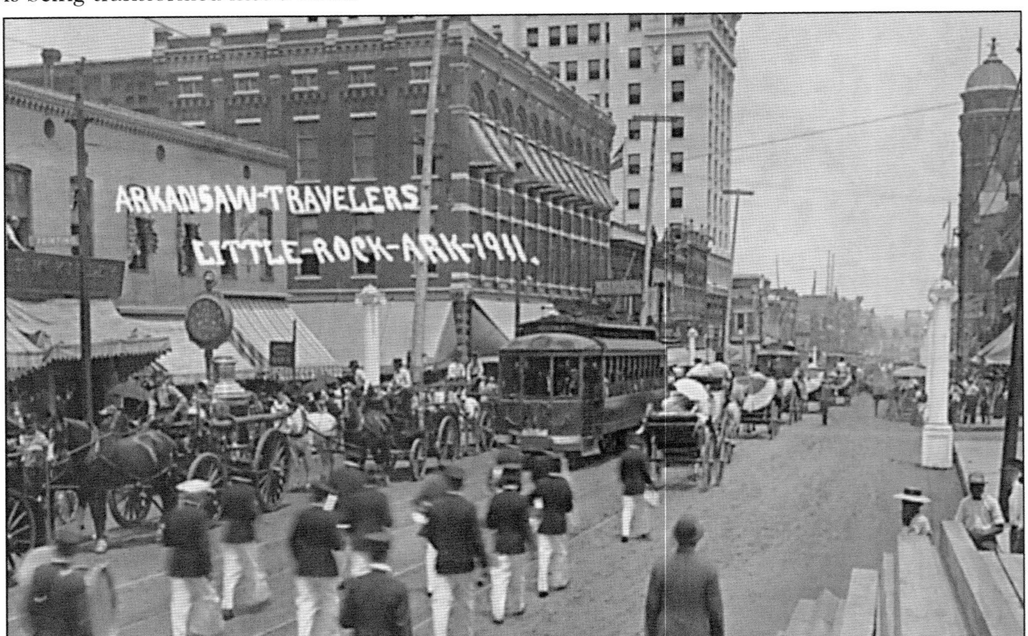

The Arkansaw Travelers marching band parades north through the 600 block of Main Street in 1911. Sharing the parade route were streetcars, buggies, and a steam pumper fire wagon (left). The same route would be used within a few days for a parade by the United Confederate Veterans' reunion, for which the white plaster columns at right were erected.

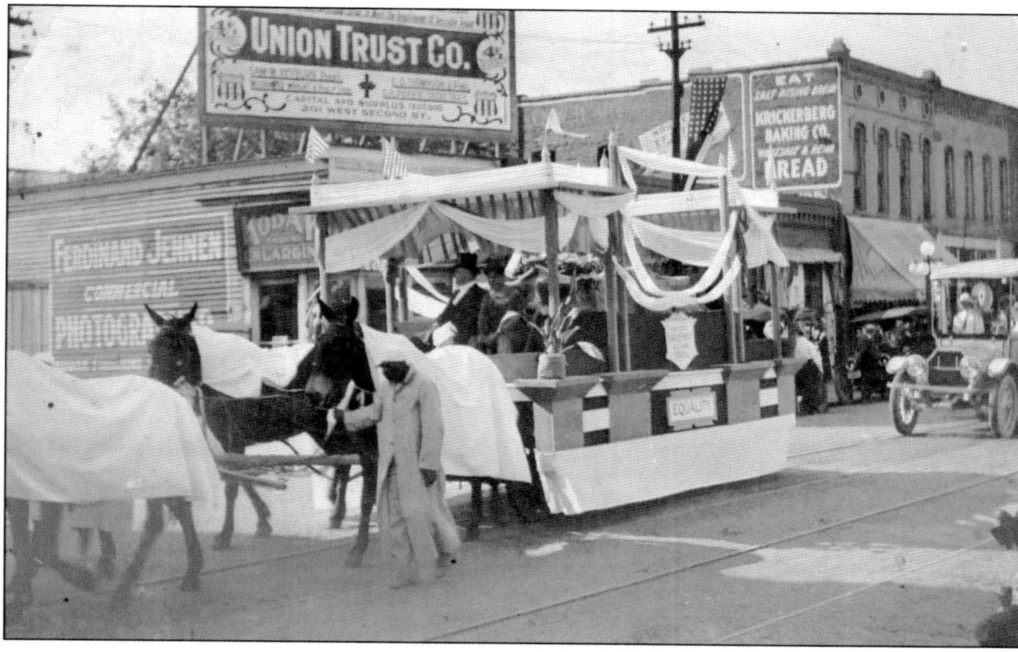

On perhaps the same day in 1910 as that of the previous photograph, the Elks Parade moves down South Main Street past smaller business enterprises that lined the street farther from the main commercial district. Guided by men clad in long coats, the white-draped mules pull floats marked "Equality" (above) and "Liberty" (below), with perhaps "Fraternity" pending in the queue. At that time, the African American assistants might have been struck by the irony of the labeled floats.

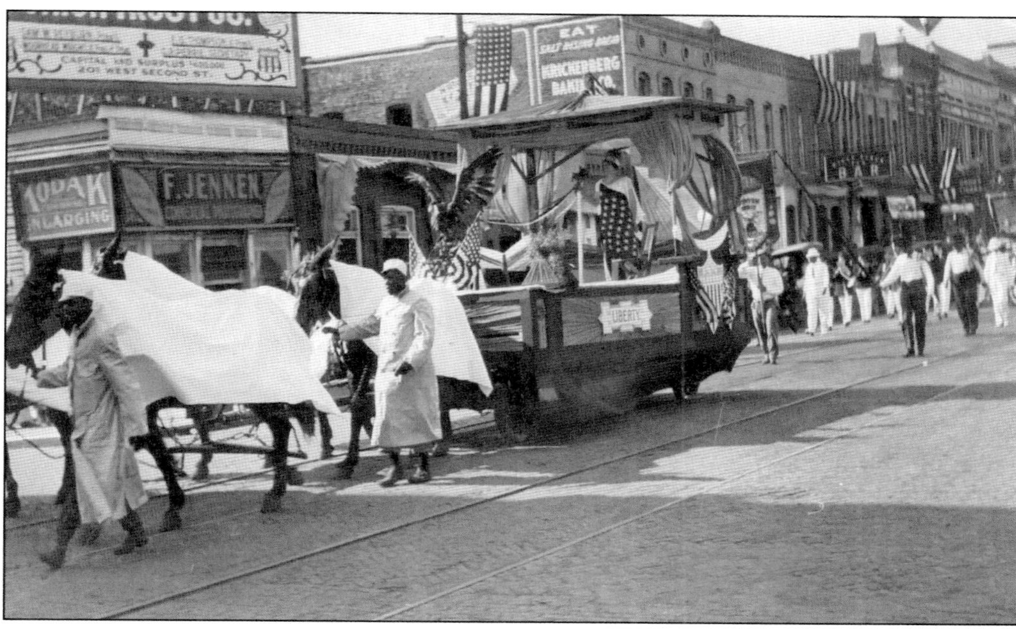

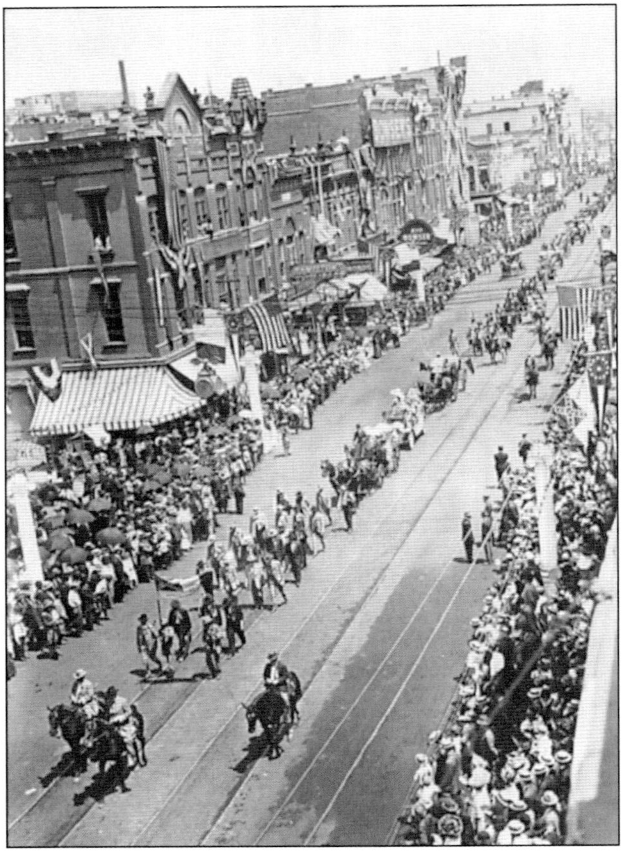

The grandest parade in Arkansas history took place on the final day of the United Confederate Veterans' reunion, hosted by Little Rock in 1911. Some 12,000 aged but determined gray-clad soldiers marched on a round-trip from the Old State House to City Park and back again in a parade that took two hours to pass any given point.

The United Confederate Veterans parade included remnants of the famed cavalry corps of Gen. Nathan Bedford Forrest, the charismatic and mercurial Confederate officer. These men, who 50 years earlier had endured great hardships, grueling marches, and deprivation in order to secure a number of Confederate victories, mounted up for one more ride together.

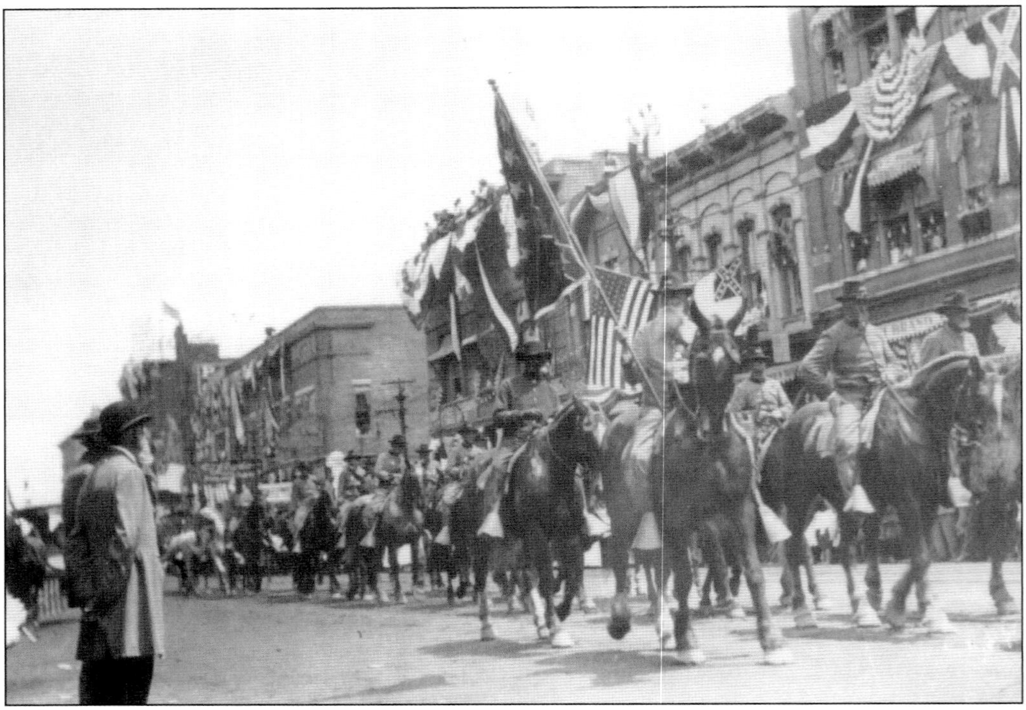

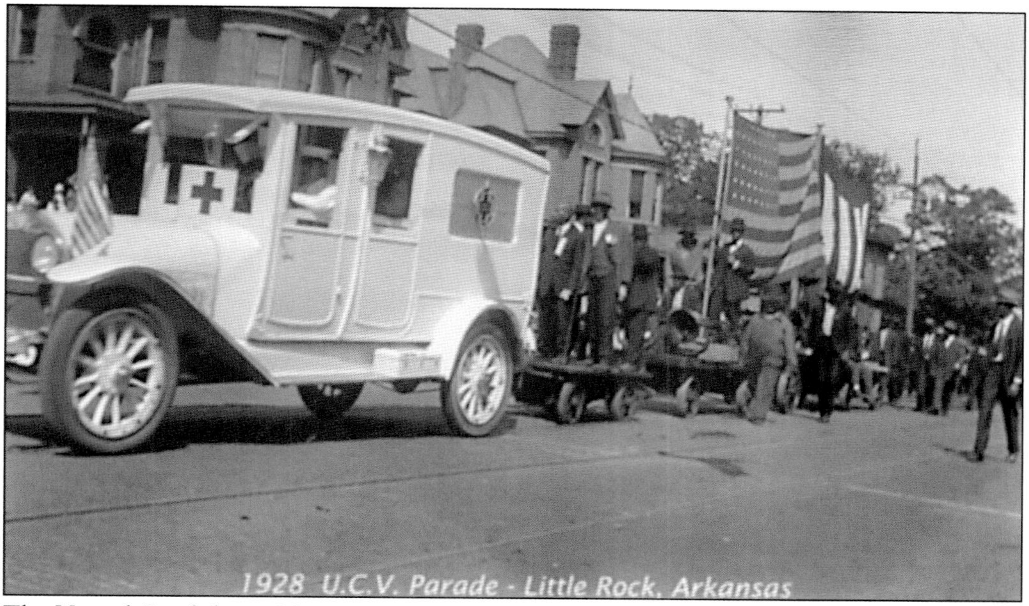

The United Confederate Veterans returned to Little Rock in 1928 for another reunion, but by this time only 1,100 were registered. As in 1911, the event concluded with a parade, this time running from North Little Rock's Park Hill onto Little Rock's Main Street and then up Capitol Avenue, as seen here. The old rebels who had marched in 1911 now rode atop railroad baggage carts. (Courtesy of Jim Smith of Little Rock.)

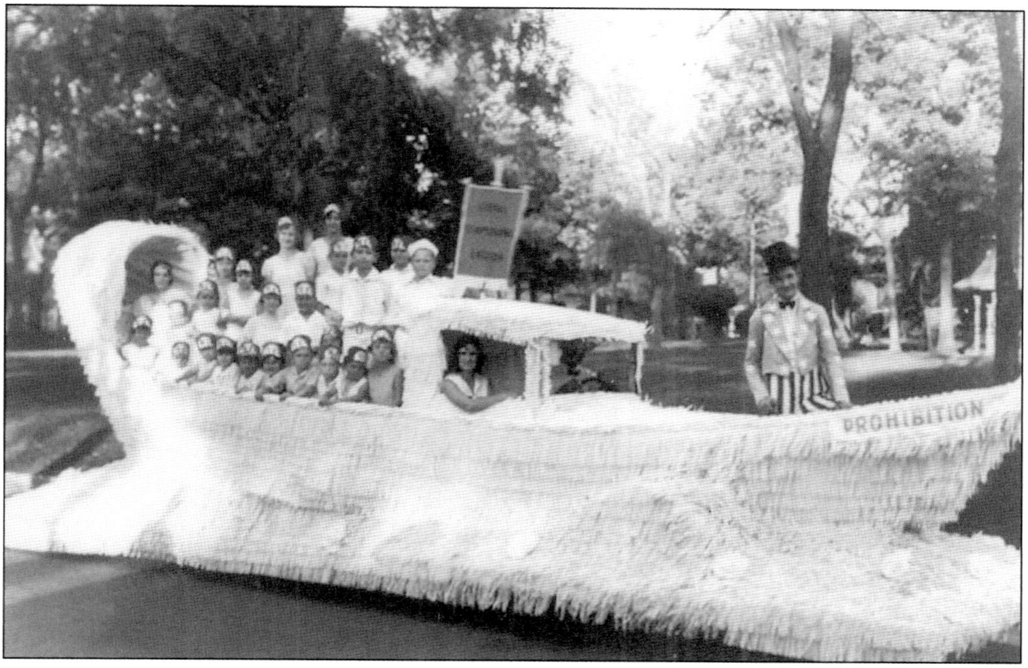

In 1930, twenty-five children in City Park (later MacArthur Park) are set for a ride on a parade float constructed around an early-model automobile. The theme of the float appears to be support for the prohibition of alcohol, which was the law of the land at that time. Uncle Sam appears to be steering the ship *Prohibition*, bearing fresh-faced youngsters into the future. (Courtesy of Butler Center for Arkansas Studies.)

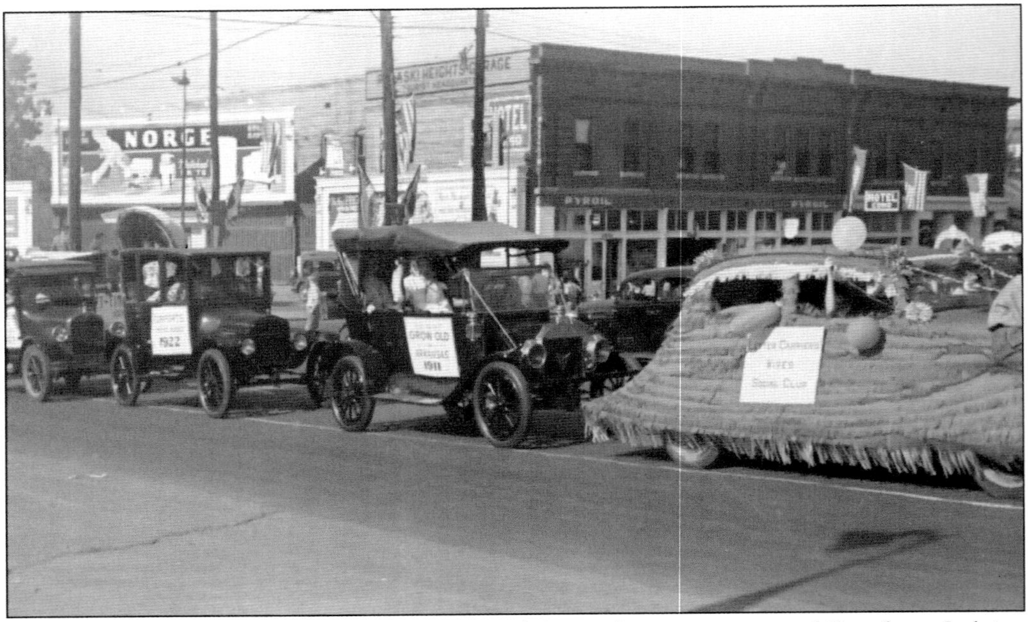

Around 1940, this parade moves east on Second Street, having just crossed Broadway. Judging from the bunting on the electrical poles, it may have been an Independence Day celebration. The segment of the parade shown above appears to be giving a history of transportation, presented by the Letter Carriers Wives Social Club in the lead car, draped with paper fringe and balloons. The following three cars bear signs indicating their vintage, from 1911 ("One Might Grow Old in Arkansas"), to a 1922 Model T ("Comforts Were Added"), and then 1927 ("We Grow With Arkansas"). Drivers and passengers appear to be wearing period costumes. Also included among the cars in this parade was the stagecoach below, complete with an "armed guard" seated atop the strongbox.

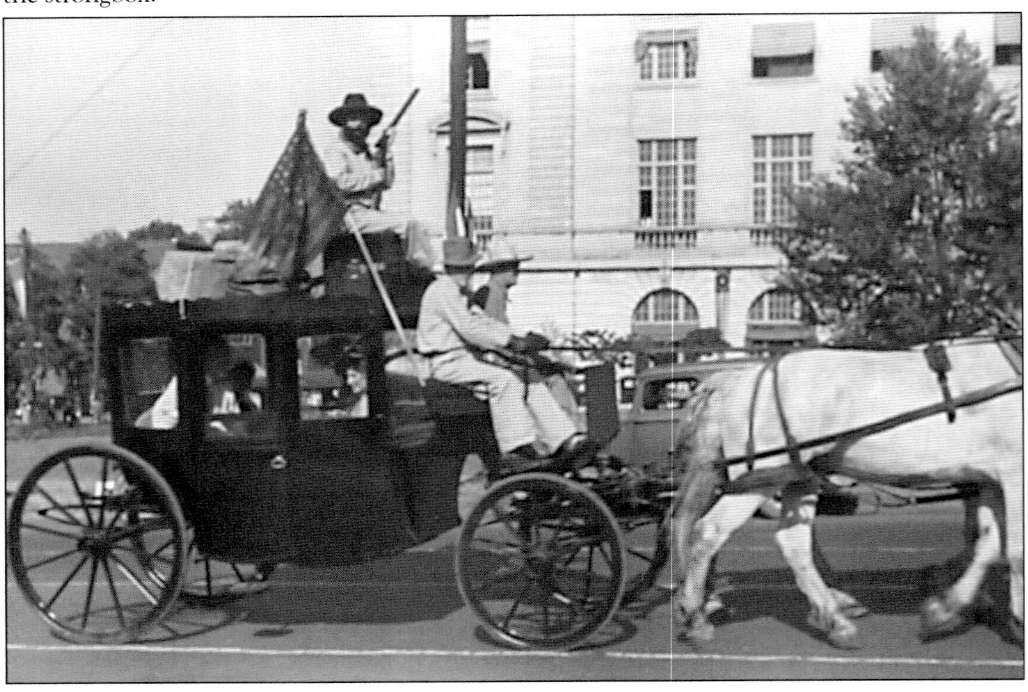

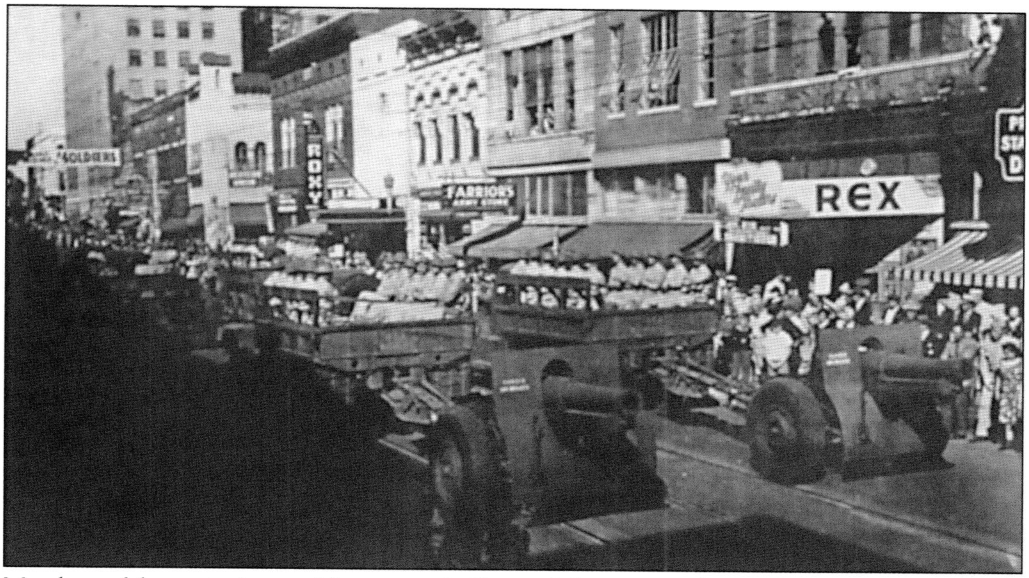

Members of the nation's armed forces paraded beneath banners reading "Welcome Home Soldiers" strung over Main Street sometime after the conclusion of World War II. The troop carriers, towing artillery pieces, make their way past the Rex Movie Theater. The Roxy Theater is just beyond, on the 200 block of North Main Street. Ironically, Farrior's Army Store was located between the two theaters.

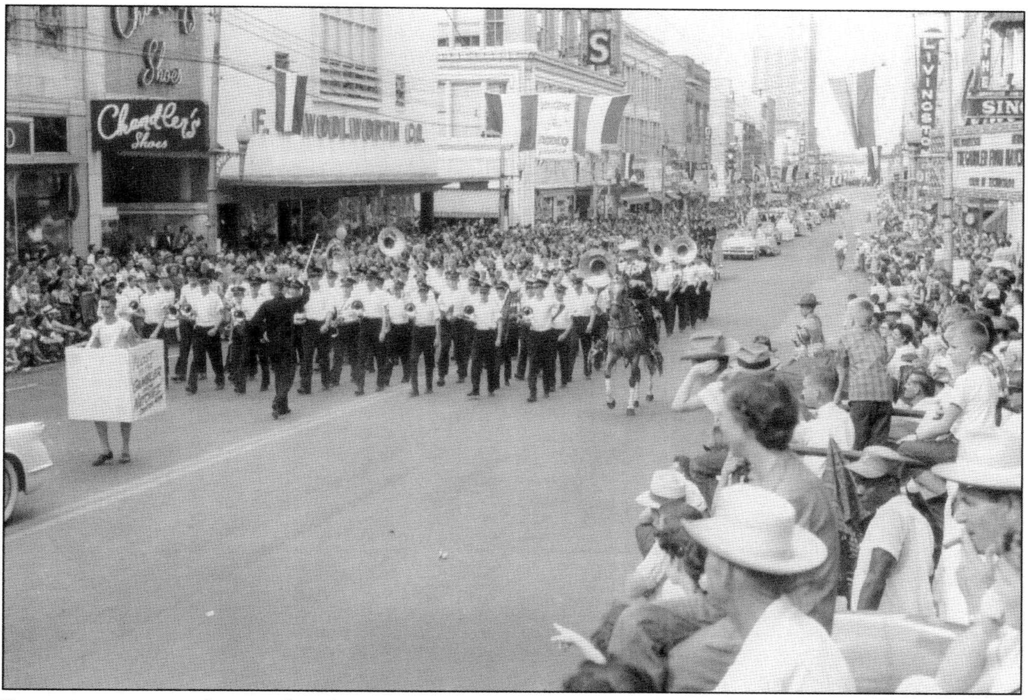

Sometimes, a parade gave local movie theaters an opportunity to promote their current fare, as was the case in 1954 in the Rodeo Parade on Main Street. As an advertising stunt, a man walks the parade in his underwear with a box promoting the movie *The Gambler from Natchez*, starring Dale Robertson and Debra Paget. Coincidentally, the Center Theater marquee (right) shows this very movie playing there.

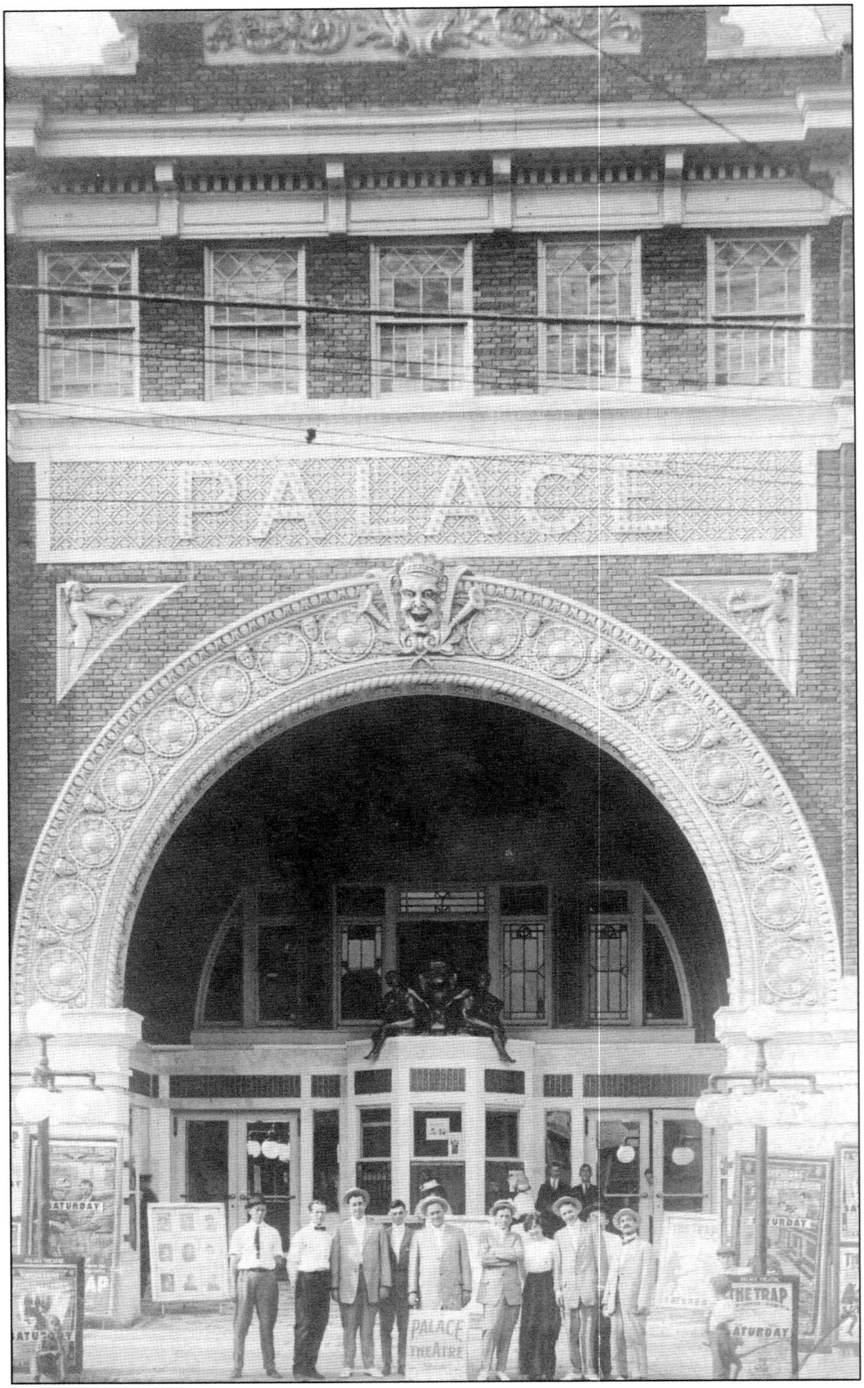

The Palace Theater opened on Fifth Street (later Capitol Avenue) between Center and Spring Streets around 1910. The grandly appointed theater boasted an ornate frieze and life-sized statues over the doors. It would have first hosted minstrel shows and traveling vaudeville productions before moving on to silent films. The many signs announced that on Saturday the theater would be showing *The Trap*, apparently a cautionary tale from Keystone on the dangers of "the bar room." Happy young people pose before the Palace, while several street urchins look on.

The original Palace Theater would later be renamed the Capitol after a theater of the same name was closed on Main Street. In this 1954 photograph, the current feature at the Capitol is *The Robe*, a biblical epic starring Richard Burton and Jean Simmons, presented in the new Cinemascope technique. The Capitol Theater was razed in the 1970s to make way for the First National Bank tower.

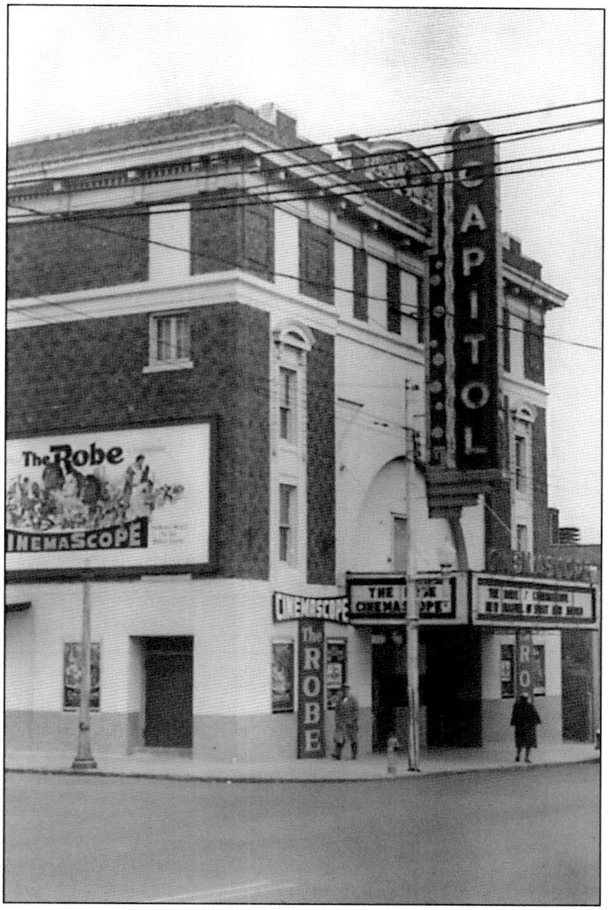

In 1915, the Savoy Theater at 509 Main Street was showing the silent film *The Prisoner of Zenda*, starring James K. Hackett. The Canadian-born actor had first played the role on stage in 1913 and was then lured to film. Also promoted was a series of short films displaying the new technique of Kinemacolor, recently developed in Great Britain. The Savoy was gone within a few years.

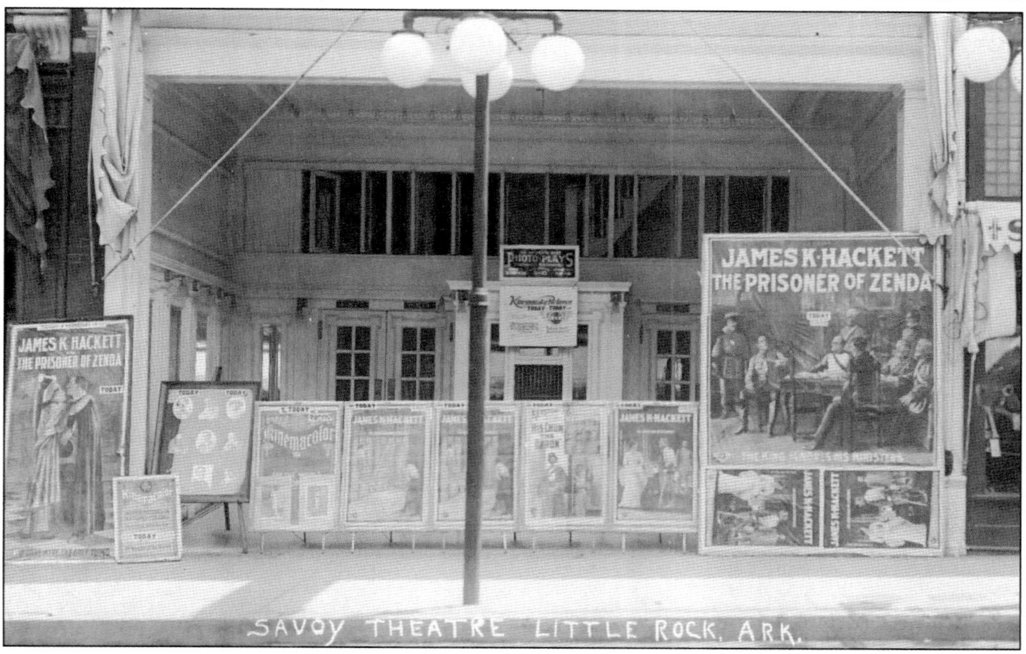

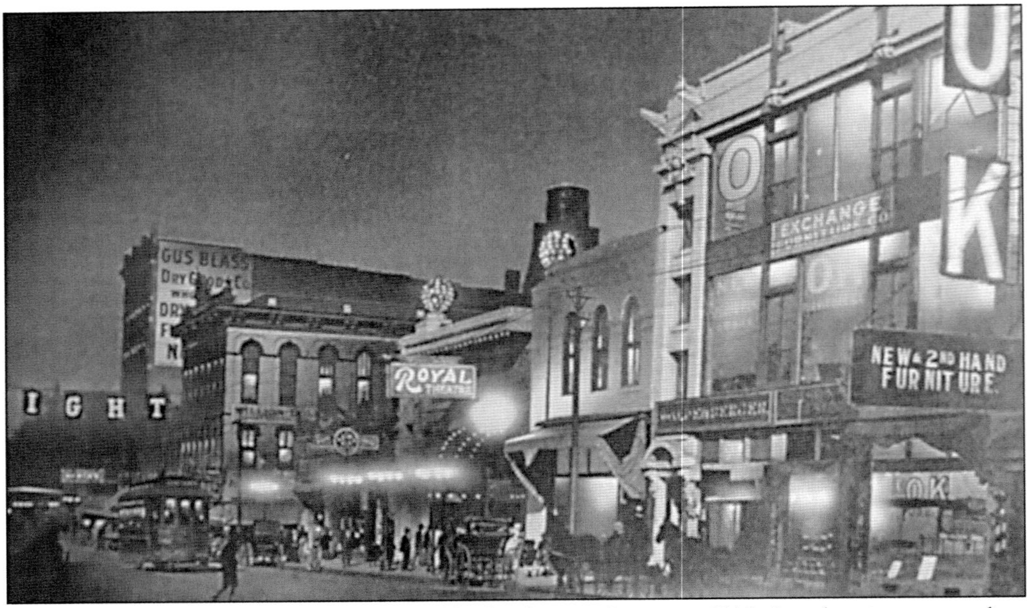

The Royal Theater opened on the 400 block of Main Street in 1910, first hosting stage plays and then moving to silent films. Seen here in a "night" view around 1915, the theater sports large illuminated spheres to attract customers, who perhaps arrive at the theater by streetcar, automobile, or even horse and buggy. The Royal shared the block with the OK store, selling new and second-hand furniture.

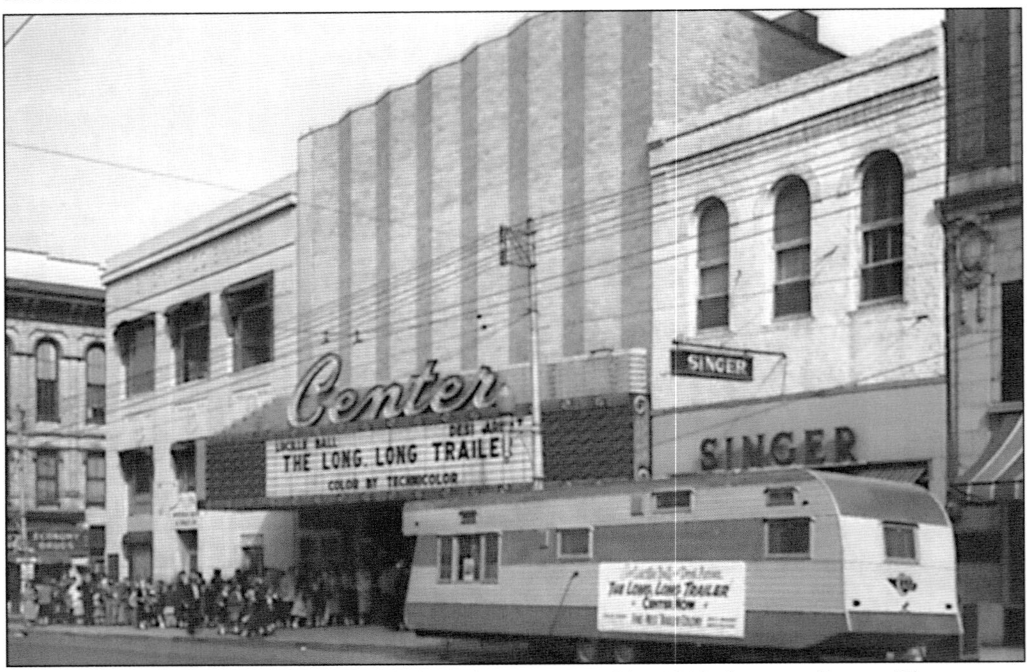

The old Royal Theater was dismantled in the 1940s, and by 1949 the new Center Theater was built, holding 1,252 seats to accommodate larger crowds before its single screen. One of the hits of 1954 was Lucille Ball's comedy *The Long, Long Trailer.* To promote the movie, the theater owners had a real travel trailer parked at the curb. The historic theater was razed in 2009, and today the site is a parking lot.

The Majestic Theatre opened on the 800 block of Main Street in the early 1900s as a small brick playhouse decorated in red, white, and gold, with a small lighted sign but no marquee. In 1912, topiary trees flanked the entrance, and a sign seemed to promote the day's matinee of a blackface comedy. Among the stage stars who performed there over the years were Will Rogers and Vera Gordon.

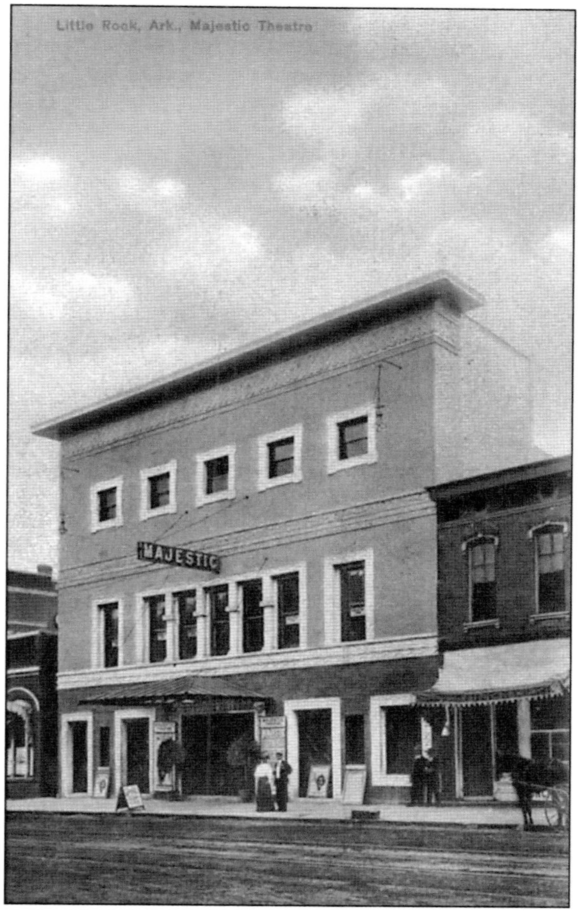

The Majestic Theatre was hosting "Vaudeville of Quality" the week of January 16, 1911. The detailed advertising bill headlined the Rathskeller Trio, which had played for long runs in New York and Chicago before coming to Little Rock. Also featured were the "Bicycle Eccentrics," the 3 Dooleys; two Australian comedians; and a demonstration of "Majestograph—Flickerless Motion Photographs." The Majestic burned down in 1930 and was not rebuilt.

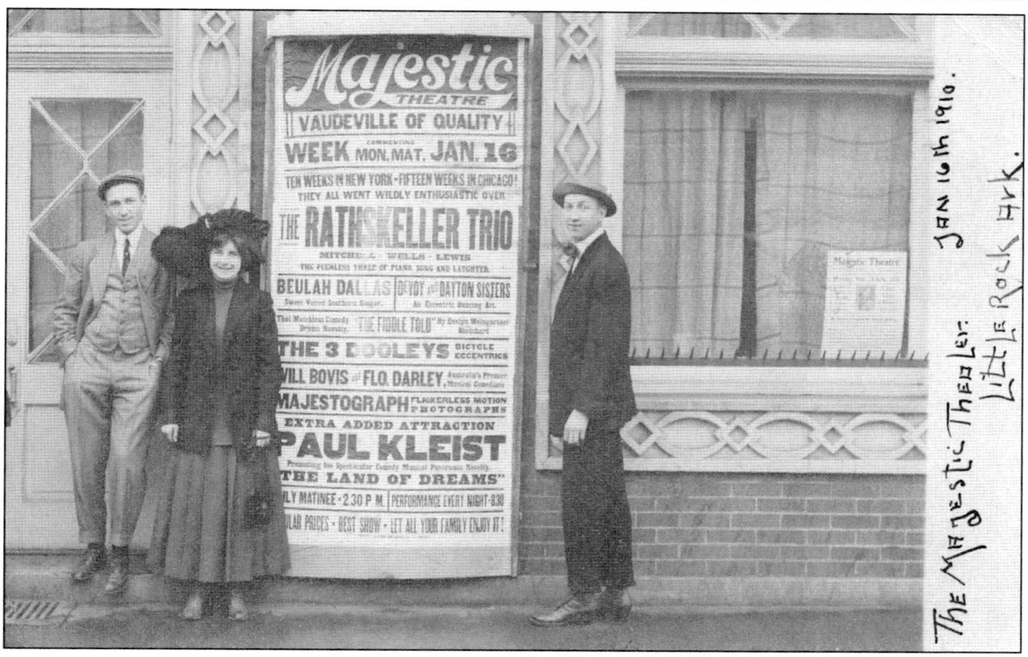

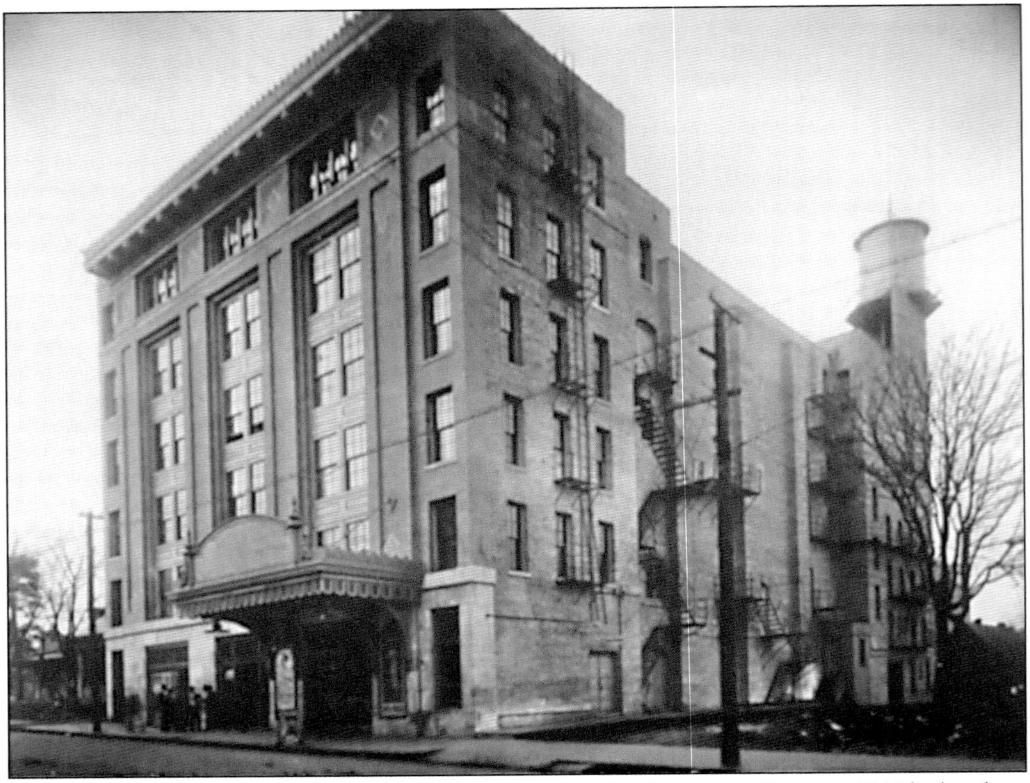

Seen here around 1912, the Kempner Theater was opened on Louisiana Street in 1910 by brothers Ike and Dave Kempner. It played host to minstrel shows and hundreds of traveling acts, including such celebrities as William Jennings Bryan and Sarah Bernhardt. In 1929, it was renamed the Arkansas Theater, playing movies on the big screen until it closed in 1977. Efforts to save the historic building failed; today, its site is a parking lot.

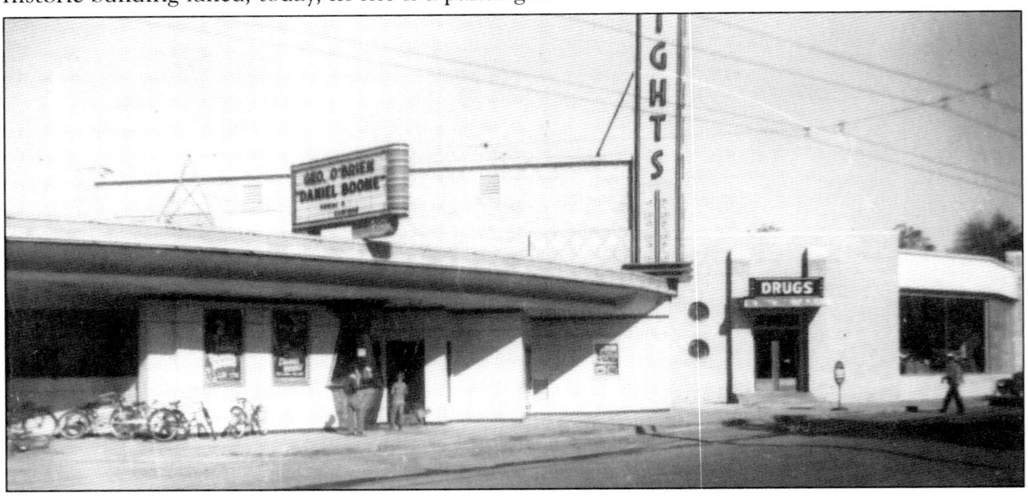

The Heights Theater opened at 5600 Kavanaugh Boulevard in 1946 on the spot where streetcars were turned around to head back downtown. In this 1940 view, boys have left their bicycles while they attend *Daniel Boone* starring George O'Brien. The neighborhood movie house ended its run in 1985, with the final film being *The Last Picture Show*. The building was converted to a small shopping center and still stands. (Courtesy of Monsignor Bernard Malone.)

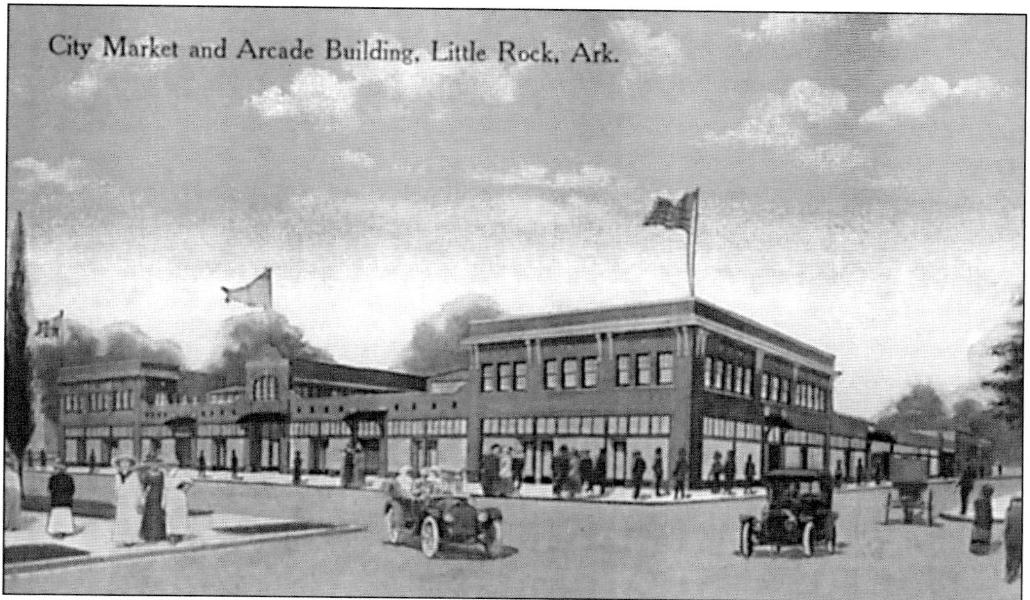

The concept of an enclosed shopping mall may have been revived in 1970s America, but such facilities are actually modeled after the indoor markets of Europe and South America. Little Rock boasted a fine facility in the City Market and Arcade Building, which opened in 1914 and filled the entire 600 block of Louisiana Street across from St. Andrew's Cathedral. It contained 100 shopping stalls, initially offering an array of meats and vegetables among the competing vendors. Later, the shops diversified to offer musical instruments, hardware, and household goods. The historic building was razed in 1960 to make way for the Downtowner Motor Inn, which would itself fall to the wrecking ball in 2004. Today, the site is a parking lot. (Below, courtesy of Butler Center for Arkansas Studies.)

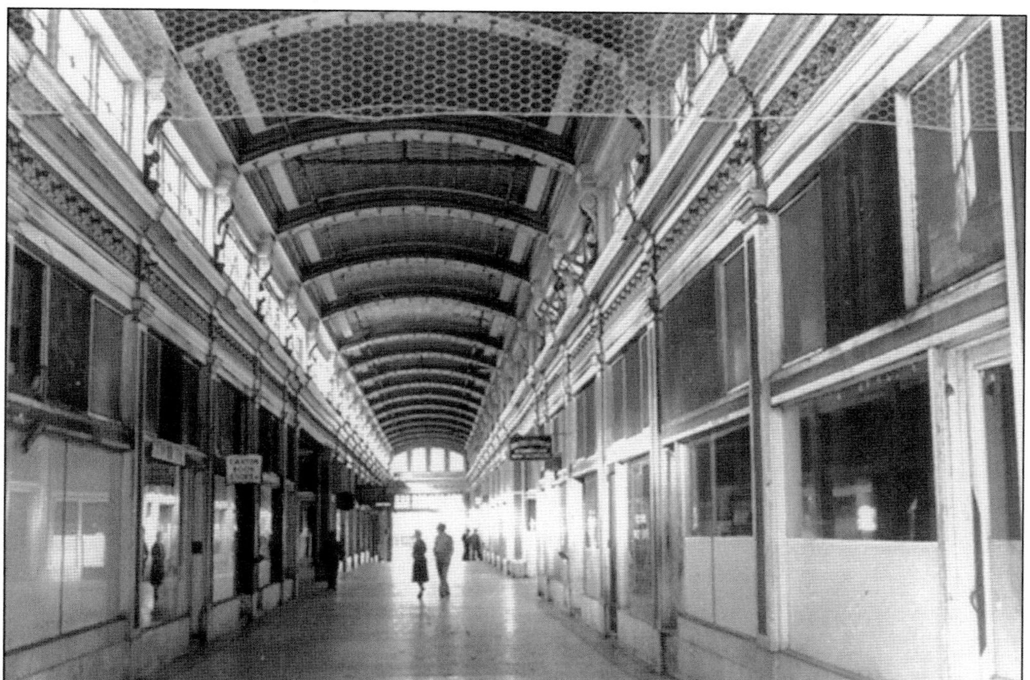